"I've been waiting for somec   :y
and inner healing in an integr   le
has described how interact   in
transformation into Christ-likeness."

– Jan Johnson
>   Retreat speaker and author of *Invitation to the Jesus Life*

"A superb presentation about the healing power of truth. One of the beauties of this book is witnessing the author's own personal journey towards transformation. David talks with you, not at you, while at the same time challenging you to come and be made whole. His sincerity, wisdom, and practical applications will show you, his reader, how you, too, can live in the truth that will set you free."

– Todd Oakley
>   Lead Pastor Gate City Vineyard Church,
>   Area Leader Vineyard Mid-Atlantic Region

"David Takle knocks the ball out of the park with this insightful book about the insidious power of lies – not the kind of lies that we all recognize as false but the deeply held internal assumptions about how life works and who we are that seem true, yet have malformed our soul. No one escapes."

"These often hidden lies have warped our souls making it hard to believe that we are truly beloved children of a good God. The nagging sense that we will fail, that we are not good enough, that we will never have the love we long for are all rooted in these kinds of lies. David not only succinctly describes the problem but he provides the solution, experientially engaging with God so we can receive his forgiveness, let go of self recrimination, and let him restore our whole heart."

"This book is a must read for all who seek to grow in intimacy with God. If you apply the wisdom within, it will change your life."

– Elizabeth Stalcup, Ph.D.
>   Executive Director of Healing Center International

"Many years ago when I was a teenage boy and at the beginning of my spiritual journey, I left the safety of my liturgical church family to go and listen to an elderly English preacher. I don't recall the texts used in his preaching, but I do remember how his words touched something deep in my heart. He said, "*Be careful what you believe, because what you believe rules you,*" meaning that all of us make decisions and interact with God and others in accordance with our own internalized values and beliefs, no matter how much those beliefs may or may not agree with how God views things. While these words have had a life-long impact on my life, initially I was left primarily on my own and then eventually in community with dear Christian friends, to seek and develop an experiential relationship with God that could heal many of the bumps, bruises, and wounding in life that had resulted in my own wrong believing, and over many years eventually replaced many of my distorted beliefs with his truth."

"As I read *The Truth About Lies and Lies About Truth*, I found myself reflecting on this journey with the predominant thought of, "Boy do I wish I'd had this book forty years ago!" It really would have eliminated much of the trial and error in my own spiritual formation. In this book, David Takle does a masterful and thorough job of describing the problem of deception and how it results in our spiritual malformation, as well as the power of beliefs and how they drive our lives. But then he offers incredibly practical solutions, which leads to an experiential relationship with the Spirit of Truth. This relationship with the Spirit of Truth causes the exposing of deception, the alignment of our beliefs with his truth and results in being transformed into the image and mind of Christ. In my mind, this book and study should be a must for anyone who is serious about Christian discipleship."

– The Rev. Canon Andrew Miller, LCSW
Founder of HeartSync Ministries

(for comments by **Dallas Willard**, see the Preface to the Revised Edition)

What some of our readers are saying:

"A must read … I love this book and recommend it highly."
– Reader in Lawrenceville NJ

"I am better as a Christian and as a person for reading this book."
– Reader in Boston, MA

"One of the best pieces of writing and wisdom that has ever come to the Body of Christ."
– Reader in Spring Hill, TN

"A really terrific book for anyone who doesn't understand why it's so hard to be as good as they want to be; why they react so often with fear/anger/defensiveness in situations; why they don't live in the joy and victory that they expected in the Christian life."
– M. P. (Amazon review)

"A wonderful book … hard to put down. I plan to reread this book, it was so good!"
– Kindle reader (Amazon review)

"The concepts and information in this book will stick with me the rest of my life.."
– R. K. (Amazon review)

"I love it! This is a book that I will read over and over again."
– Amazon review

"This is one of the most profound books I have ever read. It is a must read for every Christian who wants to walk in freedom and victory."
– S. R.

The Truth About Lies
and Lies About Truth

A Fresh New Look at the Cunning of Evil
and the Means for Our Transformation

by David Takle, M.Div.

For Jan

The Truth About Lies and Lies About Truth

Revised Edition

David Takle, M.Div.

david@KingdomFormation.org

Available from
www.KingdomFormation.org
www.TruthAboutLies.info
www.Amazon.com

First Edition 2008 – ISBN 0-9674357-9-4 (Pasadena: Shepherd's House, Inc.)
Revised Edition 2017 – ISBN 978-0-9890069-5-8 (NC: KFM)
Kindle Format 2017 – ISBN 978-0-9890069-6-5 (NC: KFM)

Published by Kingdom Formation Ministries
High Point, NC
www.KingdomFormation.org

Table of Contents

Part 1 – The Truth About Lies

An Invitation to The Abundant Life..21

1. The Problem is Worse Than We Think...31

2. The Truth about Lies..57

3. The Destructive Nature of Deception...73

4. From Deception to Malformation..87

Part 2 – The Power of Belief

5. My Beliefs May Not Be What I Think I Believe.......................101

6. How Beliefs Drive My Life..117

7. True Belief is Hard Work...135

Part 3 – Lies About Truth

8. Lies We Believe About Christian Development.......................145

9. Truth is More Than True Information......................................163

10. Internalizing Truth..185

11. Realigning Our Christian Development.................................217

Addendum..239

Group Discussion Guide...253

Above all else guard your heart, for it is the wellspring of life

(Prov.4:23).

Acknowledgments

In many ways this book has been a lifetime in the making, and there is no way that it would have been possible but for a long list of people who have helped me come to know the inestimable value of truth. Because of that, I cannot name them all here. However, there are a few who stand out, to whom I owe a tremendous debt of gratitude.

Jay McGown comes to mind here, whom God brought to me at a very desperate moment in my life to mentor me for nearly eight months in 1970. His best gift to me, and there were many, was the understanding that my search for truth had only begun and that God had many things yet to teach me. He was more right than I ever imagined. Wherever you are, Jay, thank you for caring and for the mark you left on my life.

I need to mention the people of We Care, who taught me by example that truth was relational and experiential, and not just a thing of the mind. More recently, the teachings of Ed Smith paved a way for the power of truth to set me free me from the depression that had held me in bondage all my life. His understanding of the cunning of evil solidified much of what I had suspected to be true about lies and deception. And from 1999 to the present, the writings and teaching of Dallas Willard have had a profound impact on both my understanding and my experience of the Christian life. His wisdom and insight are in many ways evident throughout this book.

It would be impossible to express the debt of gratitude I owe my professor Julie Gorman, whose patience, guidance, encouragement, and thorough critique of this work have been invaluable. Were it not for her support of this effort, the present book probably would not exist.

I also want to thank all of those who proofread the manuscript and offered so much helpful feedback, from spelling and grammar to structure and content. Your comments have greatly helped to strengthen the message in these pages.

Finally to my wife, Jan, who has taken much of this journey with me, my love and gratitude for the many talks long into the night, the prayers for healing and light, and your own love for the truth that has encouraged me to stay on the path that leads to life.

Preface to the Revised Edition

A lot has happened in the last nine years, prompting me to revisit this text and update it. Perhaps the greatest motivation has come from the amazing response we received from those who have read the book. We also received a very meaningful email from Jane Willard, wife of world-class philosopher Dallas Willard, my favorite author. Here is what she wrote:

> *I've been seeing your book lying around and moving around with Dallas' mail and few books that are out. Today I picked it up and saw that he had marked the eighth chapter. So later in the day I said, "I see you have David Takle's book out – have you been reading it?" He said yes, he'd read it. I asked, "Well, what did you think?" He said, "It's wonderful. I have it out to remind me to write him about it." Then he added, as he walked away, "It's an excellent book."*

It would be impossible to say how much that has meant to me. More than anything else, those encouraging words have been my primary motivation to review the text again and make the improvements I have outlined here.

First, from a purely practical standpoint I have learned more about formatting a book and preparing it for publication. The 2008 edition was my first published book, and I was still quite new to the process. Hopefully, this edition will be much easier on the eye and easier to read. We have also corrected a few typographical and grammatical errors previously missed.

Second, I wrote the original draft in 2004, just four and a half years after starting my own journey of healing by truth as described here. Since then we have continued to learn much about how God transforms lives. While truth is perhaps the most accessible means for our transformation, it is not the only way God changes lives. When we address truth from this larger point of view it has a way of enhancing some of the discussions about transformation, and that is reflected in this edition.

To help put this in perspective, I have added an introduction titled, *An Invitation to the Abundant Life*. My intention there is to cast a clearer vision of where we are going and to better set the stage for the larger picture of how truth brings about transformation.

Another note which was not entirely clear before, is that all of the stories in the book are about real people. Names and other details have been altered where necessary. But all of these examples of transformation have actually happened.

Finally, the group study guide that was developed after the first printing is now incorporated into the book, making it easier to discuss these ideas in a group setting.

While the first edition has been enthusiastically received, my hope is that these new additions will strengthen its message even further.

A Note About Gender Syntax (my disclaimer)

Due to the limitations of our language, every English author has to decide how to address the issue of inclusiveness regarding gender when using pronouns. Reading the phrase "he or she" all the time can be very cumbersome; using only "he" or "she" sounds very biased in modern literature; and randomly switching between the two is often disorienting.

One solution is to refer to "you" all the time, but that generally comes across as too preachy. Another approach is to use "I" and "my," but after a while that begins to sound a little too self-referenced.

By way of compromise, I have often opted for the convention of using inclusive plural pronouns, despite the fact that this results in grammatically incorrect sentences. So instead of, "When a person sets aside time to be with God, he or she needs to quiet his or her mind and focus his or her heart," I will tend to use, "When we set aside time to be with God, we need to quiet our mind and focus our heart."

My assumption is that since we hear this kind of grammar all the time, most readers will have little trouble with the license I have taken with the language. I hope you will find this to be an acceptable solution.

Preface to the First Edition

"We must teach about the nature of belief."[1]

We are witnessing today what may well be the single most important development in the Western Church since the Reformation – a rediscovery of what it means to build a relationship with God that has enough vitality in and of itself to change who we are from the inside out. Often referred to as "Christian Formation," it is nothing less than the recovery of transformation and intimacy with God as a way of life. At long last we are beginning to emerge from the *deeply flawed strategies* of "try harder" Christianity that have been so destructive to the body of Christ for so many years, and move on to a truly God-centered, Spirit-driven process of spiritual development.

Interwoven throughout these fresh life-giving perspectives, an incredibly important recurring theme has emerged that lies at the very heart of our Christian experience. This one theme explains both how *the evil done to us* injures our soul, and why *we ourselves do evil things* which violate our own values. And coming to terms with this issue is vital to restoring the broken places in our lives as well as stimulating new growth and change. Briefly put, our very hope of transformation is heavily dependent upon *the power of truth to bring life, the power of deception to cause death, and the means by which our lives are shaped within this context of Deception, Truth, and Belief.*

The hardest part in writing about this phenomenon is knowing where to begin. The more I discover about the insidious role deception plays in disabling our lives, the more convinced I become that it is by far one of the most significant, if perhaps one of the least understood, aspects of Christian growth and recovery. Whether or not the full import of that conviction can be conveyed within the pages of a book remains to be seen. As for myself, it has taken over forty years of life as a Christian to gain a glimpse of the crucial nature of belief and why it is so central to the process of

---

[1] Willard, *The Divine Conspiracy*, p. 309.

transformation. In the spirit of the quote at the beginning of this preface, I am more certain than ever that we *desperately* need more teaching about the nature of belief in order to better live as God intended.

Why I Wrote This Book

After a devastating personal and spiritual meltdown in the mid-1980s, I found myself among a group of friends who were all trying to rebuild their lives, relying on each other for the support and encouragement needed just to get from day to day. As we picked over the pieces of our lives together attempting to make sense of the mess we were dealing with, we began to notice one particular thought that kept surfacing in our discussions, one idea that captured for us the part we all seemed to have played in our own demise: *"There was so much that we did not know, and what you don't know can destroy your life."*

Of all the things I learned during that period of recovery, none were as surprising as the sheer number of things that I had been deeply mistaken about. These were not simple errors in judgment, but severe misconceptions at the core of my being regarding my own identity, the character of God, the nature of relationships, and what sorts of things actually drive our lives. Most of all, I came to realize that we can be very hurt by what we do not know, and that much of my pain was caused by my own lack of understanding of life. What made this so disorienting was that most of my life I believed I had a superior grasp of things because of my extensive Christian and theological background. Yet none of that had been sufficient to keep my life from coming undone.

Then in January of 2000 I was introduced to the work of Ed Smith, a Christian counselor who not only had an incredible grasp of the relationship between emotional pain and the lies we believe, but who had learned much about how the damage caused by lies can be healed by engaging directly with the Holy Spirit.[2] His work had such an unmistakable ring of truth to it that my wife and I began to pray with each other for God to restore the broken places in our lives in this way. Within a very short time the depression that I had lived with all of my life began to lift, and in its place was a rapidly growing sense of hope and joy. After having been a

---

[2] Smith, *Beyond Tolerable Recovery*.

Christian for well over forty years, I was for the first time experiencing God's direct work in my life to change my heart and mind day by day.

As I witnessed what God was able to do in my own life, I had to wonder why the Christian world is so terribly ineffectual much of the time in the face of life's difficulties. It was in attempting to make sense of this tragic state of affairs that this book was written. And while I have borrowed from a number of authors and speakers who have addressed elements of this issue very eloquently, I am unaware of anyone who has drawn all of these elements together in one place to form a coherent picture of why the Christian life has become so much more elusive than it needs to be. I believe this book is a step in that direction.

One of the many results of this journey has been an ever-increasing awareness of the depth and pervasiveness of deception, as well as the power of truth to set us free. More recently I have begun to see the extent to which the interplay of truth and deception provides an integral framework for much of Scripture, theology, and life. This single framework equips us with a powerful means for breaking the bondage of the sins we feel stuck with, for breaking the bondage that comes from the wounds we have suffered, for developing a genuine relationship with God, and for growing proactively in our walk with Him. By way of contrast, the extensive theology and discipleship training I received years ago (and taught to others) did very little to rescue me from the brokenness I lived with inside me. My meltdown did not come from disobedience or lack of repentance or any moral lapse. It came because doctrine is no match for the lies we learn from life experience. And those who trust their doctrine and willpower to keep them afloat are in far greater danger than they could ever imagine.

Most important of all has been the change in my relationship to God. My encounter with truth has been made *through* God, and has led me to a relationship *with* God that is authentic, tangible, and substantive. To be precise, it is my *experience of God* that has changed my life so significantly. I only speak of it as an encounter with truth because that is the aspect of His character that has so profoundly affected my life. My experience of God and His truth has, in turn, opened the door to the Kingdom that I have been searching for my whole life. I feel a bit like John McCarthy when he wrote in a letter to Hudson Taylor, "I seem to have got to the edge only, but of a sea which is boundless; to have sipped only, but of that which fully satisfies."[3] My prayer is that this exploration of the nature of belief may touch others who have also yearned for more of God or struggled with how to move forward in the Christian life, and that this will provide both the hope and the means to break free of whatever holds them back.

---

[3] Edman, *They Found the Secret*, p. 19.

Part 1

The Truth About Lies

"What? Are we blind too?"
(Jn.9:40)

Part 1 – The Truth About Lies

Introduction – An Invitation to the Abundant Life

The only way we can possibly live the Christian life as described in the New Testament is if God transforms our heart and mind in ways beyond our own ability. Understanding how God transforms will set the stage for the rest of the book.

Chapter 1 – The Problem is Worse Than We Think

Everything that matters in life has been corrupted. What's more, every possible measure has been taken to prevent us from seeing what has happened to us and to our world.

Chapter 2 – The Truth About Lies

Nearly every page of Scripture reveals the extent and power of deception in the world. By comparing the words of the text with the way we internalize life experience, the true nature of the problem that we face begins to take shape.

Chapter 3 – The Destructive Nature of Deception

The reason the Bible says so much about the nature of deception is that mistaken ideas of life are sufficient in and of themselves to destroy what is good.

Chapter 4 – From Deception to Malformation

Deception not only causes us to sin, it is also responsible for the festering wounds we carry from the bad things that happen to us. And both of these problems corrupt our soul so that it no longer functions well.

Introduction

An Invitation to The Abundant Life

All throughout the New Testament we see glimpses, even panoramic paintings, of a life so filled with the Spirit of God that trust in Him seems as natural as breathing, where healing our soul is as common as waking up in the morning, and victory over sin is our normal Christian experience. Here is just one example:

> *"Whoever drinks of the water that I shall give him shall never thirst; but the water that I shall give him shall become in him a well of water springing up to eternal life ... from his innermost being shall flow rivers of living water." (Jn.4:14; 7:38, NASB)*

What an amazing promise – and only one of many! Jesus had quite a bit to say about the kind of life His followers would have. He promised us "an abundant life" (Jn.10), rest for our soul (Mt.11), and that He would be with us and reveal Himself to us so that we would never be alone (Jn.14).

From a treasure hidden in a field to abiding in Him, Jesus described life with God in terms that were almost too good to be true. And that is not the end of it. Paul picked up on the wonder and beauty of this life as well:

> *"Blessed be God, who has blessed us with every spiritual blessing ...*
> *according to the riches of His grace which He lavished upon us ...*
> *I pray that you would know the hope of His calling ... and how incredible His love is toward you" (Eph.1:3,7,8,18; 3:18-19, NASB paraphrased).*

This is the life we have always wanted, the life we were meant for. But there seems to be a problem.

How Do We Get There?

Many Christians who have attempted to take these verses seriously have been grievously disappointed, to say the least. The promises sound good, but attempting to make them a reality has proven to be more challenging than anyone would have guessed. This way of life seems so far off in the horizon it is barely visible at all. Many have even dismissed this image of life as impossible in this present age. We struggle year after year with the same old sins, we haul around emotional wounds that never seem to heal, and we rarely see any real change at all except that which comes with getting older.

Why is that? Why did Jesus and the New Testament writers give us a hope that so many of us never seem to find? How is it that we have missed the abundant life?

We go to conferences, read the latest books, and pray until we cannot stand to pray any more. Still we are haunted by the thought, "Surely there has to be something more than what I've known so far. This cannot be all that God meant for me to have."

Rest Assured, There is a Way

No doubt you have heard promises of the abundant life from time to time, and right now you may be wondering whether this book is just one more in a long list of those that make outrageous claims. But here is the whole problem in a nutshell.

What if the main reason we have so much difficulty experiencing life as described in the New Testament is because we have been misled on how it all happens? What if God never really intended for us to try our best to live up to His standards – because no one can? *What if transformation does not come from trying hard to be different, but rather, being different comes from transformation?* What if we have it backwards? What if God could change us more and more into the kind of people who live the abundant life by virtue of our transformed character?

Personally, I am convinced that this is precisely the radical process of transformation that has been lost to us. And to whatever extent we can recover the means by which we are changed more into the image of Christ, we will experience the abundant life that Jesus promised to His disciples.

How God Designed Transformation

When God set out to create a path toward Christ-likeness, He did not leave it up to us to crank it out by sheer effort, nor did He decide to dole out transformation in rare life events. Instead, God provided a number of predictable, dependable means for us, so that we could reliably pursue the changes we so desperately need. The better we understand these sources of transformation and the means by which we can participate with them, the more we will experience life in the Kingdom as God intended.

While we cannot provide a comprehensive study here on the theology of transformation, if we step back and look at the big picture there are three overarching aspects to transformation that work together to bring about the sort of character change which brings us closer and closer to the image of Jesus. They are:

- *Direct causes* or means of transformation which originate outside of us.
- Ways in which we can engage and *participate* with these means.
- Certain contexts which *foster* this process.

Doing minimal justice to each of these three aspects would require another volume. My goal in this book is to cover one particular element, namely, how *truth* brings about transformation, and how we can participate with God so that truth can do its work in us.

Among other things, what will become evident along the way is the fact that while much of the Christian world is deeply concerned about truth as an objective matter and truth as it pertains to doctrinal purity, there appears to be very little understanding about *how to internalize that truth* so that it becomes *truth in us* – a part of who we are.

For at least a couple hundred years now, we have operated under the illusion that if we just said the truth often enough, loud enough, and with enough rationale behind it, people would be better for it and do what is right. But propositional truth, it turns out, is simply not sufficient in and of itself to do the work of transformation. As important as objective truth is to our sanity and our well-being, hearing true words will never be enough to enable us to live in that truth or live out that truth day to day. Something is missing – something vital.

Truth as a Cause for Transformation

Imagine trying to get around Cincinnati when all you have is a map of Columbus, which is mislabeled so you don't realize the mistake. Nothing makes sense, you cannot get to where you want to go, and you feel lost at every turn. Now imagine that someone explains the problem and hands you the correct map! Suddenly, many things are clear and life in the city takes on a flow it never had before. Truth has a way of doing that.

For many Christians, this is what happens when they first find Christ and begin to follow Him. Suddenly, the world makes more sense to them than ever before, and they joyfully realign many aspects of their personal life to be more in line with what God says is good for them. Whatever truth is readily accessible to them and gets all the way into their heart propels them forward, provides new levels of healing and freedom, and encourages them in their journey. But this is only the beginning.

What we need to understand is that truth is a lot more than having the right ethics, good doctrine and making good choices, as important as those are. Truth includes all that God knows about everything – the best way to handle problems, the reasons why we have stubborn habits, why we have difficulty letting go of old wounds or trouble forgiving someone, as well as everything else we might encounter in life.

More to the point, we have all been overrun by the corrosive effects of this hostile planet, our sick culture, and our flawed family systems, usually in ways we are only partially aware of. As we learn how to engage with God to receive His truth into all these areas of our life, we begin to see things more the way God sees them, and each revelation brings us more freedom, more life, and more hope. Truth is transformative almost by definition. Because what we do not know can destroy us.

Our Means of Participation

Given that God is the author of truth and has given us the Spirit of Truth, one has to ask why so many Christians find real change to be relatively rare. I suppose there is more than one reason for this state of affairs. But mostly it comes down to not knowing how to participate with God in ways that allow truth to alter our very way of perceiving and understanding our own life.

In addition to relying heavily on Christian education to produce spiritual growth, people have tried at least three other primary avenues for change, all of which have led to fairly disappointing results. First, there is sheer willpower, the attempt to follow the truth by making all the "right" choices. More often than not, this results in legalism instead of transformation.

Second, a lot of people have focused their efforts on changing the culture, trying to get everyone to think and behave in ways that are more Christian in nature. But this misses the more serious problems that exist in the heart of every individual, and again, transformation does not happen. Third, there are those who believe that transformation should be completely effortless, resulting from just the right prayer, said in just the right way. But none of these approaches are how real change happens. Rather, they are all failures to participate well, to actively engage in the process of being restored and discipled by Jesus.

Knowing how we are involved in fostering transformation is crucial. We cannot be transformed without proper participation any more than we can learn tennis or Russian without participating in the necessary learning experiences.

Building a Context for Transformation by Truth

Effective participation in God's way of transformation involves several things, including a workable context. Again, we cannot go into all of the different elements included in a transformative context. But two of these elements stand out when we talk about transformation by truth.

First, we need to fully grasp the idea that we actually have an inner life that is capable of being transformed. While that should be obvious, many segments of the church are loaded down with practical theologies of Christian identity which actually put transformation out of reach. Some even teach that as Christians we have been given a new nature that is already perfect and does not need any change, and this new nature has moved in alongside our old nature which is irredeemably sinful and incapable of change. Well if our new nature does not need change and our old nature cannot change, it is virtually impossible to develop any coherent theology of change! And we need to be honest about the fact that learning how to use our willpower to encourage one and repress the other bears absolutely no resemblance to the New Testament's descriptions of transformation.

Whatever our theory of Christian identity, it has to make room for Paul's declaration in Colossians: "Seeing that you have stripped off the old self with its practices and have clothed yourselves with the new self, *which is being renewed* in knowledge according to the image of its creator" (3:9-10, NRSV, emphasis mine). We have a nature that is in the process of being renewed. Real change is possible, even expected in the Christian walk.

Not only do we have an inner life that is capable of transformation over time so that we become more and more like Jesus (1Jn.3), but the truth is we are in far more need of this transformation than we think we are. Growing in grace is not a matter of tweaking a few things here and there that seem to give us difficulty. Most of us need dramatic and significant reforming of some of our most basic ways of approaching life and others. That is why Jesus talked about death and resurrection as a daily occurrence for His followers.

Once we understand the radical nature of the work that needs to take place inside our own heart and mind, we have the beginnings of a context that can foster transformation. Until we grasp this process, we will continue to rely on our willpower to make minor adjustments in our behavior or to suppress whatever awareness we might have of an inner conflict that cries out for resolution. Transformation is about changing our very character – not our environment, not the people around us, not even our behavior – it is about changing who we are from the inside out.

The second major element of participating well involves our receptivity. As apprentices to Jesus, we must see ourselves as perpetual students of life in the Kingdom. We will never exhaust what there is to learn and discover about how this all works and how Jesus wants us involved. Nor will we in this lifetime ever finish the work of transformation needed in our own soul. So in order to participate in this process of change we need to be fully receptive to whatever God wants to do in us.

In order for us to move forward, we need not only truth about God and His Kingdom, but also truth about who we are and where we are at any given moment in this journey toward wholeness. That means learning how to be totally transparent before God without any sense of shame or disgust for being an unfinished work of Christ. We must learn to be totally honest in the presence of God about our unhealed wounds, our emotional triggers, our flaws, our bad habits, and our sinful urges. Because only then will we be able to receive what God has for us in those places; only then will we be open to the work He wants to do in us.

Furthermore, this is a work only God can do. We need to learn how to become receptive to His work because it is a job we cannot do. Our will was never designed to be able to force our heart to change. Our best efforts are not the solution we need. Instead, we must learn how to engage with God in ways that allow Him to do in us what we cannot – change our heart and mind to be more like His.

Once I am willing to admit that I do not know nearly as much about life in the Kingdom as I would like to think I do, I become teachable and receptive to what the Spirit wants to show me and do in me. Without that, my efforts toward transformation will be hindered by my own mistaken notion that I can live this kind of life if I try hard enough.

A Simple Example

Transforming moments do not have to be earth shattering or life-changing in order to feed our soul. They can be as simple as renewing our vision in some area where we need help seeing what God sees.

While working with a man who wanted to learn more about how God could speak into his life, I suggested that we spend some time together in prayer and bring a life-issue to God in order to see what He might reveal in regard to that area. I proposed the following question for our consideration: "God, how do You view my relationship with You?"

Immediately, I saw an expression of fear cross his face and he said he would rather not go there. He was not at all sure he wanted to know God's thoughts about the kind of relationship they had. So I suggested an alternative: "God, what could you show me that would make it safe enough to ask that other question?" My friend said he thought he could do that.

We then began listening and journaling, and over the next few minutes an amazing revelation came to us both. *We do not have to perform well enough to earn a relationship with God, because grace means we get the relationship first – and then we work on the stuff*!

My friend was so relieved he actually laughed! What a wonderful way to grasp the glory of grace! That God wants to have a relationship with us so we can then work with Him for our own restoration! We even noticed how this is exactly what Paul was saying in Romans 5:8,10. Our God removes the barriers between Himself and us so that He can then do for us what we could never do for ourselves. Such a simple idea – yet so profound! This is why we need truth to live, day by day, year in and year out, truth from the heart of God tailored just the way we need to hear it in that moment.

Where We Go From Here

The abundant life is one in which God is always with us, working *in* us day after day, *to make us more and more into the image of His dear Son.* This is so important, I want to restate my initial premise.

All throughout the New Testament we see glimpses, even panoramic paintings, of a life so filled with the Spirit that trust in God seems as natural as breathing, healing the soul is as common as waking up in the morning, and victory over sin is the normal Christian experience. This can be *your* life.

Again, there are several major causes of transformation. The reason I have chosen to focus on how *truth* transforms is because of this one thing: of all the direct causes of transformation, truth is by far the most accessible. And since our need for relearning how to learn and how to live is so extensive, truth also offers us an almost unlimited avenue for transformation and growth.

You must know up front, however, that we will not get there directly. Before we can describe the means by which we are to be made whole by truth, we must first clear away the many layers of misinformation and misunderstanding that have obscured this issue from one end to the other. Because only when we have successfully deconstructed our mistaken views of the spiritual journey will we have any chance of re-constructing a coherent strategy for engaging with God in ways that allow us to receive what we need for life.

So please bear with me as we re-examine the prevailing views about how truth is involved in our spiritual growth and restoration, and as we redefine a foundation that we can truly stand on with confidence. Once we know how God actually changes lives by means of truth, we can then participate with Him in ways that foster that transformation. And when we begin to see our own life changing before our eyes, our hope will be renewed, and our desire to be whole will re-awaken to the joy of moving forward in this life, and we will learn how to participate with God to impact others and to flesh out the Kingdom in this present age.

Let me invite you now to walk through this process with me, and see perhaps for the first time how possible, how accessible, this abundant life really is!

Chapter 1

The Problem is Worse Than We Think

One of the most important revelations embedded within the pages of Scripture is the single fact that there exists a direct correlation between bondage and deception on the one hand, and between freedom and truth on the other. When Jesus called Himself the Way, the Truth, and the Life, He was making a statement not only about Himself, but also about the relationship between truth and the life that He made possible. We cannot have life apart from truth, and many of the destructive elements of this world lose their power in its presence.

The basic premise of this book is that *a proper understanding of belief, truth, and deception is absolutely essential to the development of a coherent approach to Christian growth and recovery, because it leads directly to one of the most practical means available for dealing with both the causes of sin and the effects of sin.*

We grossly underestimate the power of deception both in regard to the extent of its presence in our lives and in regard to its effects on our heart and mind. As a result, we find ourselves spinning our wheels and unable to put our finger on the nature of the problems that so beset us. This is true even if we know a lot of theology or are heavily invested in a great deal of religious activity. Once we come to appreciate the nature of the relationship between belief, truth, and deception, the entire Christian venture begins to take on a new dimension of clarity and purpose that brings freedom and hope to our lives.

Ironic as it may be for a religion based on faith, most Christians have a rather poor understanding of how belief drives their life – which is precisely why deception has so much power. Unmasking the strategy of the enemy and engaging in the appropriate means for our restoration are absolutely essential to developing an effective approach to life as a Christian. That being the case, let us begin where this all began.

The Greatest Lies Ever Told

When Satan first decided to derail and destroy the human race, he did not come to Adam and Eve with some trivial temptation, trying to get them to do some bad thing in order to disobey God. Instead, he coughed up two of the most bold-faced lies ever crafted for evil intentions – a distorted image of God and a distorted image of the human self.

"You can be like gods" (as direct as could be).
"God is not to be trusted" (implied by his challenge).

Thus the enemy played his best hand. In response, Adam and Eve doubted God, desired what was unholy, and acted out of that desire. All this was possible even though they knew God, talked with him daily, and lived in a world completely free of human evil. They had none of the previous experience with sin, fallen nature, and unmet needs that now characterize our world, and yet they sinned.

How does that compare with where are we today? We now live in an entire culture of deceit, where the truth is made to stand on its head, evil is called good, and those who speak for truth are hated. Pervasive darkness covers the earth[4] making us easy prey for deception at all levels of life. The Bible speaks endlessly of the perils of being led astray, believing false teachers, and being blind to the truth.[5] From nearly every vantage point we see that deception is still the primary tactic used by the Father of Lies. Shocking as these two lies were to Adam and Eve, we now find ourselves in the tragic position of needing proof in order to *not* believe them.

Understanding that deception plays a central role in virtually every spiritual struggle admittedly requires a radical paradigm shift. But that one shift makes all the difference in how we are to be made whole. Because as long as we continue to focus on faulty behavior as our biggest problem, we will expend all of our energy trying to deal with the *effects* of sin without ever coming to grips with the underlying *causes* of sin.

Looking at this from the other side, deception's pivotal role in our lives is precisely why the Holy Spirit has the ministry of teaching truth to us and

[4] e.g. Mt.6:23; Jn.3:19; Rom.1:21; Eph.4:18.
[5] e.g. Mt.24:4-5,11; 2Cor.4:4; Eph.5:6; Col.2:8; 2Th.2:9-10; 2Tim.3:13.

why He is called the Spirit of Truth (Jn.16:13-15). It explains why Paul talks extensively about the need to renew our mind and our understanding,[6] and why Jesus claimed that the truth would set us free.[7] We can only act out of what we believe in our heart and out of the character that has been formed by the practice of those beliefs. Virtually everything about our life rests on the core beliefs we hold in regard to who we are, whose we are, and how we are meant to live.

When we are genuinely converted, the Holy Spirit cancels the contract we had with death and breathes new life into us that is not bound by the sin of our past. Instead of remaining on a downward trajectory, we are given a life of renewal and movement toward God.[8] But unless we get an idea of how pervasive deception is and how poor our current vision remains, we will continue to live in a perpetual state of confusion about how to grow up as Christians. That is why our old patterns continue to assert themselves.

In his book, *The Screwtape Letters,* C. S. Lewis gave us a wonderfully vivid picture of how pervasive this problem really is in our lives.[9] A demon apprentice named Wormwood was being trained by his demon uncle in the art of deception and temptation. By following Wormwood's education, we can observe a very narrow set of methods that are repeated over and over: *distract, distort, confuse, and misrepresent all elements of reality* to the person being targeted. There are dozens of examples of this strategy in the book, which is what makes it so enjoyable to read. We can all relate to the distortions presented by the demons which are meant to keep people off balance. But the book's real value is its comprehensiveness. It portrays deception as *a matter that affects every aspect of life*.

Now that all sounds rather dark. But the good news is that deception is a problem for which God has a solution – one that is not only highly effective, but is also amazingly accessible to all who will learn how to engage with God directly in order to renew their mind.

---

[6] Rom.8:5; 12:1-2; Eph.1:17-19; 4:17-24; Col.1:9-10, 21; 3:9-10.

[7] Jn.8:32; 17:17-19.

[8] "You have taken off your old self with its practices and have put on the new self, *which is being renewed* in knowledge in the image of its Creator." (Col.3:9-10, emphasis added).

[9] Lewis, *The Screwtape Letters*.

A Brief Overview of This Book

Throughout Part 1 of this book we will focus on the pervasiveness of deception, both as a theme in the Bible and as an everyday experience in our darkened world, including a detailed look at the destructive nature of deception and its impact on our lives. In Part 2 we will explore in depth the complex nature of belief, its relationship to truth and error, and why these things have so much power in our lives. Finally in Part 3 we will look at the nature of truth and some of the means by which we can deliberately pursue truth in ways that transform our soul and liberate us from bondage. In particular, we will examine some of the ways Christians have misused truth in the past, and why those approaches to change can actually hurt us as much as the problems we are trying to cure.

Identifying Deception as a Pervasive Force in Life

To begin our discussion, we must first lay out the extent to which our experiences in this world are altered by deception, and call attention to the incredible array of language that we use everyday to describe its impact on our lives. Although we do not always think of it this way, ***deception includes all of our perceptions or interpretations of reality that are incomplete or distorted in some way***. This goes far beyond the basic notion of being tricked or being tempted to sin. It includes nearly everything we think or believe that is in any way flawed, any misplaced emphasis on life issues or the various aspects of relationships, any foundational matter about which we are uncertain or confused, and even things that we simply do not know that we ought to know for the sake of a life well lived.

For example, if I believe that it is cool and fun to get blind, stinking drunk with my friends as often as possible, or that the rush of shoplifting is really a blast, everyone would probably agree that I lack some basic understanding. But I am also deceived if I am so overly-committed toward some worthy goal that I do not realize my marriage is suffering under the load, or if I think I am more important than I really am, or if I am convinced that God can barely stand me as a person.

Perhaps the most amazing thing about deception is that it is *so pervasive* and *so invisible* at the same time, saturating literally every aspect of human existence, yet we hardly notice it. *We are so accustomed to deception that we take it completely for granted, like breathing.* That is why its effects are so baffling to us, why we often feel so powerless, and why we assume that our perceptions of life are more accurate than they really are.

Deception takes a great many forms and we have many words to describe its various dimensions. The following is a very short list of some of the ways in which we experience this phenomenon.

• outright lies	• double standards
• mistaken goals	• false assumptions
• self-deception	• false dichotomies
• confusion	• misinterpretations of our experiences
• being led astray	• distorted images of God
• doubt / unbelief	• distorted images of self
• denial	• what I don't know about life
• misinformation	• twisted or distorted reality

References to deception permeate our language. Sometimes we focus on the absence of truth (which can be quite the same thing as believing a lie) while at other times we may speak of confusion or not knowing how to proceed. But to fully appreciate the extent of deception one must simply observe how truth and belief are interwoven with nearly every element of life. For example, the hope or despair we feel about the probable outcome of an event is heavily driven by and dependent on our sense of values, our judgment about the influence of various factors, and our beliefs about the likelihood of anything good happening to us. Hope and despair do not arise inevitably out of our circumstances, but primarily from the perceptions and interpretations we have of our life.

> Deception is pervasive yet invisible at the same time.

The entirety of our value system is dependent upon what we *believe* to be good and bad, either ethically or practically. And our discernment in any given situation is dependent upon those values as well as other beliefs regarding our options and the potential outcomes. If our beliefs are accurate, then our judgment will tend to be better. To the extent that our beliefs are distorted or poorly formed, our discernment will be faulty. Nearly every decision we make and every interaction we have with another person is related in some manner to what we believe about the various components of that event.[10]

Darkness Has Many Forms

Even a brief survey of our world demonstrates that deception is a major factor in a great many elements of life and thought for both Christians and non-Christians. We highlight here some of the more prominent ways in which deception presents itself. While this list is by no means exhaustive, hopefully it is sufficient enough to demonstrate the point that deception is everywhere we look and has a tremendous impact on all of us.

Philosophical. The history of philosophy is marked by tremendous shifts in thinking, many of which have been terribly misguided. From Plato's dualism to Nietzsche's nihilism and Marx's dialectical materialism, people have thought about ultimate reality in many ways, often with terrible consequences for humanity. Modernism is almost synonymous with faith in the power of science to solve the ills of society, a belief that has been seriously challenged only in the last generation or so. The more recent postmodern understanding of reality has often bordered on the absurd. Whatever validity postmodernism may have as a critique of modernism, many of its outrageous claims about the nature of truth and reality are in practice complete nonsense. Yet it has been treated as a credible interpretation of the world in many academic settings. Even more revealing is the fact that the whole debate between the modern and postmodern worldviews is a great example of a false dichotomy, which is another way of distorting the truth, since neither one is able to explain the meaning of life or establish the criteria for finding God.

Keep in mind that those who have little interest in formal philosophy cannot legitimately claim they are unaffected by it. Many people are under the mistaken assumption that they are free to choose their own worldview

---

[10] These nuances of truth and deception are also deeply embedded in the vocabulary we use to discuss many theological concepts. For a list of faith-related terms and how they relate to truth and error, please see the addendum.

without any interference from what others think about those things. The truth is that we are so inundated by the ideas that have been hammered out before we were born, that we are not even aware of their influence. All we need to do is look at how the materialism and hedonism of Hollywood have inundated much of the popular culture. Or notice how the near total absence of any mention of God or Christianity in the public sphere has bestowed a virtual agnosticism upon an entire generation.

Like any other ideas that propagate throughout a culture, philosophical distortions have a profound impact on how we think about life.

Ideological. Common ideologies that we take for granted are often quite flawed. For example, most of us in the West have been raised from birth with a deep respect and admiration for *individualism*. Most of us believe that the primary indicators of maturity are independence and self-sufficiency. If offered the opportunity to live in a community where meals and goods are shared, most people have very strong negative reactions and voice concerns about finances and privacy. Yet living in a highly relational community was the norm throughout most of history. Only in recent decades have we begun to appreciate the great cost we have paid both individually and corporately for the loss of community. Unfortunately, we have been so thoroughly shaped by our pervasive individualistic ideology that most people are completely unaware of how much of their internal belief system is at odds with their own basic need for interdependent relationships.

Three other ideologies that are closely related to each other also dominate the Western worldview – secularism, pluralism, and relativism. The complete *secularization* of public life is today considered normal and preferable. We have elevated the state to the place of a religion and banned all others from having a voice in critiquing society and government. While no one wants to resurrect a medieval version of Christendom, there is no reason why Christian thought should be banned from public debate. After all, Western culture as we know it would not even exist without the influence of Christian ideals, and the wisdom of Christianity has much to offer our confused and wayward society.[11]

---

[11] See D'Souza, *What's So Great About Christianity* for a thorough analysis.

Pluralism has grown in complexity and meaning over the last couple of centuries into a belief that now has all the force of Newtonian physics. The politically correct view of religion today is that they are all equally meaningful or meaningless, depending on your point of view. But under no circumstances can one religion be held to be more correct, or a better reflection of ultimate reality, or the only way to God. The one thing that is intolerable in religion today is any claim to be the one true faith. It is considered extremely offensive to speak of one's faith in such a way, about on par with lighting up a cigar in a California restaurant.

Relativism is the belief that no absolutes exist at all, that there is no such thing as absolute truth, or at most, such truth is unknowable. Everyone has their own interpretation of ultimate reality, and it is impossible to arbitrate between them or determine the accuracy of any one of them. One of the most significant consequences of this belief is that human morality no longer has a norm, because there are no timeless principles that can be known or applied in order to determine what is good and right.

Combined, these ideologies form a pervasive spirit of disbelief that blankets our world and not only blinds people to the truth, it encourages active resistance to what is true, especially to the claims of Christianity. As a result, Christians are often afraid to speak about their faith for fear of humiliation, rejection, or worse. And for many, the underlying fear of being attacked or ostracized can actually erode confidence in their own beliefs.

Materialistic. Materialism is clearly one of the most powerful forces in Western society. People spend many years beyond high school preparing themselves to compete for a share of the goods and services that are available only to the very successful. Investments, portfolios, holdings, and earnings – we have literally hundreds of terms for wealth and how it is managed. It drives our choices, feeds our lust, and determines our social status. Yet it is largely a false hope for happiness, because it cannot deliver much of what it promises. One very competent entrepreneur recently told me, "More than anything else, my success at making money has brought me the fear of losing money."

Materialism has always been a major distortion of what it means to have a good life. It bends our perception of the world and distracts us from those things that truly matter.

Religious/Spiritual. A great many types of deception also fall under the category of religion, apart from the religious pluralism described above. In the general culture, a common form of religious deception is the idea that everyone has the freedom to decide what is true about the 'god' he or she wants to believe in. One often hears comments such as, "My god is not like that, he (or she) is much more [fill-in-the-blank]" as if God were no more and no less than what some person would find acceptable. The idea that there might be things about God that are true whether a person believes them or not, is either inconceivable or offensive. A god who meets my felt needs or who affirms my desires is permissible, whereas a God who has the authority to define what is good or a God who wants to change my life is not allowed to exist. And this problem is not limited to non-Christians. Even believers have a tendency to reduce God to various categories, such as someone who primarily takes care of their happiness, comfort, or afterlife, or as a cosmic policeman who sets up and enforces the rules.[12]

One of the more pervasive religious distortions regards our general accommodation to the world. An alarming number of Christians are very prone to viewing their faith much like a cafeteria plan. They pick and choose which values they wish to adopt from Scripture and which they will adopt from the dominant culture. This eclectic approach to faith is only possible because of the unexamined assumption that *we* are in charge of our doctrine, dogma, and morals rather than God. Much of its appeal lies in the ability to blend in with the surrounding culture, minimize our discomfort, and still hold the illusion of being Christian-like in one's behavior.

At the other end of the spectrum is another problem that has plagued Christianity from its inception, and that is *legalism*. Properly understood, the Christian life contains a great deal of tension between the now and not-yet, between the seen and unseen worlds, between what we have been called from and what we are called to, between being *in* the world but not *of* the world, and so on. There is a strong tendency to reduce these tensions to a set of rules or narrowly defined principles rather than to do the continuous work of navigating through the complexities of life day after day.

However, these rules can easily lead us to a moralistic religion of self-effort dependent upon a strong will. Everything is then interpreted in terms

---

[12] see J.B. Phillips, *Your God is Too Small.*

of whether it is absolutely right or wrong. And once there, it is extremely hard to get out of that mindset because everything else looks like relativism. If "being right" is the highest priority, then not only do these rules make some kind of perverse sense, any competing model of following Christ would have to prove itself to be *more right* in order to be acceptable. In contrast to that way of thinking, true Spirit-led living requires a complete shift toward another way of approaching life, not just better answers. Thus the need to be "right" can paradoxically become a form of blindness.

Then there are religious distortions regarding what we can expect from our Christian experience. Occasionally, I encounter Christians who are waiting for God to take *total control* of their life. By this they mean that their will would virtually evaporate as God took possession of their body, making every thought, action, and word an inspired event. But this is a false hope that is destined to failure. No such complete takeover exists anywhere in Scripture. God does not violate our will. In fact, the continual desire and choice to engage with God is precisely what we are called to learn. Waiting for God to pull the strings is an abdication of the responsibility He has given us, and a major distortion of what the Christian life should be about.

Another area of deception can be seen by the way in which Kingdom life as it is portrayed in the Gospels is commonly dismissed as merely visionary or as an impossible ideal. Relatively few churches teach that such a life is actually possible, or that ongoing personal transformation is supposed to be a normal part of the Christian experience. Few can explain how transformation occurs at all, apart from abstract references to some vague work of the Holy Spirit. Fewer still can demonstrate or live out this life we are promised. The confusion around this issue puts spiritual growth virtually out of reach for the vast majority of Christians, at least when growth is defined in terms of character change and not reduced to acquiring ministry skills or mastering Christian doctrine. It is yet another symptom of spiritual deception permeating the Christian world.

Still other forms of spiritual confusion exist that get in the way of true spiritual development. For example, anyone who has tried to listen for the voice of God knows full well the difficulty of telling the difference between God's voice and their own internal tapes from self, parents, and teachers. It is also difficult to insure that one's own motives and desires are not being interpreted as confirmation from God about some issue.

Regarding spiritual practices that can aid our spiritual development, until recently relatively few Christians could correctly explain the nature of spiritual disciplines and how they differ from self-effort or religious habits.[13]

Religious distortions abound, and we have only scratched the surface. These lies are particularly insidious, because they masquerade as the truth and present a misshapen image of the gospel to the world as well as to the people in our churches who are sincerely looking for answers.

> Religious lies are particularly insidious.

Personal or Subjective. Several types of deception are best categorized as personal distortions of the world. One example is our ability to hold *double standards*, or to condemn others for the very things we ourselves engage in. This is a form of self-deception that we have all practiced and manage to accomplish through various levels of rationalization and simple blindness.

If we look closer we see that the ability to hold double standards is really a special case of a much larger problem, one that is crucial to understanding Christian character formation. One of the most important aspects of deception is *our ability to believe two or more conflicting things at the same time*. The most common symptom of this is when we believe one thing deep inside while professing another thing with our conscious mind. We can do this because belief is not the same thing as confession. In many churches people are actually encouraged to profess things they do not really believe.

For example, I can hold deep resentments toward God because of things that have happened in my life which I think He should have prevented in some way. Yet when asked, I might tell myself and others that I believe God is always good (because that is what I'm *supposed* to believe). I might even be able to quote verses to support that.

If asked, I might say that God loves me so much I can come to Him just as I am without proving myself worthy. Yet when I really mess up I might spend days or weeks trying to run or hide from Him because I feel so much

---

[13] This has changed dramatically since the publication of Willard's, *The Spirit of the Disciplines.*

shame. My professed doctrine and my internal system are at odds with each other, because what we truly believe in our heart and what we think we believe can be two different things.[14]

Another important area of personal deception are those implicit beliefs that we hold deeply but are unable to name. A person who was poorly nurtured as a child may have deep underlying feelings of rejection or of being unlovable, feelings that may never be consciously expressed, yet result in many choices as an adolescent or adult that contribute to isolation and relational cutoffs. Such emotions do not arise out of nothing. They come from deeply held convictions about one's identity that may have been formed even before the person had a vocabulary with which to name the beliefs. These types of internalized implicit beliefs can make it very difficult to relate to God or other people.

> We can readily hold
> two or more conflicting beliefs
> at the same time.

Or consider the case of a person who grew up in an environment of constant physical or emotional violence. The child may have interpreted those experiences in ways that led to persistent fear or self-hatred which has been reinforced hundreds of times in subsequent events, resulting in deeply seated beliefs as an adult regarding how he or she will never fit well into any divine plan. This person's distorted sense of self then exerts tremendous influence on every interaction they have with others, even though they may be largely unaware of their own brokenness.

Virtually all of the characteristics we normally ascribe to dysfunctional families have profound impact on the identity formation of children. Which is to say that most of us grow up with distorted beliefs about who we are, how we matter, and what we can expect of life. Yet these implicit beliefs can remain unidentified for an entire lifetime, even in people who consciously subscribe to better propositions when they are old enough to recognize these problems.

---

[14] Willard, *Renovation of the Heart*, p. 88.

Holding beliefs like this can have serious implications for spiritual growth. As we shall see later, what we are convinced of internally affects our choices, feelings, and behavior. And acting on distorted beliefs releases destructive power in our life, keeps us in bondage, and disrupts all of our relationships, including our relationship to God.

Cognitive. There are many ways that we commonly think about the world that are simply poor perceptions of reality. One example is that of an *egocentric* worldview. Most adolescents have this down to a fine art, and often make statements like these:

- My parents are completely stupid.
- If I can't go out Friday night I will die.
- Why do I have to do everything?

Similar examples of faulty thinking can be seen in *black-and-white*, all-or-nothing patterns of thought, such as:

- Nothing ever goes right for me.
- Things will never change.
- I'm right and everyone else is wrong.

Distorted thinking is also quite common in our practical theology. A good example of this can be seen where sin is viewed primarily as a matter of disobedience or failure of the will. People get divided into two groups – those who are "obedient" and live up to a proper moral standard and those who are disobedient, self-centered and careless about the law of God. This is a distorted understanding of both obedience and sin. While there may be people who fit that description of sin, such a simplistic view does serious harm to those who are in bondage to addictions or other destructive patterns and find themselves unable to get free. Shaming and condemning people without offering any accessible means of change and transformation that would release them from their misery actually makes life more difficult for them. Telling a person who struggles that they can correct their problems by simply making a decision to do so is actually a form of spiritual abuse, because the truth is their will has been overrun by the very problems which they are expected to overcome by willpower.

Cognitive deception can also be the result of being presented with limited alternatives. Unfortunately, this happens quite frequently in religious literature. A writer who is attempting to make a particular point may set up a *false dichotomy* in which the opposing side is clearly a mistake, leaving the author's point of view as the only reasonable alternative. For example, there are a number of Christian leaders today who speak out very strongly against the practice of contemplative prayer. In their attempts to add fire to their critique they will often describe in great detail a number of New Age practices along with the many evils of acquiescing to New Age beliefs. The only options they leave to their readers are to either agree with them or be guilty of embracing New Age ideas.

The problem, of course, is that they have not actually described contemplative prayer at all. Instead, they have setup an ugly portrait of something else, labeled it contemplative prayer, and asked their readers to choose between the two alternatives they offer. It is blatantly a false dichotomy. A true third alternative exists, which is the practice of fully Christian, completely biblical, historically proven, contemplation with God. The psalmists talk about it all the time, as do many of the great Christians of the past two thousand years. To present it as something evil in order to persuade people to reject it is a classic example of deception at work.

Another form of faulty thinking is *rationalization.* Everyone engages in rationalization from time to time. We use it to justify our choices, to spend money unwisely, to treat others in ways we would rather not be treated, and to get us off the hook in many ethically questionable situations. These are all very clever ways of distorting reality and confusing the issues. The hallmark of rationalization is the intent to protect one's position rather than search for truth.

Summary

This brief survey is by no means exhaustive, but it does begin to demonstrate the many ways in which deception invades our lives. There is virtually no aspect of knowledge or values that is immune from its impact. It is pervasive in its breadth of influence and in the extent of its distortions. As a direct result, our perceptions of the world become deeply flawed.[15]

---

[15] Mulholland, *Shaped by the Word*, p. 103.

Darkness Has Many Sources

In the previous section the emphasis was on the many *forms* with which deception presents itself. Here we will see that its origins include nearly every corner of our world. What follows is a brief look at *sources* of deception that we encounter every day. While some of these categories will overlap the above survey of types of deception, the focus here will be on where distorted messages come from rather than on the nature of the messages themselves.

Culture. We are all naturally embedded in our own cultural context to such an extent that it shapes our thinking in innumerable ways that we have little awareness of, even when we consciously attempt to be counter-cultural. Much of what we consider to be the "normal" way of living and interacting with others is nothing more than the conventions of the culture in which we live. We grow up with the social values that we see around us and simply assume that this is how the world works. Most of these things have no moral significance at all, such as the practice of eating with a fork instead of our fingers, or cutting our hair in a popular style. But culture also holds values that have moral connotations or speak to our identity in some way, and these can be either positive or negative.

For example, some people give a lot of attention to what labels are on their clothes and think more or less of themselves depending on the labels they wear. Others are very conscious about the make and model of the car they own and the statement their car makes about their social status and level of success. Virtually all of our penchant for consumerism, self-centeredness, and self-indulgence is encouraged by the surrounding culture.

The values that most Westerners have regarding *sexuality* are derived much more from culture and the entertainment industry than from any established moral value system. In fact the messages are so strong and so deeply entrenched in our thinking that almost any attempt to address sexual values from a spiritual point of view is now regarded as ridiculous or offensive. We tend to assume complete autonomy in regard to determining for ourselves what is proper or improper sexual behavior, and for the most part we take our cues from what is considered acceptable by the larger society. I almost hesitate to bring up the issue here for fear of losing a great many readers, because these beliefs are so much a part of our emotional makeup. But the truth is that the sexual norms of our culture are a far cry from the principles we derive from Scripture.

The most that can be said for contemporary sexual values is that there exists a respect of sorts for individual consent, but then only because of our overall belief in personal autonomy. The key idea is that people should not engage in sexual behavior until they are "ready," which means when they feel like they want to. However, even this is a mixed message, because the corollary to this dictum is that virtually all well-adjusted mature adults are sexually active. Only losers and the immature are celibate.

Some time ago I saw a women's magazine on a newsstand that had a subtitle on the cover that read, "10 Dates Before Sex and Other Secrets." Apparently the editors of the magazine thought they were announcing some previously unheard-of strategy for successful relationships by suggesting that people wait to have sex until they have had at least ten dates with someone. What does it say about our culture if such a concept is considered a novel improvement in relationship strategy?

Still, that is barely scratching the surface. Consider the issue of what it means to be "sexy." Just a few years ago, appearing in public in an overtly sexy outfit was viewed as brazen and morally loose. Today it is seen as a flattering style of clothing. One of the biggest complements a young girl can receive is to be called a "hottie" by her peers.

What all of this says about our views of sex is staggering. Yet these values have become so prevalent that Christians have been carried away by them as well. Today it is the voices for modesty and chastity that are considered extreme or distorted. In our current cultural climate, feelings are sacred and sexual power is an asset to be used to gain status, approval and pleasure. The characteristics that have fallen from virtue are self-control and higher morality.

Which brings us to the greater issue of belief in *personal autonomy* that is so pervasive and unquestionable that it has all the makings of socially enforced secular religion. Although individualism was discussed earlier as a type of deception, it is necessary to make the point again in relation to the power of social pressure to form our values. At one level, we are pushed into accommodating specific values for fear of being ostracized. On another level, we are repeatedly shown by example and by the larger machinations of society that we all possess the godlike quality of deciding for ourselves what is good and evil. And it is this broader assault that seeps into the soul like a solvent penetrating the skin, until we view everything around us in terms of its usefulness for our own agenda.

Another example of this can be seen in the *social values* of pluralism and "tolerance." Christian ideals today have been largely marginalized by the tremendous social pressure to regard all religions as equal in value, and by the social condemnation that is heaped on anyone who says that God has a claim on our lives. The public charge of "intolerance" (and now "hate speech") has the power to generate instant rejection and contempt for whoever is guilty of the charge. The fact that all of this is rooted in a distorted understanding of both God and religion is not even addressable, because any attempt to clarify the issue draws more condemnation.

In very few areas does the ability of culture to *redefine terms* become any clearer than in its use of the term "tolerance," not to mention the power wielded by those definitions. The word "tolerant" *pretends* to mean that one does not pass judgment on another's views, or at least that one does not cause harm to others because of the views which they hold. However, there are a couple of exceptions that are not tolerated.

First, no critical evaluation of one worldview by another is allowed (unless you are criticizing Christianity, which is perfectly permissible). Second, no spiritual view is allowed to claim to be the sole truth because that implies a negative evaluation of other views. But notice the double standard embedded in that definition. This so-called tolerance is essentially an *imposed* pluralistic understanding of religion with the added feature that any religion that does not have a pluralistic foundation is unacceptable. No one is allowed to define universal terms except those who declare all religions to be relative and devoid of knowable truth. The irony of this situation is astounding. Those who preach "tolerance" the loudest are the first ones to use the force of government to control what comes out of your mouth. Yet they paint themselves as the ones who are making society more safe. This misuse of language and distortion of public dialogue has thus become a tremendous source of confusion and deception.

Unmasking the double standard behind tolerance is just one example of the pervasive willingness in our culture to call evil *good* and good *evil*. These distortions are not benign and they are able to impact our thinking in ways we barely notice.

The Material World. Wall Street, Fifth Avenue, and the New York Stock Exchange dominate much of our attention and energy. These icons are the very embodiment of success for all healthy, competitive-minded Americans. Financial independence is a highly coveted goal, with rewards given to the smartest, the swiftest, and the most creative. "He who dies with the most toys wins" reads the well-known bumper sticker. And we have all dreamed of what we would do if only we had a few million dollars to work with.

This great American dream is related to bigger issues including the lust for power and the need to compete in order to prove one's personal worth. Status and prestige are dependent on performance, whether in the sports arena or the board room. On the scale of relevant virtues, contentment is viewed as precariously close to laziness. Those who lack the "killer instinct" are therefore less valuable players. Almost no one is rewarded for being honorable or having integrity. Books by Steven Covey may sit in the corporate library, but most of the time the politics of profit take priority.

Not that there is anything wrong with hard work and excellence. But Western culture has turned those virtues into self-serving vices that pit people against one another and elevate covetousness and greed. Christians are in no way immune from this pressure to prove oneself in the marketplace. Most only pay lip service to the truth that life does not consist in the abundance of our possessions (Lk.12:15) or that expending all of our energy in pursuit of earthly satisfaction is a distortion of our life purpose. Mammon is truly a harsh task master, and few who make the accumulation of wealth their primary goal can avoid making it their god. We even occasionally claim the title of "good steward" in our pursuit of financial rewards. Thus the material world has become for us a tremendous source of pressure that distorts meaning and value.

Life Experience. Of all the sources of deception, perhaps the most forceful is that of our own life experience, especially in early childhood. As infants and children, we search for ways of making sense of the world. Most days bring either new things we have never experienced before or new ways of interpreting familiar people and events. And while children are great observers, they are very poor interpreters.[16] They simply lack the wisdom and experience to make good judgments about what they see and feel. So a great deal of life is internalized in distorted ways, full of misunderstood meanings and incomplete messages. This of course is made much worse by the fact that the world they are attempting to make sense of has already been badly distorted before it is presented to them.

Imagine, if you will, something as simple as a family in which the parents have grown tired of the task of parenting and have opted instead for making the children conform to the adults' needs and wants. At that point, what ought to have been creative teaching moments over childish mistakes become power encounters in which the parents' primary objective is to produce compliance. Efforts the children might make to explore new ways of interacting are discouraged, moments of excitement are crushed in favor of a quiet house, and curiosity is punished because of its inconvenience.

A child in this scenario may interpret these experiences in a number of ways. Perhaps there is something terribly wrong with himself; there is no way to be himself around other people; the needs of others are more important than his. Or he may simply remain confused about why desires that seem so innocent to him turn out to be so unacceptable to Mom and Dad. Instead of becoming more of who God created him to be, the child must expend more and more of his energy learning how to cope with an environment that is unsympathetic or even hostile to his development. Any effort to make sense of his context can distort his worldview even further.

Life events that impact us adversely can generally be divided into several categories: *intrusions, deprivations, and our own mistakes*. Almost everything bad that happens *to us* in life is experienced as either intrusion or deprivation, or even both intrusion and deprivation simultaneously. These injuries come in many forms such as physical, emotional, spiritual, or psychological traumas. For example, indiscriminately hitting a child is an intrusive *physical* assault, while never holding or touching a child in a loving manner is physical deprivation. Constantly shaming or degrading a child is *emotional* intrusion, and never showing affection is emotional deprivation.

---

[16] One of Alfred Adler's insights into the motivations of children.

We could go on. One form of *spiritual* intrusion is to involve a child in various forms of evil. Deprivation would be to withhold or limit spiritual guidance. An example of *psychological* intrusion would be to break a child's spirit, while deprivation would be the failure to teach boundaries or a balanced self-image. All of these forms of intrusion and deprivation distort children's understanding of themselves, the world, their parents, the meaning of love, and a host of other things.

> A person's entire worldview can be distorted
> by intrusions and deprivations.

The conclusions children derive from life experience are often extremely detrimental to further development and growth. Very early in life children come to believe such things as: I am only as good as I perform, mistakes are inexcusable, anything I say or do will be used against me, I don't need other people, I can manage better by myself (it's safer that way), or girls are desirable and boys are not (or the opposite). In short, a person's entire worldview can be malformed by various wounds caused by intrusion and deprivation. The result can be all manner of emotional and psychological issues, difficulty bonding or relating with others, fearfulness, distorted images of self and God, and many other problems that can last a lifetime.

In addition to the wrongs done to us, there are the wrongs that we ourselves have committed. While this area will be explored in more detail later under the topic of Malformation, we will take a moment here to look at the fundamental connection between sin and deception. First, it is important to note that the relationship is reciprocal or circular in nature. Deception will lead us to sin, and sin will breed deception. This is most clearly seen in the arena of addictions, which once they are fully active, are basically ongoing sins committed against one's own person.[17] The self-destructive nature of these actions wounds a person's own soul, while the payoff that one gets from the addiction provides the basis for self-deception. The alcoholic who drinks in order to medicate some unnamed emotional pain does so because he believes that the substance "works" in

---

[17] Please note that this does not address the *origins* of addiction, which are another matter entirely.

spite of its down side, and because it is relatively quick and predictable. But there are many lies embedded in this belief: (1) This is the best way to deal with the pain now; (2) I can always quit later; (3) I can control the negative effects; (4) the negatives are not that bad; and so on. The truth is, underlying problems are not being dealt with, more problems are being created, the addicted person is fighting reality, the body is being abused, and relationships are being damaged. These additional problems and lies can easily lead to a deeper dependence on the alcohol, and so the cycle continues to spiral downward.

This cycle is true of most sin. When a middle school girl tries shoplifting for the thrill of it, she may quickly become overwhelmed by lies. First, there are the lies that led her to make such a faulty choice in the first place – that it will be fun, that no one is really getting hurt, or that it demonstrates her daring. Then once the deed is done, she may suddenly think she is very clever indeed, or if her conscience is working overtime, that she has done something that is very nearly unforgivable. She may further rationalize her actions to downplay the seriousness of what she is doing. In any case, lies are an important part of why we miss the mark, and sin in turn can act as a vehicle for lies to penetrate one's soul.

The point is that we all become embroiled in lies through life experience, whether by things we do or the things that happen to us, and even things we have left undone or things that ought to have happened but did not. No matter what we are doing or who we are interacting with, our mind is continuously asking, "What does this mean?" And whatever conclusions we arrive at can become extremely hard to dislodge due to the nature of this experiential learning. So as adults we may find ourselves with any number of spiritual difficulties for which we are unable to identify a source cause, but which affect us nonetheless because we have internalized some very specific lies many years previously.

Family. A very powerful subset of culture and life experience as a source of deception comes from our family of origin. Of course we may learn a great many good things from our family, such as common cultural courtesies and etiquette, how to walk and talk and do many of the things people should know how to do, and many basic values such as how to share and how to make and keep friends. At the same time, our parents also teach us whatever distortions they have of life, and provide ample opportunity for us to arrive at still more faulty ideas. The more spiritually misguided or impoverished the family is, the more deceived the child will be in regard to important issues of life.

In a small child's world, adults are very nearly omnipotent and possess the ability to easily overpower anything the child can do. From these powerful adults children learn about the uses of power and what it means to have it, which can greatly influence later thinking about who God is and what He will do. These flawed adults are also the source for all sorts of values that the child must learn: what is right and wrong, what is praiseworthy and what is not, what is shameful or embarrassing, what must be kept secret and what can be said out loud.

To whatever extent a parent has unresolved issues, they will usually be transmitted to the child in one of two ways. One possibility is that the child will internalize the parents' values as if there were no other way that things should be. This can be as blatant as racial hatred or as subtle as never apologizing for mistakes. Another way in which an issue can get passed from one generation to the next is when the child overreacts in an opposing direction which may be equally flawed in other ways. For example, overly permissive parents may raise children who are so out of control that one or more of those siblings may become an overly authoritarian parent in an attempt to avoid that issue in their own family. Either way, the parents' unresolved problems cause children to internalize a great many distortions of who they are, who God is, how to relate to others, and what the main issues of life are about.

Furthermore, family is the primary source of life experience for the child, which means that the overall family system will greatly shape the child's worldview. If there is a lot of violence in the home, the children may internalize a great deal of fear and mistrust as if those were the basic building blocks of life. If the adults are continuously critical and disgusted with the children, the children will most likely assume that they themselves are defective rather than come to the conclusion that the adults in the home are in need of help. If they do make the discovery that their parents are deeply flawed, they may internalize a great deal of contempt for the world at large, or develop a deep hatred of their origins that again distorts their understanding of life.

At the very core of our development are the ways we learn from infancy to interpret and respond to significant people in our life. Since much of our identity is shaped by our attachment pattern[18] and by how we experience the ways others respond to us, any imperfections that exist in our family members can greatly distort how we interpret our own value and place in the world, as well as what we can expect from life and those around us.

A Darkened Mind. Once we have been deceived in one area, we can extend that lie by reason and inference, giving it power in other areas of our life. For example, suppose I get the message that I am not a lovable person. The next logical step might be that no matter what I do, I will never be able to make people like me. One more step might lead me to the conclusion that it does not matter how I treat people, since the result will be rejection anyway. After that, there are any number of destructive patterns of relating to others that could develop. The whole process is simply a logical extension of the first faulty presupposition.

Accepting one lie also weakens our ability to withstand others. If I am told as a child that I have no common sense, I might believe that I am defective in some way that most other people are not. Later on if I have a stressful conflict that results in the loss of a friendship, I may very well apply the same premise and assume that I am simply defective in my ability to sustain friendships.

This process can be very crippling, depending on the nature of the lies believed. For example, if a child is made to experience deep shame every time she makes a mistake of any magnitude, she may adopt any number of related beliefs and behaviors. She may become an extreme perfectionist who feels excessively anxious at the slightest imperfection. Basic self-examination may become so painful that she is unable to grow in necessary areas of life. Or she may internalize deep feelings of self-hate and self-rejection. Thus the initial distorted experiences can become a malignant lie that grows into a complex system of self-protection that becomes self-defeating and fertile ground for further distortions of life.

---

[18] Clinton and Sibcy, *Attachments*.

Christian Institutions. We may not want to admit it, but many of our churches and Christian colleges today are significant sources of deception in key areas of life. Ever since the inception of the Church, keeping the gospel pure of distortions and misconceptions has been a struggle. Paul's letter to the Galatians is filled with pleas for returning to the liberating message that he had delivered to them and to reject the legalism that the Judaizers were trying to introduce into the gospel. One and a half millennia later, Martin Luther nailed his ninety-five theses to the door of a church, exposing the excesses and outright lies that were being perpetuated at that time. Resistance to his critique was so intense that it split the Western Church and led to many years of hatred and violence between Christians.

Of course, Christian organizations today are still as vulnerable to misinformation and spiritual deception as they were then. By omission or commission, there are many false principles that are explicitly taught or implied by actual practice that cause people to spend years in fruitless confusion about how to relate to God. To name just a few examples:[19]

- Transformation is relatively rare, and I have little to do with it.
- If I am spiritual enough, nothing bad will happen to me.
- If I have God, I don't need people.
- Christians should not have emotional problems.
- Those who struggle spiritually have some moral defect.

The list of problems does not end there. Many of these beliefs have become so accepted in some places that to call them lies would disturb a lot of people who are convinced they are true. For example, there are many who believe that any true Christian can live the life described in the New Testament if they just care enough and try hard enough. If you fail in some area it is only because you lack commitment or are willfully disobedient. A person who is unable to forgive his father for being emotionally absent may be told he is simply refusing to do what God has said he must do. Little regard is given to the wound in his soul that needs the healing hand of God that would make it possible for him to forgive from his heart. This legalistic approach to life's problems has done irreparable harm to many people, and

---

[19] See also, Townsend and Cloud, *12 Christian Beliefs That Can Drive You Crazy*.

is the force behind much of the partice of "shooting our own wounded," which is more common in the church than we might think.

Another place where we find serious deception at work in the Church is in the whole area of spiritual growth and sanctification. These concepts are so poorly taught by so much of the Church that most Christians have virtually no idea how to participate effectively in their own growth. It is just assumed that going to church, reading the Bible and praying will somehow change a person's character over time. Those who discover that these approaches work for a while but usually do not deliver over time are often told they are not sincere enough or that they have some personal problem that needs attention. So we are left with a spiritually impoverished Church full of Christians who have no idea how to make the gospel more relevant. Many of them come to the conclusion that Christianity is mostly about holding to a set of doctrines and trying to be good, or at least look good. This distorted understanding of the gospel bears its ugly fruit in the form of immaturity and self-righteousness, a witness the world can only reject.

More will be said later in Chapter 8 about the problems we have in regard to spiritual growth and sanctification. For now, let it suffice to say that many of our most able theologians today have difficulty articulating a coherent understanding of how we grow spiritually and, in particular, how we can deliberately engage with God in the process. This inability to offer an understandable and accessible means for change has left our churches with Christians who are disillusioned with their lives and have no idea what to do about it. What's more, most leaders do not know how to help them.

The Enemy's War on Truth. Besides all of the sources of deception that have been examined so far, there is another that has become much more overt in recent generations – the frontal assault on truth that is being waged by the enemy. From the world of philosophy we are suffering from the aftermath of Nietzsche's nihilism and his campaign to declare that "God is dead," as well as the work of others who opened the door to the now-common belief that there is no absolute truth. We see this resistance to truth most pointedly today in the anger and contempt that gets unleashed at anyone making absolute truth claims or statements in favor of traditional values, and in the way that people adamantly demand their right to declare for themselves what is moral and what is not.

In the sociopolitical realm, we have seen the gradual adoption of the idea that government is our best hope for salvation, for solving the problems that science alone has been unable to deal with, while paradoxically at the same time our politicians seem less and less concerned about truth and integrity. We have witnessed one of the most blatant spin campaigns in history generated by Planned Parenthood and its allies, distorting and lying about virtually every aspect of the debate on abortion in order to justify their terrible agenda. And we are still reeling from the social revolution of the sixties which threw out all sense of history and centuries of classical wisdom in the name of personal freedom. These were all conscious efforts to challenge the truths that were known at the time.

More recently we have seen a precipitous rise in the visibility of the occult. Movies are released almost weekly about vampires, witches, or other paranormal phenomena. Many shows that do not deal with the occult explicitly find ways to insert Tarot cards, astrology, and the like into the lives of the characters in ways that make these things look as normal as making dinner. Satanists openly proclaim their presence and cults abound. Westerners today are clearly fascinated by evil and its many forms.

Anyone willing to view our situation objectively can see that we are experiencing what could be described as a deliberate coordinated attack on Christian truth and values. Lies and deception are used to promote darkened worldviews that are insidious, bold, and rash. Anyone who speaks against the assault is targeted and discredited. Tremendous social pressure is applied to make allegiance to the truth a costly venture, to the extent that many people will not even question the point of view being presented and are carried away by the distorted interpretations of reality.

When we take the time to stop and look at our world, the pervasiveness of deception is undeniably everywhere and affects everyone. Being a good student of Scripture offers only so much protection, as the stories in the Bible demonstrate quite well. As we will see throughout the rest of this book, we need much more than exposure to truth on the printed page in order to renew our mind and become more Christ-like. These facts did not escape the Biblical authors, and in this next segment we will look at the extent to which the issue of deception is addressed in Scripture.

Chapter 2
The Truth about Lies

From cover to cover the Bible is literally filled with the twin themes of truth and deception. We rarely call attention to this fact for two reasons. First, most of the time deception is simply assumed by the authors and therefore is not pointed out. It would be overstating the obvious, like noticing that the characters in the story were alive and not dead. The second reason is that we as Christians are blind to our own condition of pervasive unbelief and have long since convinced ourselves that we already have a corner on the truth because we believe the Bible. But when we stop to look at how extensively the Bible itself deals with the issue of deception, it becomes extremely obvious that this is no small matter.

How the Bible Views Deception

Belief and Unbelief. One of the single greatest motifs of Scripture is the interplay between belief and unbelief. The classic case is that of Israel refusing to enter the promised land after their initial contact with its inhabitants. Sometimes teachers misinterpret this event and suggest a rebellious spirit is the cause for their error, when the real reason they did not attempt to enter was because they did not believe it was possible.[20] Their unbelief was the root cause for their rebellion and disobedience.

What we often miss, though, is that unbelief is not just a lack of belief, like some sort of vacuum. It is actually itself a form of belief, specifically belief in a lie due to deception.[21] In the case of Israel's turning back from the land, they believed a number of lies: the giants are too strong, the cities are too impenetrable, we will all die if we go in there, God must really hate us, Moses has led us here for nothing, and so on (Deut.1:27-28). They believed only what they could see and figure out on their own.

---

[20] "We see that they were not able to enter, because of their unbelief." (Heb.3:19).

[21] William James, "The Will to Believe", cited by Dallas Willard (dwillard.org).

Since the basic issue at stake was their trust in God, the story is written and viewed by later authors as one of unbelief. But from a practical standpoint, this was not a matter of *whether or not* they believed, but rather *what* they believed. They were really divided between two sets of beliefs. As it turned out, the majority of them were deceived and believed a false view of their circumstances. Or to put it another way, their interpretation of the raw data was completely mistaken, yet they were convinced that they had arrived at the proper understanding of the situation. God tried to tell them to trust Him instead of their own perceptions, but they believed the faulty version of the facts.

> *Unbelief* is actually belief in a lie.

This point can also be seen in the reaction of various groups of people to the ministry of Jesus. There were those who believed Him and those who did not. Jesus expressed many times and in many ways the problem of belief among the people.[22] The central question of the Gospels, "Who do you say that I am?" is precisely a matter of what one believes about Jesus.

We know of course that belief is a primary factor in the whole issue of salvation as presented in the Gospels, Acts, and Romans in particular, as well as other places throughout Scripture. And conversely, belief in the wrong things can be disastrous. The question is not *whether* a person has "faith" but in *what or whom* that person places his or her faith. If we believe the right things and align ourselves with them, we move toward life. If we believe faulty premises and align with them, we move toward death. Given that belief and unbelief are so central to our spiritual life and that what we put our faith in is of critical importance, it becomes obvious why truth and belief are fundamental issues of Scripture.

Blindness, Light and Darkness. Closely related to the theme of belief and unbelief are the metaphors of Light and Darkness that can be found throughout the Bible.[23] Jesus said that people who are spiritually blind walk or sit in darkness (Jn.12:35,46). Paul speaks often of people's minds being

---

[22] e.g. Jn.3:10-12; 5:38; 6:36; 8:45-46.

[23] Ps.82:5; Jn.1:5; Acts.26:18.

darkened (Eph.4:18), and for whatever reason, the apostle John was completely captivated by the Life and Light of Jesus, as can be seen throughout his gospel.

Darkness in Scripture is often used as a picture of ignorance[24] and not knowing where one is going,[25] and thus provides a very graphic symbol for deception. Unfortunately, this metaphor has often been misunderstood as "living in sin." Such an interpretation severely diminishes the dynamics of the text. When Scripture speaks of darkness, sin is usually viewed as the secondary effect. The main focus is on the fact that people cannot see where they are or where they are going. This is also what it means to be *lost*: not that people are going to hell, but that they have no idea where they are or how to get somewhere else and so they end up in the wrong place.

Closely related to the theme of darkness is that of spiritual blindness which causes a person to stumble.[26] Jesus drew a relationship between the blindness of the Pharisees and their mistaken practices and teachings. At Paul's conversion Jesus brought together the images of darkness and blindness to describe the way in which the truth of the gospel would cause the Gentiles to repent.[27]

In using the metaphors of darkness and blindness the Biblical authors clearly intended to describe a spiritual condition by way of an image that communicates more than anything else the inability to see or know what is out there, which way to go, or where one is actually headed. When we lack sufficient light to see by, or when our vision is clouded by our own distorted lenses, our best efforts at making choices and discerning direction become seriously impaired. As a result we become entangled in all kinds of bondage and evil.

Seen in this way, these images of darkness and light become very effective ways to illustrate the various consequences of deception and truth.

---

[24] "They understand nothing. They walk about in darkness" (Ps.82:5).

[25] "He deprives the leaders of the earth of their reason...they grope in darkness with no light" (Job.12:24-25).

[26] "They are blind guides. If a blind man leads a blind man, both will fall into a pit" (Mt.15:14) (also Isa.59:9-10).

[27] "To open their eyes and turn them from darkness to light" (Ac.26:17-18).

Lack of Knowledge. Often the Bible addresses the issue of spiritual ignorance very directly. Lack of wisdom, truth, and knowledge are all ways in which deception is described very explicitly in the Bible. The prophets took great pains to identify the lack of spiritual knowledge as one of the major causes for national self-destruction,[28] idolatry,[29] and the exile.[30] Jesus pointed out that lack of knowledge hinders Kingdom life.[31]

In fact Jesus was constantly challenging both the disciples' and Pharisees' understanding of reality, including such things as how they understood greatness, whether all suffering was a form of judgment, the purpose of the Sabbath, and how to respond to evil. His wisdom was necessary because the people lacked sufficient understanding of the spiritual world and how God designed us to live. The Sermon on the Mount (Mt.5:3-7:28) challenged their assumptions about life precisely because they were just as deceived as we are about what is true and important. For example, the reason it was necessary to tell us that it is impossible to serve two masters was because we really think we can.

Writers throughout Scripture call the people of God to an alternate understanding of reality that defines our true purpose,[32] because true knowledge about the ultimate nature of things is paramount to holy living, and any distortion or lack of knowledge (i.e., deception) leads to sin. This theme of spiritual knowledge literally permeates all of Scripture.

Deception in Biblical Eschatology. Deception also plays a major role in teachings about the last days.[33] The fate of many people will hang on whether they believe the truth or are deceived by the anti-Christ. Jesus warned His disciples not to believe any false Christs. Throughout the major prophetic passages in the New Testament it is abundantly clear that *the reason why evil will be so strong* at that time is because the people are greatly

---

[28] "My people are destroyed from lack of knowledge...a people without understanding will come to ruin!" (Hos.4:6,14).

[29] "Ignorant are those who carry about idols" (Isa.45:20).

[30] "Therefore my people will go into exile for lack of understanding" (Isa.5:13).

[31] "You have taken away the key to knowledge. You yourselves have not entered, and you have hindered those who were entering" (Lk.11:52).

[32] Mulholland, *Shaped By The Word*, p. 74.

[33] Mt.24:4-24; 2Th.2:9-12; Rev.13:14; 20:3-10.

deceived.[34] Thus in the climax of salvation history we have a strong emphasis on the fact that *evil is utterly dependent upon deception for its success*.

An Integrating Theme. The dual themes of truth and error permeate all of Scripture, and provide a continuity of thought that integrates many other themes. For example, the enemy is above all a deceiver,[35] and just as Satan is called the Father of Lies, the Holy Spirit is called the Spirit of Truth. These titles are not given lightly. They symbolize the great tension between good and evil. Good is always associated with a *true* representation of spiritual realities. Evil must always distort and confound those realities in order to seduce people into participating in their own self-destruction.

From Adam and Eve to the problems of Israel, to the light of the gospel, to the final prophetic acts of history, a major issue at stake is the nature of the perceptions that people hold in regard to God, themselves, and their future. It is here that truth and lies clash with full force in competition for our heart. Scripture is a record of these struggles over time and these forces are a major integrating theme of all spiritual conflict.

How We Come to Believe a Lie

No one sets out to purposely acquire a distorted sense of reality by making up or believing lies about God, life, and human nature. Yet everyone manages to internalize much of the darkness that exists in the world. How does this happen? As we said earlier, children are great observers but relatively poor interpreters. So we will begin by looking at the process by which children arrive at their distorted worldviews.

Primarily, values and beliefs are caught, not taught. Most of what children come to believe about the world is discovered through a process of experimentation and evaluation with a heavy dependence upon their primary caregivers to guide their interpretations.

In many cases, these internalized beliefs may be initially held quite loosely and remain open to revision for some time. Then as similar experiences receive the same response and interpretation, eventually the

---

[34] "False prophets...false teachers...destructive heresies...will bring the way of truth into disrepute...with stories they have made up" (2Pet.2:1-3).

[35] 2Jn.7; Rev.12:9.

beliefs become deeply embedded in the child's mind. Much of this actually results in very positive constructs with which to make sense of the world. For example, repeated admonitions will make very clear where the property lines are and what constitutes "staying in the yard" and what violates that rule. Watching Mom's reaction lets a child know that eating a doggie biscuit is disgusting. Through play times with friends a child figures out that "Bobby" is nice and "Johnny" is mean. For that matter, the words "nice" and "mean" have meaning precisely because of those experiences.

Experience + Interpretation → Internalized Belief.

On the other hand, children also internalize a great many beliefs that are harmful. If every time Mom gets angry at the child she says terrible things and hits him, he may come to believe that anger and violence are always related, or that underneath all of her warm affections Mom really hates him, or some other explanation for what he is experiencing. If most of the time his requests for attention are denied, the child may eventually decide that his needs do not matter as much as other people's, or more broadly that his needs will never be met. If he then observes other people getting their needs met, he may decide that the problem lies with him, and that no one values him or would want to spend time with him. This scenario can be played out endlessly, resulting in all sorts of distorted beliefs.

When we say children are poor interpreters, we mean that the explanations they come up with often fail to reflect reality. They also see that those who are "bigger" know a lot more about things, so they look to them for clues. When little Susie spills her milk at the table and Dad goes ballistic, she does not say to herself, "Wow! Dad sure has trouble managing his emotions over simple upsets. He should get some help with that." Quite the contrary. Instead she thinks, "I did something terrible! I'm really sorry! I didn't mean to spill. I can see I'm the only one who ever does that here, so there must be something terribly wrong with me, judging by Dad's reaction. I don't mean to be so awful, I just am. I will have to try real hard not to make so many bad mistakes, or Daddy might hate me." Even though this thought process is most likely non-verbal, she may very well internalize a false perception about herself as a result of what should have been interpreted as a commonplace event of little real significance.

Lies also get compounded over time so that they become harder and harder to dislodge. A friend of mine was a child of missionaries in Africa, and her earliest memories of her parents are that they never had any time for her because they were so busy taking care of the local people. By the time she was old enough to go off to boarding school (which was five!) she had already internalized deep rejection and negative beliefs about whether she mattered to anyone.

To make things worse, when she was getting on the plane to go away to boarding school, her parents tried to put on a good front in an effort to cheer her up. She herself was feeling very distraught, and looking out the window at her smiling parents was incredibly confusing. Everyone looked so happy that she was leaving! Was she supposed to be happy? Was there something wrong with her for not getting it? Were they glad to be rid of her so they could concentrate on their "mission"? The distorted interpretations that were added that day penetrated deep into her soul and added considerable support to the doubts she already held regarding whether she was really loved or wanted and whether others were to be cared about at her expense. This is how our misunderstandings of life build on our prior experiences and compound with each new event.

As adults, we usually continue to see life through the lenses that we developed in childhood. Every rejection we experience confirms our suspicions about being unlovable, every unforeseen disaster reinforces our belief that God does not care, and every dull church service adds to our conviction that Christianity is not very practical in the real world.

We even add new lies from time to time as we watch life unfold over the years. If we are more or less successful, we may come to believe the illusion that we can manage life quite well on our own. If we learn a lot of theology, we may drift toward the assumption that knowledge of doctrine is what separates good Christians from the mediocre. Or a sudden break in health may shatter whatever faith we previously held.

The point is that we are continually interpreting our experiences, at both conscious and subconscious levels, and *these interpretations become so deeply internalized that they define who we are and how we relate to the world around us.*

The problem is that we arrive at most of those interpretations by means of our own faculties apart from the light of truth to give us an accurate assessment of the situation. And as our own best wisdom about life becomes malformed by prior misinterpretations, we tend to layer error upon error over time, without ever knowing how far astray we have gone.

Imagine a doctor who has examined all of the evidence to the best of his ability, yet arrived at an inaccurate diagnosis of the disease. Once he becomes convinced of his conclusions and begins treatment, the problems begin to compound. Not only is he failing to address the underlying problem, he may be introducing still more challenges by his choice of treatment. As symptoms continue to worsen, his treatment becomes more radical and more removed from the real issue. And the more dedicated he is to working things out from his current perspective, the worse the prognosis. Now multiply that by a hundred different ailments that need attention, and the problem begins to look insurmountable. This is precisely the condition that exists in our soul.

Lies We All Believe

Since lies are internalized from experience, they tend to be very personal, tailored to our own life and history. Our lies are rooted in memories and images that are unique to each one of us, and the way in which we might express our faulty interpretations of life tend to have specialized meanings. At the same time, there are some common threads that run through most of the lies we hold, and virtually all of our spiritual struggles involve distorted ideas and images in regard to one or more of the following:

- Who God is, whether He cares, how He is involved in our life.
- Who we are, how we have value or find significance.
- How life works (especially relationships).

Within these over-arching categories there are dozens of lies which are extremely common. More people than not struggle with these invasive beliefs at some level. Some present themselves as personal vows, others as attitudes or orientations toward life, and some as blatant propositions, even if we have never verbalized them.

- I will never really be free.
- Evil has the last word in this world.
- I can't forgive myself for [fill in the blank].
- God is waiting to free me so I can learn humility.[36]
- God will never get over His disappointment in me.
- If you knew me better, you would reject me.

Such lies are not only common, they are legion. We all walk around with hundreds of these faulty premises driving our lives, quite unaware of why we feel like we are at war with ourselves, with God, and with life in general.

Once we begin to see how pervasive deception is in our own mind, we can begin to make sense of the confusion we live with all the time and where it is that we need real help.

The Pervasiveness of Deception in the Human Mind

It would be hard to overstate the impact that deception has on the human mind. As demonstrated so well by the demon Screwtape,[37] every question we can ask has a myriad of possible answers that are all terribly misleading. If a person sees the flaw in one lie, then he can be deceived by another lie at the opposite end of the spectrum. If he sees the flaw in both extremes, he can be deceived by a false dichotomy or a deceptive middle ground. People can even hold conflicting lies and believe them all at the same time. And this problem cuts across virtually every area of human existence.

The chart at the end of the chapter will attempt to summarize some of these areas and the ways in which people are kept in the dark by the labyrinth of lies that exist in their own mind. The first column lists various categories of belief. The second column highlights the kinds of thoughts that reflect our most negative self-understanding within each category. The third column lists contrasting beliefs that we subscribe to in our moments of exaggerated self-adulation. The fourth column is an example of human wisdom attempting to resolve the lies in the previous two columns. While it

---

[36] This was actually suggested by a pastor, supposedly as a liberating thought about spiritual bondage, and published in a leading Christian magazine (June 2008) supposedly in order to be helpful to others.

[37] Lewis, C. S., *The Screwtape Letters*.

may contain some grain of truth, it can end up being yet another clever distortion. The final column attempts to put each category into some perspective, based on the truth of the Word.

For example, in the category of self-image, there are times when our fundamental self-concept is one of shame and self-hate, and other times when we are extremely prideful. Most people can oscillate quite freely between the two extremes depending on how life is going at the time. Psychologists and recovery organizations see the destructiveness of these two belief systems and consequently have attempted to teach a balanced view of self-acceptance, which allows for the fact that one is not perfect, without any need for self-condemnation, and that it is possible to become something better. This may be a step in the right direction, yet it still falls short of God's truth. Finally, the godly self-image is one of true humility which means we understand that we are small creatures in the hands of a big God who loves us more than we know.

The purpose of this chart is not to present an exhaustive correction to our perceptions of life, but to demonstrate the fractured nature of our worldviews. At some level, most of us are able to identify with the majority of beliefs in both the Self-Deprecation and Self-Adulation columns, and also see the elements of truth that may be contained in the Human Wisdom column. At the same time, we may cognitively agree with the perspective shown under God's Wisdom, even if we do not always experience life that way. *The fact that we can essentially hold all of these views at the same time is very characteristic of how our mind works.* And when the issues of life are neither settled nor refined, we find ourselves constantly fighting old battles, feeling overpowered by worldly elements, and confused by our inability to live out the principles we think we believe. Such is the pervasiveness of deception.

So what does all this have to do with the Christian life? In this next section we will step back for a moment and take a look at the bigger picture of how we tend to think about our own handle on truth. Then we will dig a bit deeper into the implications of living with deception.

Deceived About Deception

Perhaps one of the most common misconceptions among professing Christians is the idea that they are in possession of most of the truth, due to their understanding of the Bible (at least as a group). In order to experience the life they read about in Scripture, they are fairly sure all they need to do is commit themselves more fully to what they already know to be true. Some think they need better worship or to become more obedient, others put their hope in deliverance, some decide they need to pray or read the Word more, and some seek to perfect a spiritual gift or hope that a special encounter with God will give them the power they lack. They keep looking for the silver bullet year after year, and many eventually come to still more faulty conclusions about Kingdom life as it is portrayed in the New Testament – that it may be an exaggeration of some sort, may not apply to this age, may not apply to them, or God has decided to ignore them.

Unless we see the prevalence of deception in our everyday life, we will not focus our efforts on the right battles. Satan has relatively little real power in this world apart from the lies that he can tell and the power that is released when we believe them. More than anything else, Satan is a masterful deceiver. In order to wrestle well against the darkness of this world, we must become wise about the nature of the war in which we are engaged. Otherwise, we may become overrun completely by the enemy without so much as a clue that we are already behind enemy lines. *Recognizing the pervasiveness of deception is the first step to finding victory.*

The Paradox of Hope in Pervasive Deception

There is an interesting paradox involved in coming to terms with the scope of darkness in the world. *The more we see the pervasiveness of deception, the more hope there is that life can be different.* If deception is the root cause of our spiritual problems, then we are not failing due to some inherent character flaw like a weak will or a rebellious spirit or an irredeemable dark side for which there is no remedy.

The truth is that we have been led astray in too many areas and kept in the dark about some very important matters. If we think that we already know most of what we need to know and yet life still seems beyond our grasp, what hope do we have? On the other hand, if we have been fighting

the wrong battles because of our blindness and there really is another way
to live that we have yet to experience, a way we can learn, then we have
reason to hope.

What if we are in fact confused about nearly everything that matters –
our deep need for community, how to manage our resources, the meaning
of family, how we matter, or even about God's intentions toward us? Then
it would stand to reason that if we could clear up that confusion and learn
how to seek God's perspective on our life, we would experience a dramatic
change in our basic motives, emotions, and desires.

Instead of continually striving to perform better, we need to learn how
to engage with God for the truth that will renew our mind in ways that will
free us to become more of who He designed us to be. We have been called
to humility, to become more teachable, so that the deepest parts of our soul
can become readjusted to the values of the Kingdom and be freed from the
bondage of the lies of the past.

Summary

This has been a very short survey of some of the ways in which
deception pervades our lives. These are not rare phenomena, but the stuff
of daily existence, running through all of our thinking and feeling. Given
the little attention that this subject has received in the past, one might think
that we have been deceived about deception!

Having presented the pervasiveness of deception in the world and the
prevalence of the theme in Scripture, we now move on to a crucial question
regarding the relationship between deception and sin. *Is deception the result
of sin in our life, or is sin caused by deception?*

Since Augustine, the traditional answer to this question has most often
been that our minds are clouded and filled with faulty ideas due to our
sinful nature and the sin we commit. This is assumed to be the case not
only for the unbeliever but for the Christian as well. Even after coming to
Christ we still sin, which is seen as evidence that we are not rid of the sinful
nature we inherited at birth. If we are deceived about anything at all, it must
be due to the remnants of this old nature.

Unfortunately, this line of reasoning is deficient in several ways, with
serious implications for Christian victory over the various forms of spiritual

bondage. In the next chapter we will demonstrate from Scripture that sin is actually the *last* item on a chain of causal events, which reveals not only the destructive nature of deception, but also makes very clear why deception is the key point of intervention. Then in Chapter 4 we will show how this all ties together with the evil that happens *to us*, as well as the evil we *do*, which in turn will bring tremendous continuity to the means by which we can be set free to live more as God intended. Because the same principles apply to our restoration whether we are talking about freedom from the sin *within* us or freedom from the things that were done *to* us.

> We have been deceived about deception!

Let me clarify that I am in no way trying to argue against any doctrine of original sin here. Rather, my point is that the way in which that doctrine has been applied has resulted in very poor theologies of sanctification and has had serious detrimental impact on Christians who struggle to experience Kingdom life. A proper understanding of how deception derails our spiritual life provides not only a better explanation of the defeats that we suffer, it points us toward a very hopeful and liberating answer to many of the problems we face.

Ways People Are Kept From Finding the Truth

	Self-Deprecation	Self-Adulation	Human Wisdom	God's Wisdom
Self-Image	shame, self-hate, self-doubt, self-loathing	pride, take self too seriously	self-acceptance	true humility
Sense of Worth	contemptible	self-righteous	accepting	beloved
Hope	my life is hopeless	I don't need help	self-help	God will save me from my own ways
Sense of Power	impotent, helpless	inflated sense of power	self-directed	strength from God and a strong identity
Source of Problems	me	others	society	lies, deception
Source of Truth	irrelevant, because I'm always wrong	whatever I think or feel, I'm right	rationalism	revelation, Holy Spirit
Perception of God	condemning tyrant	distant, unnecessary	useful for morality	Father, Mentor
Relationship to God	God wouldn't want me	I don't need him	role model	intimate
Forgiveness	I'm unforgivable	I won't forgive	letting go	forgiven and forgiving

	Self-Deprecation	Self-Adulation	Human Wisdom	God's Wisdom
Significance	I'm useless	I'm indispensable	competent	given by God
Other People	better and more fortunate	less than me, foolish	both good and bad	redeemable
Relationships	no one wants me	I'm too good for most people	selective for my good	part of human design
Victimization	used, victimized	willing to use others	harmless	blessed, giving
Death	afraid of death	invulnerable	realistic	resurrection, eternal
Control	out of control	master of my environment	limited control	submission
Uniqueness	I'm weird	I'm special	diversity is good	I'm part of the Body
Change	I'll never be any different	No need to change, I'm fine	I can be whatever I want to be	transformation from God

We can easily vacillate between the four columns in any of the areas listed.

Chapter 3
The Destructive Nature of Deception

Of all the stories the Bible has about the nature of deception, few are as instructive on the subject as the very first one to address the issue, that day in the garden when Adam and Eve were taken in by the schemes of the serpent. As we shall see, this story is not just about how sin entered the world – it is about how sin happens at all!

The Greatest Lies Ever Told (revisited)

The two greatest lies ever told were also the *first* lies ever told. They were powerful enough to deceive Adam and Eve despite their close relationship with God, and they still haunt us today as the greatest obstacles we face. These lies are significant for two major reasons:

- They are truly the archetype of all lies, just as the story itself is the archetype for sin.
- They deceived our parents *before* the fall, before they could have had any "sin nature" to trip them up.

We will examine these two lies in some detail to see what they reveal about the nature of deception and why it has so much power to disrupt our lives.

Great Lie #1: A Distorted Sense of Who We Are

> *"For God knows that when you eat of it your eyes will be opened, and you will be like God, knowing good and evil"* (Gen. 3:5).

When the serpent made his final play, he came up with a lie that was so bold, so shocking, it must have hit the human couple like a sledgehammer. Up until that moment, the relationship that Adam and Eve shared with each other and with God had been based on trust and love. They had no prior experience of deceit and betrayal to prepare them for this event. We may envy their innocence, but at this moment it became their greatest weakness. The unheard-of idea that they could become like God had all the force of a revelation, a stunning new piece of mystery they had not considered before. They were intrigued. They were amazed. *They believed.*

That was the hook. Like fish after a shiny new lure, they took the bait. The rest is history. Within a few generations the world was overrun by so many "gods" doing whatever was right in their own eyes that the Creator God may well have been sorry He had started the whole thing.

As it turns out, **this particular lie** *is one of the most fundamental problems human beings face.* The belief that we can be the master of our own destiny is at the very core of much that derails our spiritual life, for Christians as well as non-Christians. This presupposition is the driving force behind the seductive individualism that shapes Western culture, which in modern times has blossomed into the "me" generation and a spirit of self-centeredness and self-importance that is tearing our society apart. It fosters relativistic views of reality, a wholesale rejection of God, and an overbearing desire for power and wealth that we see all around us.

The idea that "I can be the master of my own life" is a lie. Because it is a lie, it cannot deliver what it promises (by definition). So it must be propped up by still more lies, such as "I at least *ought* to be a god" which helps to create the illusion of god-ness. This whole distorted sense of power and ego is one of the main reasons why we so often promote *image over substance*, as well as put distance between ourselves and others so they cannot challenge our belief in our own god-ness. If the facade breaks down, we can resort to looking for "what's in it for me" which is yet another way of placing ourselves at the center of the universe. But since everyone else is doing this we are all in competition for center stage, which leads us to all forms of greed and violence in the name of protecting what is "rightfully mine."

In short, the lie that I can replace God is the consummate distorted self-image, and it fuels a whole host of distortions of who I am including my selfish and self-centered attitudes and behaviors, both self-deprecating or self-promoting. It is a boldface lie that destroys community, defies submission to the true God, and ultimately cuts us off from all that is holy and needful for a godly life.

Yet behind this lie there is another, even more destructive lie.

Great Lie #2: A Distorted Sense of Who God Is

"What God said is not true at all!" (Implying, "You can't trust God")
(Gen.3:4, paraphrased).

This lie was so vile that the serpent did not even say what he really meant. He only implied it by his audacity and his indirect use of language. From the abbreviated story we have in Genesis it is difficult to see the dynamics of the interaction between Eve and the serpent. But after she told him, "God said if we eat from that tree we will die," his comeback was loaded with implications. Using modern vernacular, his response was probably something like, "He said *what*? You can't be serious! That's not what will happen at all! He knows that!"

Now if you were Eve, what would you be feeling about that time? She must have been shocked by the idea that God might be keeping something from them, holding out on them. It had never occurred to her that God could have some ulterior motive for banning the tree. Why else would it be there? Here this serpent is saying that this is the most ridiculous thing he ever heard. *Maybe God is not who He claims to be!*

This is the most foundational level at which we have all been deceived. To one extent or another, we all hold distorted images of God. We fear His disapproval, we do not trust Him with our futures, we doubt His love, and we run away from Him when we have failed. God for most of us is either too distant, too disappointed, or too uncaring.

In one of his many excellent books on the Christian life, David Benner poses an interesting question.[38] "When God brings you to mind, what do you suppose He thinks and feels about you?" As it turns out, the answer which a majority of Christians will give is, "Disappointment." One can only wonder why that is, and it would take another book to explore that issue in depth, which is why I heartily recommend Benner's treatment of this problem. The point here is that many people suffer terribly from self-hate, which is in part a fleshed-out disbelief in God's love for them. They want another life, either because they are sure they have failed at this one, or because they believe God short-changed them from the start. Many others have experienced enough evil in their life to cause them to thoroughly

---

[38] Benner, *The Gift of Being Yourself*

question God's presence and goodness. Still others are so successful in their lives that they see little need for God at all.

As a result of these misinterpretations of life, people internalize deeply distorted images of who God is and the nature of His relationship toward them, or what they believe that relationship ought to be. What's more, these doubts about God can be extremely painful to consider. John Eldredge and Brent Curtis capture this sentiment very eloquently in one of their books:

> *"Do you care for me, God?" ... What's under that question is our personal stories, often punctuated by the Message of the Arrows: parents who were emotionally absent; bedtimes without words or hugs; ears that were too big and noses that were too small; others chosen for playground games while we were not; and prayers about all these things seemingly met with silence. And embedded in our stories, deep down in our heart, in a place so well guarded that they have rarely if ever been exposed to the light of day, are other grief-laden and often angry questions: "God, why did you allow this to happen to me? Why did you make me like this? What will you allow to happen next?" ... "Do you really care for me, God?"* [39]

For Adam and Eve, it was the doubt about God that made the other lie plausible, that perhaps they ought to determine their own destiny. Only by calling the character of God into question could the serpent hope to convince them that they should consider looking out for themselves. If God could not be trusted, they needed to take matters into their own hands. These two lies – a distorted image of God and a distorted sense of self – are the starting point for most other forms of deception and the foundation for all kinds of evil in the world.

The Great Lessons of Eden, and Why We Miss Them

Unless we are careful we will miss the significance of this story, on account of both its familiarity and its long history of misinterpretation. Let us begin by reviewing the facts as we have them.

1. Eating the fruit of that one tree was the first human sin.

---

[39] Curtis and Eldredge, *The Sacred Romance*, p. 49.

2. Prior to that sin, Adam and Eve were free of any form of sin, including pride or lust or any defect of character that would predispose them to sin.

3. The option to make this choice had always existed. No doubt they had seen the tree before, without ever having desired the fruit. *They had no problem being obedient to God's instructions.*

4. The only thing that made this moment different was the conversation with the serpent in which *they were lied to* about power of the fruit and God's reasons for keeping them away from the tree.

5. The lie would have had no power if they had recognized it for what it was and believed that the serpent was wrong.

6. It was because they believed the lie that they made a choice they had not made before.

We conclude then that they sinned because they were deceived. There is no other plausible explanation, despite attempts by theologians throughout history to find some form of "concupiscence," pride, or natural desire to which the serpent might have appealed. Such explanations truly cloud the issue. With their trust in God severely challenged, Adam and Eve wondered if there was any validity to the serpent's proposition that there was something to be gained here. They then concluded that the only way to know was by experimentation (rather than trust!), and that is when they wanted the fruit. Their desire and their action both followed from their confusion and mistaken belief. Getting the chain of events in the right order here is absolutely crucial. From these observations we can draw several conclusions.

First and foremost, *being deceived is sufficient enough in and of itself to cause a person to miss the mark*. No prior predisposition toward evil or other defect of human nature is a necessary prerequisite. This is an incredibly important truth that should not be trivialized or brushed aside. Believing the wrong things leads to failure.

Second, if a lie was sufficient to derail perfect humans and cause them to sin, *how much more of a problem do we face*, given both a flawed soul and a climate of pervasive deception? Without some sort of divinely ministered truth, we would be completely without hope! The significance of this one truth is utterly staggering, and if it were not sufficiently emphasized one might brush past it without recognizing the weight of the matter. Deception was sufficient to cause Adam and Eve to sin. For we who live in a world of darkness, it takes so much less.

Unfortunately, the real value of Adam and Eve's story has long been obscured because we have focused on the outcome and minimized the process. Grenz is typical of many theologians when he characterizes the story of the fall as a divine test in which Adam and Eve chose to disobey God. His focus is on *the failure of the human pair to do the right thing*. The closest he comes to identifying the role of deception is to say that the serpent "subtly raised doubts" which really fails to do justice to the story.[40]

This whole preoccupation with performance criteria and whether or not we get it right or wrong is pervasive in Christian thought, and it has a way of twisting the relational fabric of the Christian life into a moralistic evaluation of behavior. As a result, we end up with interpretations of this story that tell us how their sin damaged the relationship between Adam and God, and completely miss the point that *it was actually the doubt cast upon the relationship that led to the sin*! We keep making the relationship conditional upon our performance, when it might be much more accurate to say that the relationship with God is what makes or breaks everything else.

> Being deceived is sufficient enough in and of itself
> to cause a person to sin or live poorly.

Genesis 3 provides the quintessential explanation for the presence of sin in the world. But more than that, we are given the model for *how sin happens at all*. Since Adam had no sinful nature, we cannot blame some predisposition to sin. If we say that he chose to rebel by the free exercise of his will, we still have not answered the question as to *why* he made that choice. No doubt Adam and Eve had walked by that tree many times before and had never considered taking the fruit. Why not? And why this particular time? Clearly the only thing that makes this day different is the conversation they had with the serpent.

---

[40] Grenz, *Theology For The Community of God*, p. 191.

The critical point around which the whole story revolves is that Adam and Eve were *deceived*. Prior to the deception they never considered disobedience to be an option. It was the lie that took them in, perhaps naively, and led to their error in judgment.

Deception as the Initial and Primary Means of Sin

Given that *Adam* could be deceived enough to fall into sin without any prior inclination toward evil, there is every reason to think that deception might be a major cause of stumbling for *us*. Raised by flawed human beings, assaulted by mistaken values and goals, and left to our own resources to sort it all out, we do not stand a chance against a foe who is far more clever than we can imagine.

Although this connection is often ignored while other theories of sin get center stage, Scripture actually contains overwhelming evidence which demonstrate that sin is the direct result of being deceived. Israel was often led astray by lies.[41] Moses warned that a misinterpretation of circumstances would lead to sin.[42] Isaiah taunts the ignorance of idol worshipers and concludes that only a "deluded heart" could indulge in such folly (Isa.44:9-20). Paul meticulously connects the *loss of truth* to the descent of human morality, repeatedly using phrases like "futile in their speculations," "their heart was darkened," "exchanged the truth of God for a lie," "a depraved mind," and "without understanding" (Rom.1:18-31). These are all listed as progressive *causes* of sin.

Sadly, Christian teachers have often turned this completely around. For example, passages that clearly state spiritual blindness will lead to sin are sometimes read to say exactly the opposite,[43] despite the obvious intent of the metaphor which is that *blindness causes us to stumble*, not the reverse. Conversely, having clear vision is always about knowing the truth. Truth opens the spiritual eyes of people so that they can believe and be changed. If people are blind, they fail to see the truth: "the god of this age (notice,

---

[41] "They lead my people astray with their reckless lies" (Jer.23:32).

[42] "Be careful, or you will be enticed to worship other gods" (Deut.11:16).

[43] Grenz, *Theology For The Community of God*, p. 135, 185.

the Father of Lies) has blinded the minds of unbelievers, so that they cannot see the light of the gospel" (2Cor.4:4).

The direct consequences of spiritual ignorance are pointed out quite frequently in the Biblical record. Jesus corrected the disciples' thinking time and again, because their wrong presuppositions would lead them into wrong attitudes and actions. When the disciples were arguing about who would be the greatest in the Kingdom, the disagreement arose directly from the ideas they held about what it means to have power and status – ideas they drew from the world around them. That is why Jesus never bothered to chide them for arguing. Instead, He went to the core of the problem and challenged their concept of greatness, redefining a great person as one who serves others in love. They were operating out of a distorted understanding of greatness, and that faulty concept resulted in a desire for dominance and self-glorification. They were also confused about their identity as disciples. They saw themselves as replacing earthly rulers and wielding power and controlling lives. But their true identity was that of servants in the household of God. Jesus knew that if they could grasp the truth of Kingdom greatness, there would no longer be any reason for the strife and competition among them.

And they were not the only disciples to get things wrong. Throughout history we can see the damage that has been caused by Christians who were committed to the wrong things. Taking just one small example, for years missionaries were told that as long as they dedicated themselves to their mission, God would make sure their children would be fine even if they had to be raised by the natives or sent off to boarding school when they were five years old. Of course for many of those children the consequences were nothing short of devastating. Because no matter how well-intentioned we may be, believing the wrong things can lead to disaster.

Imagine a single point with two lines coming out from it at such a close angle that the lines are virtually on top of each other at the start. Only part way across the page is there any space discernible between them. If one line represents the truth, and the other line represents the slightest deviation from the truth, it might seem like little harm has been done. Now extend those lines out a few hundred feet and the space between them will become quite significant. So it is with deception – it always leads to the wrong place.

Of course, there does exist to some extent a circular relationship between sin and deception, in which each fuels the other (2Tim.3:13). Even Romans 1 is a bit ambiguous about which is the starting point. But as we shall see throughout the rest of this book, there is sufficient reason to identify deception as both the initial cause of the problem and the proper point of intervention to stop the cycle. The interrelationship between sin and deception is especially apparent when we take into account the impact of *malformation* that results from deception, a topic that we will take up at the end of Chapter 4.

The Power of Deception to Cause Sin

The story of Adam and Eve is a clear demonstration of the power of deception and the damage that can be caused by believing a lie. That is only the beginning. The Bible repeatedly portrays deception as a fundamental cause of evil. In this section we will look at a few of these examples.

One of the longest and most powerful passages connecting these two elements theologically is found in the fourth chapter of Ephesians.

> *You must no longer live as the Gentiles do, in the futility of their thinking.*
> *They are darkened in their understanding and separated from the life of God*
> *because of the ignorance that is in them...having lost all sensitivity, they have*
> *given themselves over to sensuality.   (Eph.4:17-19)*

This passage says several things about how people reach the point of self-centered living. Primarily, it is because they are hopelessly confused about spiritual things. Confusion speaks to mental disarray. They are perplexed and cannot make sense of spiritual realities. Paul goes on to describe their confusion as the "futility of their mind...their understanding darkened." And once their hearts are blinded they are necessarily "alienated from the life of God."

By way of contrast, when talking about spiritual growth, Paul connects maturity with spiritual stability and the ability to withstand deception.

> *Then we will no longer be infants, tossed back and forth by the waves, and*
> *blown here and there by every wind of teaching and by the cunning and*

> *craftiness of men in their deceitful scheming. Instead, speaking the truth in*
> *love, we will in all things grow up into Him.   (Eph.4:14-15)*

A major sign of maturing spiritually is the ability to discern between truth
and error, and to not be taken in by deceit. Instead, the truth is known and
promotes our growth. Paul clearly understood the connection between our
spiritual understanding and the way we live.

One of the criticisms Jesus made of the Pharisees was that they were
blind, despite their extensive "spirituality." More than that, they and their
followers would all stumble and fall as a direct result of their blindness
(Mt.15:14). A related criticism that Jesus leveled at the Jewish leaders was
that they prevented people from entering the Kingdom. How did they
accomplish that? By hiding the truth about the Kingdom. Without that
truth, the people were lost (Lk.11:52).

A similar sentiment is seen many times in the Old Testament prophets
who made a direct connection between the exile of the nation and the lack
of truth.

> *My people are destroyed from lack of knowledge...you have rejected*
> *knowledge...a people without understanding will come to ruin. (Hos.4:6,14)*
>
> *Therefore my people will go into exile for lack of understanding. (Isa.5:13)*

We could go on. The Galatians believed a faulty presentation of the gospel
and lost their way. Paul was concerned that the Corinthian church was
breaking into factions because of distorted ideas about various church
leaders. The Pharisees missed their Messiah, not because of a weak will or a
lack of willpower or any other character defect, but because they had
another image in their mind of who their Messiah would look like. And it
was that mistaken perception that kept them from seeing Jesus for who He
was. Over and over we see that faulty beliefs lead directly to making errors
in judgment and practice.

Much of this should be fairly intuitive. If I am counting on a particular
map to help me find my way, the less it bears any resemblance to reality the
more hopeless will be my condition. And the more dedicated I am to a
distorted map, the more out of touch I will become. Apart from
internalized truth, we are destined to be deceived and led astray.

Distorted Images of Self and God

Of all the forms that deception can take, the most fundamental are those that deal with a distorted view of who God actually is and who we are in relation to God. By the time we reach adulthood, most of us have already internalized a great many false beliefs in regard to God and self of which we are not even aware. We simply assume certain things about life and how it works. Uncovering these misperceptions and transforming them is one of the major tasks of the Christian life.

There are almost an infinite number of ways in which we arrive at a deformed image of God, such as rarely or never experiencing His presence, seeing what He did for the people in the Bible but never experiencing anything like that personally, wondering why God did not stop some terrible thing from happening to us, trying to come to terms with the intrusions and deprivations of childhood, or suffering for doing good.

One of the most common ways we acquire distorted views of God is by projecting various aspects of our earthly parents onto God. Whatever flawed characteristics that our parents possessed, whether overly critical, authoritarian, too easy going, emotionally unavailable, or perhaps even mean, we may consciously or unconsciously apply those attributes to God, like placing a mask over His face that looks much like our own parent.

J. B. Phillips wrote an excellent book, *Your God is Too Small*, that looks at a variety of distorted images of God. He discusses these in detail, giving each type a name. God may be seen as a Residential Policeman, a Parental Image, a Perfectionist, or some other image that is less than who He really is. The point of Phillips' book is that when we embrace a diminished view of who God is, our lives are diminished as well. "We shall never want to serve God in our real and secret hearts if he looms in our subconscious mind as an arbitrary Dictator or a Spoil-sport, or as one who takes advantage of his position to make us poor mortals feel guilty and afraid." [44]

Quite often our distorted images of self and God result from our mistaken perceptions about how life works for us. Consequently, we are warned in Scripture to be careful, lest we misinterpret our life experience and think of ourselves in ways that are not rooted in truth and reality. God

---

[44] Phillips, *Your God is Too Small*, p. 63.

foresaw this potential in ancient Israel when they came in to the promised land. In Moses' farewell address to the nation, he laid out step by step how their thinking might gradually become distorted until they no longer believed the true nature of their deliverance.

Notice how subtly and almost innocently deception creeps in, unnoticed at first, growing like yeast in a loaf of bread, until it comes to full maturity as a tremendously bold lie, "My power and the strength of my hands have produced this wealth for me."

> *When you have eaten and are satisfied, praise the LORD your God for the good land He has given you. Be careful that you do not forget the LORD your God...Otherwise, when you eat and are satisfied, when you build fine houses and settle down, and when your herds and flocks grow large and your silver and gold increase and all you have is multiplied, then your heart will become proud and you will forget the LORD your God, who brought you out of Egypt, out of the land of slavery...You may say to yourself, "My power and the strength of my hands have produced this wealth for me." (Deut.8:10-17)*

Such a belief has so much power because of its interpretive function. *It appears to explain why things are the way they are*. But it also has power because it is believed even before it is expressed! The words are only an expression of what is already in the heart. They are not the creation of the lie, only an affirmation of it.

God created us with the capacity to interpret our experience and make sense of the world. That ability is essential to the process of discernment and making choices that affect our life. However, we live in a darkened world where values are clouded and meaning is obscured and we fail to see much of the truth we need for life. So we are certain to arrive at the wrong explanations for our experiences. And once those interpretations are internalized, they guide our life just as surely as if they were true.

Furthermore, we misinterpret both bad experiences and good ones. Just as the Israelites were prone to distort the meaning of God's blessing in the promised land, they also tended to misinterpret adversity. When they came to the land the first time and checked out the strength of the inhabitants, they were completely dismayed at the danger they faced. One of the conclusions they jumped to was that the Lord hated them and had brought them there to die (Deut.1:27-28). They attributed faulty motives to God (that He hated them) and faulty responsibility to themselves (that everything was up to them). Neither of these conclusions were true, but they believed them and acted on them as if that was the reality of their situation.

When lies are believed, they always have serious life consequences. The Israelites believed that the giants in the land were too big, so they failed to enter the land. And when they finally settled in the land, they were prone to think of their good fortune as the result of their own effort, and so lost their sense of dependency on God.

> Deception *causes* failure.

When today we experience our own achievements such as good grades in school, scoring points on the field, or making a good income, we tend to think we are quite self-sufficient and powerful, and we tend to push God into the background of our life. When our health fails, or when we are unable to pay the rent, or when we are deeply wounded by those who should love us, we decide that God is against us or should have shielded us, or that someone owes us something, or that we ourselves are terribly deficient. So we eject God from our life or strike out at others. Either way, in good times and bad, we misinterpret reality and believe the lies that come out of the darkness.

Why All This Matters

There are at least three reasons why it is so important to hammer down this concept. First of all, without this perspective we tend to fight the wrong fights and use the wrong tools in our efforts to grow or find victory. It is not uncommon to hear some writer or preacher issue a call for "obedience" to the Word and teach that this is what is needed in order to bring about revival or restore the church. But this approach is rooted in a persistent myth that assumes we could be obedient if we just cared enough and tried hard enough. And when we discover that our heart refuses to love our neighbor or to forgive seventy times seven times or to rid itself of all contempt, we must either fall under the weight of condemnation, or pretend self-righteously that all is well, or give up following Christ altogether. As we will show very clearly in Chapter 8, until we learn how to change our heart we will continue to put our efforts to grow into other approaches that simply do not work.

Second, unless we understand how serious deception truly is, there is the danger that we will continue to repeat this cycle of defeat by rededicating ourselves to trying harder, only to fail and rededicate again. This can be incredibly dangerous to our spiritual health because the more committed we are to a distorted map, the worse it will be for us and the more miserable we will become (or the more miserable we will make those around us).

Finally, once we discover that many of our greatest difficulties are due to our own misunderstanding of life and our lack of experience in how God helps us renew our mind in regard to those things, our journey becomes a joyful experience of God at work in us to form us into the person He created us to be.

Chapter 4
From Deception to Malformation

People often think deception is about being tricked into doing something they would not have done if they had known better. But as we have seen, deception is far more comprehensive than that. It includes every aspect of our understanding of spiritual realities that is in any way deficient. That is why deception is not only the primary source of the sin that *we* commit but also the reason why we suffer so much from the evil we encounter from *others*. In this chapter we will look at these two sides of deception with a view to understanding why truth can be so life changing. For if the evil we do and the evil done to us are both deeply interwoven with lies, then truth becomes an obvious answer for both our healing and our purification.

Deception Causes The Evil We Do

When considering the problem of sin in our lives, there is one very important question we must ask. *Why* do people sin? Or more importantly, *Why do Christians sin*? Whatever answers we come up with for this question will have serious implications for how we pursue Christian growth and development.

Part of the answer has to do with how we define our basic identity. Are Christians essentially sinners who have been pardoned, or are they saints who still sin? In many segments of the Christian world this issue is still debated with some passion. If we are fundamentally sinners who have been fortunate enough to experience certain graces of God, then most likely we believe that sin is to be expected because of who we are, and that our best recourse is continual repentance. If on the other hand our core identity has been changed and we are now new creations of God, then sin is a malfunction of our basic identity, and there must be some means available to us for real liberation and victory. Either way, it is clear that our hope for freedom is directly dependent upon how we understand Christian identity.

There are a number of approaches to explaining sin in the lives of believers, but three stand out more or less as prototypes of the rest. The first is that the only thing which truly changes at conversion is our legal standing with God. All of the promises about being given a new nature are essentially future promises. We still have the same basic nature that we had before meeting God, but we have entered into an arrangement with God that will eventually result in our complete transformation. The reason we continue to sin is because we are still sinners. There is some hope of doing better because we have the Spirit of God who can bring some pressure to bear on our will, though for the most part, we are stuck with the spiritual nature that we had at birth.

Aside from being so pessimistic, this explanation has several significant shortcomings. To begin with, it fails to do justice to the many statements of Paul regarding regeneration and resurrection to a new life. The image of being given a new nature is quite explicit and should not be trivialized. Second, continued subservience to sin cannot be reconciled with the New Testament model of the victorious life. Every reference to overcoming sin would have to be qualified and minimized in order to sustain this theory of Christian nature. And finally, it fails to explain why Adam and Eve sinned. Prior to their first transgression they were not sinners in any sense of the word. So to sustain this defeatist view of Christian identity, one must postulate one set of causes for humans to sin *prior* to the fall and a separate set of causes for humans *thereafter*. Overall, this view has so little Biblical support that we must wonder why it has been so persistent.

The second theory on why Christians still sin acknowledges that we have indeed been given a new nature that is perfect, but alongside the new one we still retain the old nature that is depraved and defective. Jesus did not change our old nature. He gave us a new one that coexists with the old one. Consequently, we will live with an internal struggle between the two natures until we die. We continue to sin because the old nature often asserts itself, and we have not yet succeeded in subduing it with the new nature.

At first glance, this model offers more hope than the first one, because we have been given a nature that is created in righteousness. The problem is primarily one of will. If we just care enough or try hard enough, we should be able to yield to the longings of the new nature and resist the desires of the old. This is very similar to an ancient Jewish doctrine which taught that we all have two basic urges: the urge to do evil and the urge to do good. Our task is to suppress the one and encourage the other. A modern version of this model can be seen in Classical Dispensationalism, which teaches that the old nature is depraved and incapable of change, while the new nature is already perfect and needs no improvement. The challenge for spiritual growth becomes primarily one of training the will to give priority to the new nature. [45]

Unfortunately, this theory of sin suffers from the same problems as the one that said nothing has changed except our standing before God. In addition, the two-nature theory has very limited Biblical support and suffers from the difficulty of trying to explain how the will can function independently of the two natures and how it is that a person can actually grow in sanctification. [46]

The third explanation for why Christians sin begins with the idea that Christian conversion is essentially the birthing of a new life which makes a whole new way of living possible. However, this new birth is a bit like being rescued from a toxic waste dump, after which we may need a lot of help as we recover and become healthy again. We still have a long way to go to unlearn our old internalized ways of seeing the world, ourselves, and God. The process of sanctification is (among other things) the eradication of old life patterns that derail us, and the incorporation of new beliefs and practices that bring life. We still sin because the task is incomplete and we still suffer from areas of disbelief and misbelief, as well as an under-developed Christian identity. As the Spirit of God teaches us about who God is and who we are in relation to Him, truth replaces the lies and we gradually live better out of a renewed mind (Col.3:9-10).

---

[45] Primary support for this view comes from an incorrect understanding of Romans 7:14-25. For an excellent explanation on how this has been terribly misinterpreted, see commentaries on Romans by either N.T. Wright or Douglas Moo.

[46] Although this is a very popular understanding of Christian identity, and often defended very passionately, it is so deeply flawed that a complete rebuttal would take many pages and distract significantly from this discussion. Suffice it to say that proponents of this view are truly unable to formulate a coherent theology of sanctification. See Dieter, et. al., *Five Views of Sanctification*.

This theory fits better with reasonable models of how people make choices. It harmonizes better with the explanations of conversion in the New Testament, and it is more consistent with the promises of victorious living that come from following the Way. Best of all, this approach opens the door to transformation at our very core, both at the time of conversion and in the process of sanctification. We are given a balance between victorious living and our present situation that does justice to the now/not-yet aspect of the gospel, without undermining the real possibility of change. And finally, this theory brings a sense of continuity to the nature of the Christian experience.

We are saved when we receive the truth of the gospel,[47] and we are sanctified by truth received from the Holy Spirit.[48] On the other hand, we sin because we can only act on what we believe, and our implicit beliefs have not been fully renewed. With the Holy Spirit as our mentor, we finally have the means by which our internalized beliefs can be changed to reflect the truth of God and thereby live more fully as He intended.

This brings us back to the basic cause of sin in the life of a Christian. As noted earlier, unbelief is not just the absence of belief. When we use the word "unbelief" we generally mean that one does not believe the truth. But that does not mean that one believes nothing at all. Something else is believed instead – a lie. And *just as righteousness is an act of faith in the truth, sin is generally an act of faith in a lie*. Both righteousness and sin are fundamentally matters of faith. The difference is in what we believe at the core of our being; that is, what we are prepared to do in any given situation. What we need to understand is that faith and behavior take their value from the *objects* of our faith, whether good or bad. This is why faith and belief are so foundational to the Christian walk, and why they are stressed so much in the New Testament.

Seeing life the way God sees it (truth) is a necessary prerequisite for living as He intends. It is therefore axiomatic that any deviation from the truth will manifest itself in some form of unbelief and sin. The more our heart and mind are clouded or distorted, the worse we will live. The more

---

[47] Eph.1:13;   Col.1:6.
[48] "Sanctify them by the truth" (Jn.17:17).

our mind is renewed by internalizing truth, the better our attitudes, perceptions, and responses to life.

Regrettably, most Christians have come to the conclusion that truth is insufficient in and of itself to bring about many of the changes we need, because they encounter truth all the time without internalizing it. That in turn leads them to trivialize the problem of deception.

> Sin is an act of faith in a lie.

But once we learn how to internalize truth in ways that are life-changing, then the significance of deception and the power of truth become amazingly self-evident. And more importantly, we then have available to us a means of deliberately fostering our spiritual growth by engaging truth for the purpose of transforming our heart and mind!

Deception Keeps Us in Bondage to the Evil Done to Us

The other great question regarding sin is, "Why is it that the evil done to us can be so destructive to the human soul? Why do the wounds of traumatic events or circumstances continue to affect us so long after the experiences themselves, sometimes for decades?"

First of all, why do we separate behaviors into categories of good, benign, and evil? Partly because the way in which these things can impact people for their good or ill. Hitting, degrading, humiliating, using, or otherwise violating another person all have the potential for being both hurtful and destructive. The very term *evil* means that either the motive is wicked or the result is harmful, or both. "The thief comes only to steal and kill and destroy" (Jn.10:10). Conversely, an act of love is one that comes out of the will for the good of another. It has the potential to assist, bless, heal, or restore another in some way. Thus, evil and righteousness are very *relational* in nature because they impact our soul and the souls of others.

But evil is more than just a painful event. Even in its least corrosive form, evil carries with it a meta-message of disregard for the other. At its worst, the message is one of hate and the will to harm. As noted earlier, the means by which these messages are conveyed can be various forms of assault and withdrawal. Both of these aspects of evil imply a rejection, a disdain for the other. Just as acts of love carry with them messages of value and worth and regard for the person in mind, so acts of evil carry devaluing messages of disregard and worthlessness. When these messages overwhelm our sense of self, we are diminished as human beings. When our identities are too fragile or the evil is too strong, the messages can be devastating.

In addition to the initial impact, our attempts to interpret evil or pain apart from God's perspective will cause us to internalize faulty assumptions about our life that in turn affect our ability to live as God designed us. Examples of destructive messages we commonly internalize from life experience are:

- God does not care about me.
- No one cares about me.
- Evil is more powerful than good.
- I will never be loved the way I need to be.
- If you really knew me, you wouldn't like me.
- I am a failure, a mistake, an embarrassment.

Then as a defense against the pain of these implicit beliefs, we often develop additional explanations that are equally flawed, adding still more layers to our distorted worldview. Here is a small sample of ways we get confused about reality:

- My problems are bigger than anyone else's.
- Most people have no idea what it is like to be me.
- My first intuition is almost always right on.
- My needs take precedence over everything else.
- I don't need people.

Such lies are not benign, because ideas have consequences. When these lies become part of our basic presuppositions, all of our relationships are affected, all of our decisions are clouded, and our means of dealing with spiritual realities severely impaired. Lies cannot lead us to the resolution of any of life's problems because they do not correspond to who we really are or to the way things actually work in the Kingdom. Consequently, our internal deception becomes self-defeating. The harder we try to live by what we really believe, the worse life becomes. This is what it truly means to be spiritually blind. We mistake a lie for a workable road map and sooner or later run into a brick wall. And when we have no other interpretation of reality, we keep trying the same strategies over and over, hoping that things will turn out differently.

How Deception Causes Malformation and The Development of Evil Impulses

Of course we must still acknowledge that as Christians we have all experienced evil impulses. The question is, where do they come from? Can the evil within us have another source besides deception?

A fundamental truth that we must come to understand is that everyone is continuously engaged in spiritual formation at all times, for good or evil.[49] All of our thoughts and actions and reactions to life work their way into our character over time and become part of who we are. From the very early days of infancy when we begin to develop a way of responding to those around us and continuing throughout all of life's experiences, we are being shaped spiritually – sometimes in ways that are life-giving and sometimes in ways that are destructive to the human soul. How we have been formed then in turn impacts how we respond to life from that point forward, which then continues to form us in a never ending cycle.

Again, the process of addiction can be instructive here as an example of how wrongful formation occurs. Initially, a person may be able to manage the addictive substance or event and choose it more or less at will. When the benefits are seen as desirable (another level of deception) and even functional (internal pain can be deadened for a while) the person gravitates more toward the addiction. Eventually he comes to believe he cannot live without it and may become physically or emotionally dependent. The mind then develops such a strong association between the pain relief and the addictive substance or event that it literally substitutes one for the other. At that point the person may even fail to identify the original pain whenever it surfaces, and instead interpret such feelings as a desire for a buzz.

---

[49] Mulholland, *Shaped By The Word*, pp. 25-26; Dallas Willard (many sources).

In a broader sense, all of the ways we live and cope in the world work their way into our implicit beliefs in very much the same way that finding relief in a substance alters the way we feel our own pain. We gradually change our understanding of who we are and how life works, often with no real comprehension of what is happening to us. We do not arrive at such conclusions "by nature," we get there by a formational process.

The power of spiritual malformation should not be underestimated. For example, when Trevor was a young boy, his family environment was often quite toxic, characterized by pervasive contempt for nearly everyone and everything, commonly fleshed out in the form of soul-rending humiliation of one family member or another. Most of the time he felt like he was living in an emotional minefield – one false move and he would become a living target. During his early years his primary reaction was one of being hurt and shocked at every incident. Gradually he learned to cut off his feelings to minimize the pain, because feeling nothing at all around other people seemed like the safest strategy. This grew to the belief that privacy is crucial to survival, and all mistakes must be hidden or fixed before anyone else knows about them. If problems do surface, try denial. If that fails, blame someone or find some compelling defense to explain your error in judgment. If that fails, yell back, or find a similar fault in your accuser. Thus one faulty strategy led to another, mistaken goal upon mistaken analysis, until the lies were so deep he did not know how it all began.

Trevor's first realization that he had a deep-seated problem came when his wife confronted him about his pattern of defensiveness over the simplest questions. He always assumed that he was under attack. When asked something as benign as "Have you seen my keys?" he would snap back with a remark about how he was completely innocent in regard to any keys she might have misplaced.

After spending some time reflecting on this, it became obvious that his defensiveness was a highly exaggerated reaction to his own implicit belief that everyone around him was a potential enemy. This internal vigilance and readiness to defend himself was of course supported by a great many unconscious beliefs about the injustice of his early life and his depression over a host of unresolved personal problems. As he began to get healing for his early wounding from the humiliation he had experienced and uncovered the faulty beliefs behind his hyper-vigilant self-protection, his defensiveness began to dissolve into more respectful communication. His anger and lashing out were *not* symptoms of an untamed old nature, they were the natural result of malformation that came from years of life in a family system that was deeply invested in a distorted set of values.

Spiritual formation is, in part, the process by which beliefs are internalized until they begin to drive our feelings, thoughts, and actions. This goes on all the time, whether we are conscious of it or not. By the time we reach early adulthood, we can no longer distinguish between our malformation and any negatively charged innate urges we might have had by nature. We experience formational characteristics as if they are part of our very being. What feels entirely "natural" to us may very well be a way of being that has been formed over time.

We are also constantly in the process of interpreting our life experience. Each interpretation in turn affects our underlying beliefs and presuppositions for the next event. The process is very incremental, and can have widely varying results given the same raw experiences. Trying to sort out what was inborn and what was learned from life experience is virtually impossible.

This perspective is really good news in regard to our battle with sin. *Most of what we have attributed to the old nature is in fact malformation from deception and can be quite amenable to change once we learn how to internalize truth!*

Whatever influence the old nature may still have in my life, and however that influence manages to effect me in the present,[50] the death of the lies that surround the flesh will effectively disarm those passions, expose them to the light, and end the alliance I have with them. In this way, the opportunity for victory is opened up and the means for purifying the flesh is made available (Rom.8:13). An all-out assault on the lies we believe is our best offense for purging our soul of its sinful malformation. Truth can set us free, precisely because it is the lies we believe that form the cords of bondage.

---

[50] Different theological traditions have quite different thoughts about the how much influence the old nature has. Dealing with deception is necessary regardless of which theological position you take.

To be clear, other things contribute greatly to our malformation as well, such as unresolved trauma, painful losses, various forms of deprivation, and lack of bonding and attachment. Consequently, we may need a variety of resources for our recovery over and above the work of truth that we are exploring here. At the same time, there are very few, if any, ways to be malformed that do not involve some distortion of spiritual realities. Which is to say that nearly all of our restoration involves at least some renewing of our mind by truth.

How This Points the Way to Transformation

Some of the greatest evidence that deception is at the heart of Christian defeat and stagnation can be seen in the way that great saints of the past have often described their most momentous breakthroughs. Many of them attribute the changes they experienced to "moments of realization, of extreme clarity of insight into profound truth." [51] Their stories are highly inspirational and encouraging, and give us clues about how truth is one of the most important means of transformation.

J. Hudson Taylor, the famous missionary to China, tells of a letter from a friend that was used "to remove the scales from my eyes, and the Spirit of God revealed the truth of our oneness with Jesus as I had never known it before." [52] Samuel Logan Brengle of the Salvation Army testified to a sudden opening of his understanding in which he was "enabled to believe without any doubt that the precious Book cleansed my heart, even mine, from all sin." [53] Charles Finney, the great nineteenth century preacher, felt very strongly that God had given up on him until a particular passage of Scripture flooded his mind and he realized, "I had intellectually believed the Bible before, but never had the truth been in my mind that faith was a voluntary trust instead of an intellectual state." [54] That revelation opened the door to an outpouring of the Holy Spirit in his life that changed everything about him and impacted thousands of those who heard him preach.

---

[51] Dallas Willard in Larson, *Indelible Ink*, pp. 50-51.

[52] Edman, *They Found The Secret*, p. 20.

[53] ibid, p. 27.

[54] ibid, p. 62.

These men were all devout Christians at the time of their revelatory experiences. What can only be described as *an encounter with truth* changed them forever from the inside out. They experienced greater freedom, less burden, more of God, and more of His love. Temptations they struggled with for years were suddenly diminished in force. And their ministries flourished as never before.

Now if an encounter with truth was the cause for transformation, then what was their situation just prior to that encounter? It can only be described as an absence of that particular truth, or the prior failure of that truth to penetrate to the core of their being. That is what we mean by the nature of deception and living in a darkened world, and how the power of deception keeps Christians from a more abundant life.

These breakthroughs stand as evidence of the power of darkness to keep us bound as well as the inherent weakness of darkness in the face of truth. Such moments of clarity can become quite common in our life, although much of the work of truth is slow and methodical, like a plant sending its roots deep into the soil.

Simply taking stock of the weapons of the enemy ought to be evidence enough that deception is one of the greatest obstacles we face in our journey toward victorious Christian living. Satan has put a great deal of energy into his attempts to sidetrack the people of God, from Adam to Abraham to Paul and us, and the entire kingdom of evil is built on lies. That is why Satan is called the Father of Lies.

> *The devil was a murderer from the beginning, not holding to the truth, for there is no truth in him. When he lies, he speaks his native language, for he is a liar and the father of lies. (Jn.8:44)*

He cannot violate our will or *make* us sin. But he can offer us distorted perceptions as if they were foundations for life, or twist the truth until we no longer know which end is up. We greatly trivialize the work of the enemy when we say that his primary activity is to tempt us to do bad things. That is only a small part of his strategy. If he can keep us from hearing the truth, or keep us from internalizing the truth once we hear it, if he can fill our heart with all sorts of distortions about spiritual realities, then we will go off and self-destruct on our own without any need for constant harassment or temptation. This is the stuff of which the kingdom of darkness is built.

Once we grasp this reality, we have within our reach a phenomenal weapon, because *light has all the power*. Wherever light enters, darkness is obliterated. There is no contest, no struggle. Light wins, hands down. The kingdom of darkness is built on a sham, and one thing it cannot tolerate is exposure. The only thing standing between us and life-changing truth is a meaningful grasp of the nature of belief, exposure of the lies we believe, and the means for internalizing truth in ways that are truly transformational.

Part 2

The Power of Belief

"The righteous will live by faith."
(Rom.1:17)

Part 2 – The Power of Belief

Chapter 5: My Beliefs May Not Be What I Think I Believe

Confusing *belief* with *doctrine* is a common mistake. What the Bible means by belief is another matter entirely. Not only that, but the fact that we are quite capable of holding two or more contradictory beliefs at the same time helps to explain how we can appear to violate our own values, when in fact we are being consistent with them.

Chapter 6: How Beliefs Drive My Life

Here we introduce a model of how we interact with the world which shows how beliefs clearly drive our lives, and it provides clues as to how the faulty beliefs we have internalized might be exposed. This model will also be used in Part 3 to make sense out of the lies we have all been taught about truth.

Chapter 7: True Belief is Hard Work

Learning to separate what is true from what I *think* is true requires a teachable spirit, a great deal of trust, and an understanding that the biggest problems we face are our own internalized implicit beliefs.

Chapter 5

My Beliefs May Not Be What I Think I Believe

In Part 1 of this book we discussed the pervasiveness of deception and the significance of its role in keeping Christians in bondage. We now turn our attention to the actual means by which internalized beliefs drive our lives. A thorough understanding of this process will clarify why deception is so essential to the success of evil in the world, and point us toward the means for internalizing truth.

The basic reason behind why truth and error are so vital is one simple principle: *human beings live primarily out of how they have been formed, and their formation is heavily intertwined with their implicit beliefs.*[55]

Believing God is able to bring good out of any situation will drive us to Him when things go wrong, while believing He is distant and unconcerned will cause us to rely on our own resources and keep us from anticipating His involvement in the situation. Believing that you and I can work through any rupture in our relationship will give me the courage to stay present while we work things out, whereas believing that ruptures signal the end of a relationship will send me out the door. Beliefs drive behavior.

If we start with the outcome and work backward, we will often find that our behavior has its source in one or more implicit beliefs that are rooted in our experience. Consider, for example, a college student named Sheryl who is facing a difficult exam in a class where her grade point average is at risk. In her consternation she decides to cheat in order to pull up her grades, and when she is confronted by the professor, Sheryl tells a little lie to cover up her behavior. All of this in spite of the fact that she knows what she is doing is wrong.

But looking back at Sheryl's past reveals some interesting insights. It turns out that the most important thing in her family was to look good and succeed. Failure was not acceptable. Admitting to failure was even worse.

---

[55] This will be discussed in detail in Chapter 6.

Over time, she learned how to hide whatever was going wrong and to make sure everyone approved of her, even if it meant making little compromises along the way. Internally, Sheryl harbored a worldview that allowed her to compromise herself and her values whenever it became expedient to do so. She was able to cheat on her test and lie about it because of the tremendous pressure her previously formed beliefs put on her choices. Yet if you were to ask her whether it was alright for people to engage in unethical behavior for personal benefit, she would have given you the right answer.

Christians often think about these kinds of experiences in exactly the opposite way. They tend to view sinful behavior as the result of fleshly desires *overriding* their "beliefs." However, in most cases these actions actually arise out of deeply internalized beliefs that are much stronger than a person's theology or ethical standards. Although we may only be aware of these implicit beliefs as emotional urges, they exist nonetheless.

As we encounter life experiences, there is a part of our mind that is constantly at work trying to make sense of it all. When it arrives at a conclusion about an event, our brain stores the information in the form of internalized beliefs about how life works for us. These implicit beliefs are then subconsciously called upon and applied when we encounter other events that are similar in nature, and we use them to interpret our experience and suggest possible responses, all of which fuel our emotions.

Within this process, there is no guarantee that our mind will arrive at the correct conclusions or internalize beliefs that reflect how God sees our experience. For example, after Jonathan had been married for a while, he began to resent his wife's requests, no matter how trivial. His Christian training told him that he should be a giving, sacrificial husband, but he secretly resented everything he had to do for her.

In searching out what was causing his resentment, it became clear that he had internalized some faulty beliefs about fairness and consideration long before he met his wife. Growing up in a family where girls always got what they wanted and boys routinely did without, Jonathan had internalized a picture of how giving and receiving worked in relationships that left him angry and bitter. Giving as a virtue was still mostly an idea about how things *ought* to work, but no where near strong enough to override the internalized beliefs about giving he had learned from his own experience.

Consequently, he found it very difficult to freely give to his wife or respond in love to her requests. Without meaning to, Jonathan had arrived at the belief that giving and receiving had a lot to do with gender, power and entitlement, and it was driving his negative feelings toward his wife.

Belief is not just a rational proposition you hold. A belief is *the degree to which you are ready to act as if something is true.*[56] Jonathan was prepared to act as if every request made by his wife was a statement about who matters and who does not. Long before his conscious mind had a chance to consider the possibility of giving to her willingly and joyfully, his internalized beliefs had already informed him at a visceral level that it was unfair for her to ask.

In this way, our implicit beliefs impact our emotions, influence our perceptions of the social context within which we find ourselves, and provide the presuppositions we use to make our choices. Whether or not this is done consciously does not change the fact that our implicit beliefs are a major driving force in our lives.

> **Belief:** the degree to which one is ready to act
> as if something were true. (Dallas Willard)

What the Bible Means by Belief

Part 1 emphasized the cause-and-effect relationship between deception and bondage, and this relationship holds true for both the sin we commit and the sin done to us. At this point it is important to clarify that relationship a bit further.

It is not the lie per se that causes the bondage. It is when we believe the lie that bondage occurs. Conversely, when we believe the truth, we are liberated.

That brings us to one of the foundational premises of this work. *Internalizing a belief is the means by which the power of a truth or lie is released into our life.* For this reason, Scripture is filled from one end to the other with stories and statements about belief and its impact on our lives. To get a better picture of this connection, we will look at a few key passages here.

---

[56] Credit goes to Dallas Willard for this definition.

Perhaps the most sustained argument regarding the relationship between what we think and how we live is found the book of Proverbs. Those who *have wisdom* find life, while those who *lack wisdom* become self-destructive. That is Solomon's whole reason for writing the book. Notice here how tightly he weaves together *cause* and *effect*.

> *For wisdom will enter your heart, and knowledge will be pleasant to your soul. Discretion will protect you, and understanding will guard you. Wisdom will save you.   (Prov.2:10-12)*

> *Do not forsake wisdom, and she will protect you; love her, and she will watch over you. Wisdom is supreme; therefore get wisdom. Though it cost all you have, get understanding. Esteem her, and she will exalt you; embrace her, and she will honor you.   (Prov.4:6-8)*

Wisdom and Folly are repeatedly contrasted as the way of truth versus the way of lies and deception. Solomon clearly understood the nature of wisdom and its relationship to life, and that what we believe at the core of our being affects the way we live.

As we have seen previously, Paul had a similar understanding of the relationship between thoughts and beliefs on the one hand, and our experience of spiritual realities on the other.

> *I pray, that your love may abound still more and more in real knowledge and all discernment, <u>so that</u> you may approve the things that are excellent, in order to be sincere and blameless.   (Phil.1:9-10 NASB)*

> *That you may be filled with the knowledge of His will in all spiritual wisdom and understanding, <u>so that</u> you may walk in a manner worthy of the Lord, to please Him in all respects, bearing fruit in every good work...for He delivered us from the domain of darkness.   (Col.1:9-13, NASB)*

> *So I tell you this, and insist on it in the Lord, that you must no longer live as the Gentiles do, in the futility of their thinking. They are darkened in their understanding and separated from the life of God because of the ignorance that is in them.   (Eph.4:17-18)*

This last passage from Ephesians is particularly instructive, as Paul is in the middle of making an impassioned plea for holy living. He contrasts the lifestyle of the Christian with that of the pagans, and focuses in on how truth necessarily causes us to live differently. Within a span of thirteen verses, he collectively refers to teaching, knowledge, truth, and deceit at least twelve times. There can be no doubt that *what* a person thinks and *how* a person thinks is a matter of central importance to Paul.

Jesus, of course, had much to say about truth. His whole ministry was about bringing to light the truth of the Kingdom and its new availability to those who believed, and He spoke a great deal regarding the nature of faith and truth. Sometimes He used metaphors and parables to make His point, and other times He was fairly direct. Here are a few typical statements along these lines.

> *But when He, the Spirit of truth, comes, He will guide you into all truth. (Jn.16:13)*
>
> *Your eye is the lamp of your body. When your eyes are good, your whole body also is full of light. But when they are bad, your body also is full of darkness. See to it that the light within you is not darkness. (Lk.11:34-35)*
>
> *If you hold to my teaching, you are really my disciples. Then you will know the truth, and the truth will set you free.   (Jn.8:31-32)*

Taken together, these verses tell us that:
- The Father, Son, and Spirit speak life-giving truth.
- God directs that truth toward us, training us in how to live.
- When we thoroughly incorporate that truth in our heart,
    we receive the life that is inherent in that truth.

From this sampling of Jesus' teaching it can be seen that He linked belief and truth together with life in the Kingdom. Either the absence of truth or the lack of belief in the truth would cause a person to miss the life that Jesus was offering.

Belief in what is true is a major integrating theme throughout all of Scripture. As we shall see, belief is the fundamental means of submitting to God and participating in His work in our life. But in order to make sense of belief, and to separate it from education about true things and our intellectual assent to those things, we must take a closer look at what belief actually is.

Types and Levels of Belief

Everyone has a basic internal model of reality that we sometimes refer to as a *worldview*. Such a model may have varying degrees of certainty and detail, and even some very ill-defined areas that have not yet been worked out. Still, a worldview is the totality of one's beliefs about things, both seen and unseen. These beliefs cover a broad spectrum from deeply held, internalized beliefs to more loosely held, surface-level thoughts about the world. We will examine a few of these categories of belief in order to demonstrate their relationship to truth and error.

Values. Beliefs are often expressed in terms of our value system. Our awareness of these beliefs may be primarily emotional at times, but such feelings are expressions of belief nonetheless. For example, we may feel a fondness for some personal item that was given to us by a dear friend, and sadness or anger if it is lost or broken. We have these feelings because of the value we place on the object and the person who gave it to us. It means something to us beyond the fragile elements that it is made from. These emotions and values are connected to the underlying meaning that we ascribe to the object, meaning that is rooted in such things as how we think about our friend and our expectations of the relationship, all of which are expressions of belief.

We value hard work, sacrifice, commitment, and a host of other abstract realities because of the complex set of beliefs we hold in regard to what those things mean to us personally and corporately. When a son or daughter makes good life choices we rejoice in part because we know that their lives will be richer for it. Or we mourn a poor choice because we have some understanding of what it will cost them.

Our values are quite inseparable from our underlying beliefs, and are indeed fairly direct expressions of them. When Jesus said, "Where your treasure is, there will your heart be also" (Mt.6:21), He was making a direct correlation between the things we value and the things we put our faith in. And when we value our work over family, isolation over community, or accumulating over sharing, these outward expressions give us clues to the implicit beliefs we hold.

Assumptions about how things work. Most people who live in the modern world have had the experience of dealing with an unfamiliar piece of technology such as a friend's microwave, for example. We approach the device with the basic notion that a relationship exists between the buttons we can press and the effects we desire, but we hold the relationship loosely because we know that the rules can differ from one device to another. Often with only one or two clues, we can adjust our ideas about how the buttons are designed to work and use that particular item with ease. We refine our assumptions to reflect the reality we are dealing with.

This process can be seen in human relations as well. On entering an unfamiliar store, we may approach an employee for assistance. If we discover through a bit of trial and error that none of the employees are going to be helpful, we adjust our expectations regarding customer service in that store. Or to extend this principle still further, we generally approach getting a job, taking a class, or building a house in much the same way. Each step along the way encourages us to reach certain conclusions about how things work and revise previous ideas that have proven to be deficient.

At this level of reality, just the slightest bit of "truth" or evidence may cause us to alter our ideas about a given situation. Our initial assumptions are easily dislodged in favor of explanations that appear more accurate or practical. Even though this kind of "belief" does not have the same force as those we have deeply internalized, the basic principle of truth and error is still observable, since *any misinformation that is trusted can result in a great deal of frustration before it is discarded and replaced with something closer to the truth.*

Doctrine. This level of belief is heavily dependent upon deliberate, rational functions of the mind, yet it includes a great deal of emotional energy in the form of deeply held convictions about how the Bible should be interpreted and the value of what it contains. What is often the case, however, is that these beliefs are initially received with very little resistance, either during early training such as a confirmation class or immediately following conversion when a new Christian has few preconceived ideas about what the Bible teaches. The explanations given by the teacher are usually sufficient to convince the student that a particular doctrine or dogma is indeed true, whether it is in regard to baptism, discipleship, life after death, the rapture, or whatever. Once these doctrines are in place, however, they are usually very hard to dislodge, and require a great deal of evidence or a strong internal sense of dissatisfaction with the implications of the teachings before someone will change their mind.

What is relevant to our study here is the understanding that many of the things which Christians are taught about human nature and the means available to them for spiritual growth and sanctification have serious implications for those who find themselves in some degree of spiritual dryness or bondage. The explanation for the bondage, the means for addressing the problem, and the potential for change are all dependent on our underlying doctrinal assumptions. If we believe spiritual growth comes from doing our best, then we may keep volunteering for ministries at church until we collapse from exhaustion, all the while wondering why our spiritual life is not improving. When our doctrine of sanctification is weak, too vague, or mistaken about the real problems we face, the harder we try to follow our teaching, the more disillusioned we will become. And unless we challenge our underlying assumptions about spiritual development, we will arrive at still more faulty conclusions in an attempt to explain why we find ourselves in so much difficulty.

On the other hand, understanding the power of truth to destroy forms of bondage that are rooted in distorted beliefs can lead us to an approach to the Christian life that really works. But this has all been greatly obscured by the many mistaken beliefs Christians have taught during the last few generations regarding the ways in which God brings about change. That is the reason why so much effort was spent in Part 1 of this book detailing the pervasiveness and power of deception. And that is also why it is necessary to point out in so many ways that our lives are driven far more than we realize by beliefs we have internalized from life experience. Unless we see this connection clearly, we may fail to grasp one of the most important means available to us for our renewal.

Explanations of Life Experience. Perhaps the deepest beliefs we hold are those we arrive at through our own life experience. As we encounter certain patterns of intrusions and deprivations over time, we begin to form internal explanations of why things work the way they do, why people behave the way they do, and why our own experience is different from that of other people.

Much of this process happens below the conscious level with little awareness of any choice in the matter or any arbitration of competing explanations. It is there that we decide whether or not God cares about our situation, how much about ourselves we will allow other people to know, when it is necessary to be protective rather than transparent, and so on. Taken together, these implicit beliefs make up much of our worldview regarding relationships and have tremendous power to direct our lives with little conscious effort. They form the foundation for many of our values and attitudes about a great many things. And most importantly, these beliefs are extremely resistant to change, even in the face of overwhelming evidence or Christian education.[57]

For example, Margaret is an adult whose life is thoroughly characterized by fear. She is afraid of her neighborhood, the people she works with, looking for a new job, committing to a church, telling anyone she is afraid, and just about everything else in her life. It would be pointless to tell her to "get over it" or that she is overly emotional. Her problem is buried deep inside a very complex system of interwoven lies from years of living in an emotionally unpredictable family environment. These lies tell her who she is, what her deficiencies are, how the world works, God's distance from her, what it means when things go wrong, and so on.

There is absolutely no way that she can talk herself out of her fears. Only when her misbeliefs are corrected and healed will there be any hope for Margaret to live without her pervasive anxiety. No doubt there was a time in Margaret's early life when this worldview of perpetual vigilance gave her the illusion of safety or control and thus kept her from complete despair in a very painful environment. But now as an adult this way of life has a decidedly destructive impact on her life. Her explanations of life are terribly flawed, yet she cannot let go of them because they are buried so deeply that she is not even aware of what is driving her life. Margaret really believes she is doing the best she can, given the danger that she sees everywhere.

What makes these implicit beliefs so intractable is that they are not only learned at such a deep neurological level, but they are also self-supporting in

---

[57] This is a well-known process, and often appears in the literature under the name "implicit memory."

nature. *Once we arrive at an explanation or belief about an event, it immediately appears self-evident to us that the event proves the belief to be true.*

For example, if a man's first few attempts at cooking are disastrous, he may well conclude that he simply cannot cook. He can point to the terrible results as proof, and his conclusion feels true. But the evidence really proves nothing of the sort, as there may be other reasons for his initial failures. Similarly, if a child decides her parents got divorced because she was bad, her dad's absence "proves" to her that it was her fault. Why else would he stay away? Beliefs derived from life-experience feel true because the evidence is real, and *our explanations feel as real as the evidence*, however faulty they may be.

> Our deepest beliefs come from life experience.

Perceptions of Life Experience. Closely related to our *explanations* of life experience are our *perceptions* of experience. The difference is in how our perceptions alter the raw data before we ever try to make sense of it.

For example, a woman who is being told by her doctor that she has cancer may have absolutely no perception that God is with her in that experience. If that is the case, then God's presence does not even show up in the raw data that she has to work with in making sense of her life at the moment. She begins with a distorted context in which God is completely missing, and the *perception* that she is alone in that experience will shape her interpretations and emotions as surely as if she were *actually* alone.

Now consider the fact that many of us live without any direct experience of God for months or years at a time. Is it any wonder that we really do believe He is distant, disinterested, or completely irrelevant to our lives? We *experience* life as if there is no God at all, even though the real problem may be that we have not seen all the data. We mistake our perceptions for the experience itself. Or to put it another way, we confuse our perceptions of reality for the real thing, and assume we have it right. And just like those beliefs that we pick up from life experience, these internalized perceptions of life are extremely hard to dislodge, even though in this case the perceptions themselves are incomplete. That is why we can continue to harbor doubts about God even when we have good Christian education that tells us He is always with us.

Chaos. Sometimes, the problem is not so much an internalized faulty belief as it is a matter of spiritual and emotional chaos that is brought about by the lack of a coherent explanation for some particular aspect of life. This is akin to being lost in the woods and in need of a compass. Often this kind of confusion is amenable to basic retraining and wise counsel. Finding the necessary truth may be as simple as reading the right book on healthy living.

A great example of this can be seen in the life of Josh McDowell.[58] He relates that there was a time in his ministry when he was greatly overextended and exhausted to the point of harming his marriage. At the height of this stressful lifestyle someone handed him a copy of *Changes That Heal*[59] and his life was never the same. Within its pages, Josh discovered the concept of *boundaries* which he had never learned in childhood. He had never before realized that he needed to be able to say "no" before his "yes" had any real meaning. It was as though he had been lost in a maze and was handed a map of his surroundings with a dot on it that said, "you are here." Suddenly a great deal of chaos was brought into order, simply because he was given some basic truth that was necessary for a balanced life.

In similar fashion, sometimes finding the right name for a problem is enough to help us clear our confusion and move forward. A woman named Susan had never finished college and had been out of school for over eleven years when she began to consider taking some classes and working toward a degree. Over a period of several months she talked with her friends about how attracted she was to the idea of school, but also how she was too busy, lived too far away, and had too many obstacles to overcome in order to resume her education. One night when she was talking about this, a friend asked her whether or not she felt any anxiety about being able to study or pull a passing grade after having been away from school for so long. Suddenly it occurred to Susan that she was actually afraid of going back to school, a thought that had never crossed her mind despite all of her consideration of the matter. All the other reasons for putting off school

---

[58] Josh McDowell in Larson, *Indelible Ink*, pp. 203-209.

[59] Cloud, *Changes That Heal*.

were nothing compared to the real one. The very next day she went down to a community college and enrolled in a class for the next term.

This example shows how truth can sometimes liberate by simply exposing what was previously unknown or unnamed. Once those things are known, we are able to make informed choices about what we will do rather than act on the pressure that is put on our will from unidentified emotions. In this particular case the problem was simple enough to be resolved by choice. Susan just needed some light to be put on what was truly at stake, in order for whatever wisdom she already possessed to be of any value.

In both of these examples, the point once again is that an insufficient or inaccurate map of life will lead to defeat and discouragement, whereas the more accurately we see what God can see, the more we will find hope and victory over the darkness.

Contradictory Beliefs and Values. One of the more interesting aspects of the human mind is the ability to hold two or more contradictory beliefs at the same time. Most Christians are familiar with what is commonly called a "head / heart" split, which means there is an internal conflict between what they "know" is right and the urges they are feeling. Rephrasing this in terms of our belief systems, this internal stress is actually caused by the pressure from a mental moral standard running contrary to the pressure brought about by an internalized explanation of life experience, both of which could properly be called beliefs.

For example, Carol is a woman who is active in her church, very articulate about the things of God, and quite capable of quoting verses that affirm the goodness and love of God. She knows all about the promises of God to believers. But when disappointment strikes she will react very much like a child who has been abandoned by God and everyone else. Why? Because so many bad things happened in her early life that by the time she was nine or ten she was convinced that God could care less about her. So even though her faith has made a big difference, her doctrines about God have almost no power in the face of more disappointment with life. If you asked her, she would say she knows God is good and that she cannot understand why she feels so down.

Or take the case of someone who has developed a very successful career and reaped substantial rewards from his hard work. His Christian training tells him that it is wrong to be self-centered and that he ought to share his abundance with others. But everything in his body tells him that he is defined by his wealth and success and that there is never enough to give it away without being diminished in some way.

These inner conflicting values are a major reason why many Christians have become frustrated in their attempts to live out the Christian life. Having been told all the right answers and how a Christian *ought* to live, they are then endlessly amazed at how uncooperative the soul and body can be in doing what is good and right. Without a thorough understanding of how implicit beliefs are formed and the means by which they can be altered, these inner conflicts can appear to be insurmountable. Such lack of hope creates tremendous bondage and causes us to dismiss transformation as merely visionary. But if the contradictory beliefs can be uncovered and realigned with the truth, then our internal war will evaporate, and we will find the freedom we long for.

Iconographic Lies. We not only internalize lies in the form of ideas, some of which we may never verbalize, we can also form vivid icons in our mind that capture for us the very essence of these beliefs. For example, it is not uncommon to encounter a person who is unable to think of God as their Heavenly Father, because the only father they ever knew was an awful person. The very word "father" calls up for them images of a rageful and abusive man, along with a lifetime of painful memories. They hold in their mind an icon of "father" that encapsulates all of their father's evil attributes along with all of their own charged emotions, and this densely packed image automatically asserts itself and derails any thoughts they might have about God as Father.

What makes these icons so powerful is their non-verbal nature. No conscious process needs to be involved in recalling them. No effort is required for them to interject their emotional content into the present context. Because of where they reside in our brain, these icons interfere with our perceptions, our thought processes, our emotional states, our discernment, and our reactions to people and events – often without any awareness on our part that an old icon is driving our boat.

In addition to their non-verbal nature, our icons are generally not pictures we choose after careful consideration, but images that emerge from our own direct experience. When I was about three years old, we lived across the street from little Alan who was without a doubt the worst brat I had ever met. For me his name was synonymous with evil. To this day I can still see him in my mind on his little green tractor, either snotting off to his mother or trying to run over the nearest child.

But what is relevant to our discussion here is how for many years after we had moved away, my gut would tighten up whenever someone introduced themselves to me as "Alan" and I would feel a sort of dread wash over me, as if I might be in immediate danger of some sort. It did not matter than I knew this person was not the original Alan. I never chose to internalize such a bad icon for that name, and I never chose to call it up whenever I heard that name. Rather, my life experience shaped that icon in my mind without any decision on my part to do so. From that point on it got in my way whenever I interacted with anyone by that name.

Which brings us to the point that the more these icons distort life as God intended, the more they will interfere with our day to day existence. Any of the levels of belief described earlier can be held by an icon, and any given icon can influence our life in ways we never wanted. And because we hold them in graphic form, these beliefs are not easily dislodged, especially not by verbal explanations to the contrary. That is why in our earlier example, we cannot convince a person that God is a "good" Father as long as their internal icon says otherwise.

Summary. As you can see from the above discussion, our worldview is multifaceted and fairly complex. More than that, this collection of implicit beliefs we hold drives much of our waking life, regardless of what we *think* we ought to be feeling or saying or doing.

Alignment, Alliance, and Consent

Most of the things we believe about life are never really verbalized. They are *caught* over a period of time by a semi-conscious process that is always running in the background of our mind, trying to protect us and make sense of the world we live in. But if we watch carefully, our implicit beliefs will make themselves known by the ways in which we cope with or align with the particulars around us. For example, if I make an above average salary and still manage to gradually slip into debt, I may be aligning myself with principles of materialism and accumulation or perhaps carelessness and disregard for the future. These principles in turn imply a set of beliefs and values that drive my behavior. I may have never set out to adopt this set of beliefs, but I have aligned myself with them as evidenced by the way that I live day to day.

Alignment with implicit beliefs also shows up in the ways in which we are prepared to act (or not act) in a given situation. If I am more or less prepared to give you an offensive hand gesture when you cut across the lane in front of my car, then I have aligned myself with cursing and revenge as basic principles (at least in certain situations), whether I would normally admit to that or not. There is clearly a part of me that believes such behavior on my part is warranted. Similarly, a person who is prepared to jump at the slightest sound is aligned with principles of fear and beliefs about the dangers around them.

Identifying which spiritual principles we have aligned with is important, because alignment is an implicit participation in those beliefs whether or not we actually act on them all the time and in spite of whatever else we profess to believe. Our alignment reveals what we really expect and believe deep down inside, the implicit beliefs we have formed into our being over time. Thus, our actual alignment may be far more relevant to the quality of our spiritual life than the accuracy of our doctrines. Being watchful of where we align our efforts can help provide us with clues as to where we need to seek help.

Another way that our internal beliefs become evident is by the things to which we lend our consent.[60] Jesus talked a lot about consent in the Sermon on the Mount when He taught how the things we desire in our heart are as significant as the things we physically act on. Sin is not just what we do wrong or the good things we fail to do. It includes those wrong things we would do if we could, those things that we consent to internally but restrain ourselves from doing for some compelling reason. For example, a thief is not just someone who steals. A thief is someone who *would* steal if he could. He has already consented to taking something, and only the fear of consequences or self-condemnation prevents him from following through.

---

[60] This concept comes from Dallas Willard.

If we begin to take notice of the things we secretly consent to, we will begin to see the ways in which our innermost desires conflict with our ethics and our theology. If we look deeper still, we will find the implicit beliefs that fuel our desires and cause us to align with faulty principles.

Chapter 6
How Beliefs Drive My Life

Throughout the book we have asserted that our lives are heavily driven by our implicit beliefs. In this chapter we will introduce a model of human behavior that demonstrates clearly the extent to which this is true. The real value of this model lies in its simplicity and its ability to portray the impact of internalized beliefs on our lives. In Part 3 we will use this model to expose the flaws in our understanding of truth and to point the way to a highly accessible means of transformation.

An Interactive Model of Belief

If we slow down the internal process of how we interact with the world, it quickly becomes obvious how much our lives are driven by our implicit beliefs. First, let's look at a simplified model of how we respond to people and life events on an on-going basis. In the diagram on the next page, the only part of the process that is outside of our own mind is the external event or person that we are interacting with. Everything else occurs inside our mind. The process goes like this:

1) We are impacted by and/or observe a person or event (*Perception*).
2) We *Interpret* the raw data to determine its meaning and impact.
3) We *Respond* emotionally, verbally and/or physically.
4) We make additional observations about the situation, and so on.

Much of the time these steps happen so quickly and automatically that we fail to realize how involved we are in the process. For example, it is common to hear someone say, "You are making me angry." In truth a person's anger comes from his or her own interpretation of what was going on. If the problem is actually a misunderstanding, the anger may have no basis in reality at all, and once things are properly explained and the person's interpretations are updated, the anger will ordinarily dissipate. In another situation where the evaluation is right on, the anger still comes from the person's value system, and is only indirectly "caused" by the other person's behavior. In fact one person can become angry while another might agree with the action entirely. The emotions and responses come out of how we interpret the situation. They are not "caused" by external events.

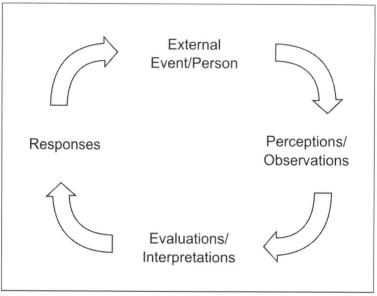

How We Interact with the World Around Us (simplified)

Just so there is no misunderstanding, before we take this process any further it is important to take a short detour and distinguish between interpreted responses and automatic reactions. To illustrate, consider walking across a campground somewhere in the Rocky Mountains. As you walk past the corner of a tent, you come face to face with a bear who is going through a stash of food. In less than a second, your sympathetic nervous system revs up, your adrenal gland gives you a shot of adrenalin, your pupils dilate, your pulse rate jumps, and your entire body prepares for action. This is an automatic reaction built into your biology to help keep you alive. It may not involve any intermediate step of interpretation at all.

Of course, we do not have to encounter life and death situations in order for us to experience automatic reactions. Hearing a loud noise, slipping on a wet surface, and many other such events will trigger these types of reactions in our body. There are also various kinds of life experiences which can get hard-wired into the sub-cortical regions of our brain that will then generate automatic reactions. For example, if a toddler has a bad experience with a large dog, they may develop a life-long phobia such that anytime they are near a dog they can feel their body ramp up into a fight-or-flight response.

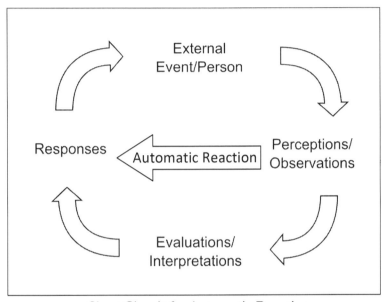

Short Circuit for Automatic Reactions

Several important observations can be made about these automatic reactions. First, as can be seen in the above diagram, for these types of external events there exists a kind of short-circuit between our perceptions and our *initial* reactions that bypasses any need for interpretation. Or to be more precise, the "evaluation" happens at such a low level neurologically, that it is involuntary and virtually unavoidable. In the first fraction of a second after we trip on a step, for example, our reactions come from basic survival instincts, not from any thought process.

But of course, we do not need healing and restoration from our survival instincts (unless we are dealing with a treatable phobia or similar problem). Those are not the kinds of reactions we are concerned with here where we are focusing on truth-based healing.

However, that does not necessarily mean these kinds of experiences have nothing to do with internalized beliefs. For example, if a person has a meltdown after every minor event (like "almost" tripping on the stairs) and they spend the next hour ruminating on how scary and dangerous everything feels for them or how clumsy they think they are, then clearly their evaluations and interpretations are involved at that point. It would not be a stretch to say that something has gone terribly wrong with their internalized beliefs about who they are or how life works for them.

So while our initial reactions to a situation might bypass any internal evaluation, within a second or two our worldview will in fact enter the picture and begin to influence our responses from that point forward. That is where our current discussion again becomes relevant.

In addition to our survival instincts, we may also respond more or less automatically in many types of situations due to whatever emotional and relational training we have had, regardless of whether that training was healthy or not. Thankfully, God has provided a number of other avenues for transformation that can help us retrain those areas of our mind as well. Again, those approaches are outside the scope of this present work. Our reason for noting them here is to clarify our position that truth is just one of one of several ways in which God heals and restores His people. And this diagram is not intended to illustrate everything that goes on in our mind, but rather to highlight the ways in which our implicit beliefs impact nearly everything else about the way our mind works.

Let us return now to our basic model and add a little complexity to make it more useful. As stated earlier, each of us has a deeply held set of internalized beliefs that dramatically impact how we see the world, what sense we make of our perceptions, what we feel, and how we respond to life. Adding these beliefs to our model offers some amazing insights.

First, our implicit beliefs act as a filter for our **perceptions**. We do not always see the world as it really is. Instead, our vision is heavily influenced by our expectations and our sense of what is possible. If I really believe that people generally do not like me, I will tend to notice data that proves my hypothesis to be correct and fail to see the rest. If I'm certain that my younger sibling is a complete idiot, there is almost no limit to the evidence I can accumulate to prove my case.

Once we have filtered the data, we rely on our **interpretations** to make sense of it. Again, our internal belief system has its say. This is where the Israelites got off track when they had their backs to the sea and interpreted the situation as proof God hated them. This is how we misinterpret illness or misfortune as evidence of God's disapproval or lack of concern. We also take credit for our successes, decide who deserves what, determine the meaning of the actions of others, and so on, all based on values and implicit beliefs that we hold from prior experience or stories of others.

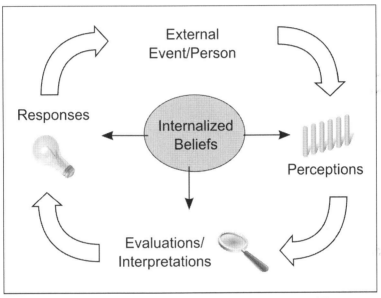

Beliefs Drive Our Perceptions, Interpretations, and Responses

Most of our **responses** then, whether emotional, vocal or physical, arise rather naturally from our interpretations, tempered by our implicit beliefs. We may or may not express our internal responses, or do so indirectly, depending on what we think of their potential impact. If I believe a display of anger would be inappropriate at the moment, I may stuff it. Or I might let it out in a humorous manner to minimize my risk. Either way, these aspects of our responses are heavily influenced by our implicit beliefs.

Putting this all together, let us look at how this process might work in a person's life choices. Take the classic case of a middle-aged businessman who has been working hard at his career for many years so that he can be the best possible provider for his family. He often works long hours to earn more and get ahead, even when it means many days and nights away from the family. Much of the time he has no awareness of the impact this has on them (a filter on his perceptions) and thinks that they are ungrateful when they complain (a misinterpretation). Over time he may even resent their demands (a response born out of his interpretations) and accuse them of "wanting it both ways" (another interpretation/response based on his beliefs). Sadly, the underlying beliefs that are driving his life may continue to persist in the face of all evidence to the contrary, until his wife announces that he has made her so miserable she is leaving. Only then does it occur to him that he may have been following an elaborate system of lies about what makes a good husband and father and how a man finds meaning in life.

We can see from this model that the implicit beliefs we internalize over time are a major driving force in our lives. They impact virtually every aspect of our interaction with life events and other people, from perception to interpretation to response. When you take into account the pervasive corrosive effect that deception has had on our belief system and how unaware we are of it most of the time, it becomes fairly easy to see how our lives can get so far off from where we think we should be. *All of my distortions of who I am, how God acts in the world, and how relationships work, all adversely impact my ability to live the way that God intends for me to live.*

> Our lives are largely driven by our beliefs
> and many of our beliefs are terribly distorted.

As we will see in Part 3, this understanding of the inner workings of our mind provides a major key to transformation. In short, if we can find a way to correct the distorted beliefs we hold, then we will see things differently, have more Christ-like interpretations of our observations, and respond more in concert with the way God designed us to live. Consequently, our life will quite naturally reflect more of the character of Christ. As the internalized beliefs become more in line with the truth, our auto-pilot responses will become more in tune with Kingdom principles.

Before we discuss that process, however, we would do well to better understand some of the ways in which our deep-seated beliefs can be exposed to the light.

Uncovering Our Implicit Beliefs

Feelings are good servants, but disastrous masters.[61]

Christian thinkers have long been suspicious of human emotion. Feelings and impulses seem to arise out of our bodies in ways that we feel powerless to control. So we are prone to think of them as either originating within an old sinful nature or else having been fatally corrupted by the fall. When the Bible speaks of "the flesh," we often associate that phrase with negative or destructive emotions we feel. Influential Christian leaders even tell us in no uncertain terms that emotions are not to be trusted. At the same time, we accept that love, joy, and hope are highly desirable and feel great. So we end up with a kind of love-hate relationship with our own nature, and wonder a bit about whether God knew what He was doing when He designed us.

At the other end of the spectrum, there is a disturbing trend today in which people believe their emotions are actually a reflection of reality, or at least *their reality*. Pluralism and relativism are partly to blame for this mistaken belief, and the misdirected desire to become *like gods* is responsible for the rest. If I feel something, it must be true; if I am afraid, it must be dangerous; if I am angry, my dignity or rights were violated; if I feel hurt, someone must be at fault; if I feel offended then someone is being hateful; if I want something, then there is nothing wrong with it. There is often little awareness that emotions are primarily an *interpretive* response which may or may not accurately reflect reality.

Along that same line, many people in recent decades seem to be losing the distinction between emotions and discernment. They tend to do what their feelings tell them to do, consider them to be sufficient reason for doing so, and are greatly offended if you suggest they are making a mistake. Feelings have become almost godlike, because when people reject truth from their lives they are left with little else to guide them besides their

---

[61] Willard, *Renovation of the Heart*, p. 122.

emotions. Even where emotions and will are understood to be separate, people often think that their desires are something that must be satisfied.

These mistaken ideas about emotions will predictably cause people to be deceived into making poor choices. A good analogy can be seen in lessons from our physical bodies. Suppose I'm a bit out of shape, and when I go for a hike on Saturday I'm sore and stiff all day Sunday. If I let my discomfort guide my decision, I will give up hiking and instead watch movies next week. But the real answer lies in hiking more often. Eventually my capacity will grow and the discomfort will end because I will have improved my physiology. Similarly, people will hide from conflict, cut off relationships, refuse to apologize, and do all sorts of destructive things attempting to avoid discomfort, when in fact seeking healing in those areas would serve them much better.

For example, a very common problem many people deal with is a fear of intimacy due to unresolved pain from past relationship failures or emotional trauma. The tragedy is that people who suffer from the fear of intimacy tend to protect themselves by isolating or minimizing their vulnerability, when the answer truly lies in the other direction. They desperately need to be *closer* to people in order to heal their damaged emotions. Dr. John Townsend has written an excellent volume on this very topic in which he addresses a long list of misperceptions and misinterpretations of life that lead to this very painful condition.[62]

The consequences of people who misuse or misunderstand emotions can be devastating, as they leave behind them a wake of damaged hearts and emotional injury. A person who has difficulty tolerating shame because he believes mistakes are unforgivable may become quite emotionally violent over the most minor issues. He may lash out at those around and attack them for whatever part he perceives they play in exposing his weaknesses. His failure to acknowledge his own part and his intent to protect his self-image result in emotional assaults that are completely unwarranted. His real need is to heal the underlying misbeliefs that drive his reactions to mistakes.

Misunderstanding emotions can distort a person's entire perception of reality. And a distorted reality can leave a person immature, unable to

---

[62] Townsend, *Hiding From Love*.

establish healthy relationships and boundaries, and permanently vulnerable to a whole range of problems like peer pressure and addictions.

Unfortunately, the "Christian" response to negative feelings has often been to tell people they just should not have those emotions and to teach them that the answer is a combination of repentance and some form of repression by an act of the will. This approach makes two major errors. First, it fails to address the *source* of negative emotions, and second, it attempts to change emotions by direct effort, which will not succeed.[63] At best it will only push them underground.

Connecting Emotions and Implicit Beliefs

Emotions do not arise out of a vacuum. They come out of our internal ideas and images of life,[64] most of which are acquired through formation, good or bad. If every minor setback I experience while working on a project results in feelings of despair and a desire to quit, it may be due to my underlying belief in Murphy's Law or some similar issue. On the other hand, if every time I encounter a problem my reaction is to pause long enough to envision another approach and then try again, it is probably due to a belief that most problems have solutions. Either way, my emotional state is dependent upon the interpretation I put on the events that I experience, rather than the event per se.

> Most emotions arise from our interpretations of life.

This principle can be seen at work in many contexts. As a child, if my mother yells at me and tells me I am really stupid, I may have any one of several reactions depending on my maturity level and belief system. If I am five years old, I will probably believe her and feel a deep sense of shame and rejection. But if I am seventeen and convinced that I know more than she does, I will probably interpret her remark as additional evidence that she "doesn't get it" and yell right back in a fit of anger.

In any case, the principle remains the same. My internal map of how things ought to work, how people ought to behave, who and what is

---

[63] Willard, *Renovation of the Heart*, p. 118.

[64] ibid, p. 128.

important to me, and my best understanding as to what meaning is inherent in an event, all contribute to my analysis of a situation and my corresponding emotional response. All this happens in a matter of milliseconds, often without any conscious awareness of the process. Even an infant who lacks the power of language will evaluate an encounter and respond according to their abilities. If the infant perceives that someone is glad to be with them they will respond with joy. If on the other hand the infant determines that someone is upset with them, they will respond with shame or fear, and may even be overwhelmed by their distress. In each instance, the emotions are largely born out of our interpretations of life, which in turn are shaped by very basic beliefs and values that we hold.

Extending this concept, we can begin to see how previous experiences influence our emotions in the present. One of the most powerful aspects of the mind is its ability to make associations on the basis of pattern recognition. That is how our prior learning helps us make sense of whatever situations we encounter. So the first time we see a particular coworker get angry, our implicit memories and beliefs regarding anger become active, and we are thus able to recognize the emotion even if this person demonstrates some unfamiliar behavior. We also know from past experience what can happen when a person gets angry and what kinds of options we may need to employ to help the person calm down or minimize our own vulnerability.

Our mind reaches back to a collective "story" of how anger works, and that story helps us interpret our present problem and formulate options. Given that the content of that story is different for everyone, and each person's relationship to this angry coworker is different, a single outburst of anger may cause one person to feel a little anxious, another mild amusement, and still another sheer terror. Each person's prior experiences with anger have a lot to do with his or her reaction to it in the present.

Understanding this relationship between feelings and implicit beliefs can provide us with a powerful tool for recovery from painful experiences and disabling patterns of behavior. Because if we can change the underlying faulty beliefs and replace them with truth, then the painful emotional response that came from those faulty beliefs will be replaced with emotions that arise from our new understanding.

For example, whenever anyone got angry with Mary for any reason, she would immediately feel intense, almost debilitating helplessness that was so powerful she would be unable to think rationally or respond coherently. Her only thought was to make it stop, and she would do anything it took to calm the person down, even apologize for things for which she had no responsibility. In seeking out the origins of this self-defeating pattern, it became obvious that Mary's basic beliefs about anger were the biggest reason why she could not control her response. During most of her early life, people around her used anger as a weapon to emotionally assault and eviscerate people. Most family members were willing to behave quite shamelessly in order to win any confrontation. For whatever reason, Mary never developed this taste for emotional violence, and always found herself completely helpless in the face of anger. The best strategy that she could work out was to diffuse the anger as quickly as possible in order to minimize the pain and humiliation that would otherwise ensue. By the time she reached adolescence, she was barely able to function in any heated exchange.

If we could find a way to reach her deeply internalized beliefs about anger and give Mary a new set of interpretations, her manner of handling anger would change dramatically.[65] In Biblical terms, this is an act of taking every thought captive (2Cor.10:5) and making it possible for her to respond in the spirit of Christ instead of a spirit of fear.

In similar fashion, when the memory of an old wound still brings up intense pain years after the event, the basic problem that the person is dealing with is probably no longer the event itself, but interpretations they hold in regard to that event. For example, Matt felt strongly called to full-time ministry while a teenager. But after only one semester of Bible college, he had to drop out due to lack of funds. He soon found himself in the military, hoping that the benefits after his tour of duty would help put him through school. Unfortunately, a year after his discharge from the service he was again strapped financially and left college to pursue a career in the business world in order to support his wife and children. Ten years later he still held deep grief about his inability to finish his theological studies.

---

[65] Her recovery may also require other resources as well, such as an increase of emotional capacity and experiential retraining in a safe community.

Upon digging a bit deeper it became apparent Matt was convinced that at some point God had given up on him and gone on to find someone else to fill the mission that had originally been slated for Matt. His greatest pain was rooted in a belief that God had abandoned him and it was his own fault. When Matt discovered that God still cared for him and had important things for him to do, much of his grief dissipated fairly quickly. It was his underlying beliefs that had kept him in pain, not the actual events.

The interpretations people develop to explain traumatic events can be very complex and non-rational, yet believed very deeply. A woman who had been wounded by sexual abuse many years earlier carried with her very heavy feelings of shame and guilt as well as the belief that she had been somehow defiled by the incident. No amount of rational re-evaluation of the experience helped her in any way, because her beliefs were too firmly entrenched. When she finally had the courage to ask God directly about how *He* saw things (she had been afraid of that, too) He revealed His heart to her in a way that broke the darkness in her soul, and she saw for the first time that she was clean and innocent in His eyes. Her entire life was transformed by this experience and shortly afterward her doctor ended her prescription for anti-depressants.[66]

In all of these examples, the person's deep feelings and reactions were clues to the underlying beliefs that fueled those emotions. Once the implicit beliefs were exposed and removed by the Spirit of God revealing truth to them, the disabling emotions dissipated without effort. The basic truth beneath all of this is that *what we believe about an event actually changes the way we experience it*, even if it occurred in the past.

Of course there are many more aspects to the nature of emotions that are beyond the scope of this work.[67] We have intentionally limited this discussion to those matters that relate directly to how belief and interpretation influence our feelings, and to factors related to inner healing and spiritual growth. But there is much more that could be said about the relationship between emotions and spiritual formation. I strongly

---

[66] Smith, *Beyond Tolerable Recovery*.

[67] Especially important is the area of regulating our emotions in a healthy manner See Friesen, et. al, *The Life Model*, pp. 11-35.

recommend Chapter Seven of Dallas Willard's *Renovation of the Heart* for a more comprehensive discussion of the topic.[68]

A Circular Relationship Between What We Believe and Why

One way in which beliefs get expressed is by how things are named and the meanings that are carried by those names. Take a very simple example. Hard as it may be for some people to accept, Calvin Klein jeans do not possess any inherent characteristic which makes them irresistible or which bestows upon the wearer some additional value. Yet a significant percentage of adolescents are convinced that wearing Calvin Klein jeans is more "cool" than wearing Levi's. Why? Some really good advertisers understood the power of implied values, and developed a strong association between their particular brand name and personal desirability. From that point on, the difference between "cool" and "not cool" could be expressed in a label.

Witness the power that labeling a junior high boy as a "nerd" has on his social relationships, or what calling a high-school girl "homely" does to her sense of self. This power of naming is used by the news media to tell us what things are newsworthy, by politicians to tell us about their opponents, and by liberal educators to tell us what is "politically correct." While naming something with its true name gives us the means of dealing with it appropriately, giving something a false name distorts both reality and our ability to deal with it.

> Our understanding of life can feel completely true
> even when it is deeply flawed.

A corollary to the power of naming is the power of misusing language to convey meanings that would not normally be associated with the thing or event. For example, as noted earlier, the word "tolerance" now actually means that certain points of view should not be tolerated! And witness how in our own time the word "Christian" has lost its common association with virtue and compassion, and has instead become connected in much of the

---

[68] Many of the insights in this section come from Dallas Willard, *Renovation of the Heart*, pp. 117-139

public mind with people who are either extremely gullible or else socially and politically dangerous. The manner in which words get used in the general press has a great impact on how people see things.

The way we name things is both an expression *of belief* and a directive *to believe* a certain way. To say this another way, the words we apply to an experience or idea reflect what we believe about it. And when we use those words in talking about that idea or experience, we reinforce that point of view in our own mind. This is the case whether or not our words are accurate reflections of reality. But truth demands that we use words which correctly identify the quality of the thing named. Otherwise we open ourselves up to ideas that are distorted and deceptive.

This same circular relationship exists between our implicit beliefs and the way we experience life. As we have seen, our deepest beliefs are drawn from our interpretations of life experience, and those beliefs then continue to interpret our future experiences. This cycle is self-reinforcing and leads us to regard those beliefs as reflections of reality itself and not separate from it. That is what makes our understanding of life feel so true, even when it is deeply flawed. Only when we grasp the extent of this problem can we open the door to real transformation by truth. Once we realize that our own malformed beliefs are some of the biggest problems we face, we can submit ourselves to the task of learning with an openness and teachability that might otherwise be severely limited.

> Our understanding of life can feel completely true
> even when it is deeply flawed.

What We Believe About Growth Can Limit Our Development

Hopefully at this point we have laid the foundations for an approach to spiritual growth and transformation that makes sense, even though it may be quite different from what most Christians have been taught. To sum up what we have said so far, we live in a very dark world where deceptions and distortions of spiritual realities are pervasive. Since we were not designed to live in such a spiritually perverse world, we are continually being malformed as we go through life. To whatever extent we interpret life on our own apart from the Spirit's mentoring, the impact of the darkness around us will be overwhelming. As we internalize faulty beliefs about who we are, who God is and how to live, we release the power of those lies into our own life and become bound by them. By definition the lies cannot deliver, so we are left empty, unfulfilled, and robbed of spiritual vitality, separated from one another and God by our distorted perceptions.

This process has an incredibly destructive effect on our soul and on our hope for getting free. Lies are deadly. Satan is above all a murderer (Jn.8:44) whose intent is to steal, kill, and destroy (Jn.10:10). Once we are entangled, the lies begin to compound, and eventually we come to believe there is no real escape, and that what we currently have is about all we can expect. A few years after a milestone encounter with God we discover that we have been worn down again by life in this dark place. We lose hope of ever seeing the abundant life we read about in the New Testament, and add still more lies to our view of life.

Yet we read that darkness cannot withstand the light. So we must ask, What is wrong with this picture? Why is it that truth does not seem to penetrate our soul and set us free? We read the Word and study its meaning, but then get up the next morning and nothing has changed. Why does the truth seemingly fail to do the transforming work we believe it ought to be capable of? What makes the difference between truth that transforms our mind and truth that does not?

The tragedy of this predicament is that people often come right up to the point of wrestling with these questions and *then arrive at still another erroneous belief as an explanation for this conflict*. One solution many have come up with is that we are reading the promises of Scripture the wrong way. Our victory is really in the future and we are stuck here now in the flesh. Another way to resolve the problem is to think the promises are for someone else, that we ourselves have quenched the Spirit or fallen too far for God to help us. Still another explanation we hear is that we just have not tried hard enough.

Unfortunately, if we buy into any of these explanations, it just adds another layer of lies to the pile! These are the means by which the enemy keeps us disillusioned and without hope. The last thing he wants is for us to discern is that *the whole scheme is a house of cards that will begin to collapse if we ever discover the way of truth.*[69]

Even hearing that, many Christians recoil and argue that it cannot be that simple. They have been trying for years to overcome the bondage in their life and they know how difficult it is to experience victory. How could anyone dare to tell them that their own belief system is what is keeping them in bondage! They want desperately to be free. How can their own beliefs be the cause of the problem?

Here at this critical juncture we must stop resisting and consider, if just for the sake of argument, the possibility that the following propositions might actually be true:

1. Evil perpetuates and complicates lies at every turn. That is its nature.
2. Satan is far more clever than we are.
3. Our own heart can be divided in many areas that are important to us.
4. We are fighting the wrong fights for exactly the same reason that we are stuck in the first place, which is, we have some serious blind spots.

What if the truth is that like all other human beings, Christians generally suffer from poor eyesight? It happened in Corinth and Galatia, it engulfed the Medieval Church, and it was predicted over and over in the New Testament. What if we too have been impacted by the strategy of the enemy to destroy every chance of restoration?

On the whole, we have largely misunderstood the ways of evil. For too long theologians have had their microscopes honed in on the spiritual DNA that supposedly came down from Adam and focused their attention on the sin problem that infests the human body. But according to Paul, the sin problem has already been dealt with by the New Adam and by our death and resurrection into the new race of Abraham's children. The biggest issue that remains is the inner renewal process (Col.3:10), recovering from the spiritual blindness and malformation that comes from living in darkness.[70]

Again for the sake of argument, we need to ask an all-important question. *What if the lies are so layered and pervasive that they are no longer*

---

[69] Willard, *The Divine Conspiracy*, pp. 230-231.

[70] Romans 5 and 6 are especially instructive here.

visible? What if we have been depending on our doctrine to grow us up, when the truth is that is something doctrine cannot do? What if we believed that we could make this Christian life work if we just wanted it bad enough and tried hard enough, and it turns out we have been taken in by one of the most popular myths the church has ever seen? And when we turn to the Bible as our one infallible source of truth, what if we find that we do not know *how to ingest* that truth so that it can become truth *in* us? The enemy has left no stone unturned in his campaign against us. One thing we can be sure of is that if there is any way to distort an aspect of Christian formation, he has found it and exploited it to the limit.

How often have you heard of a Christian who one day encountered God in a powerful way, and then two years later was struggling at a level no different than before the encounter? What causes the relapse? Some will say, "You cannot live on the mountain" and that is why life returns to what it was before. But that projects a fairly dismal picture of perpetual drudgery. Whatever happened to the artesian well that was promised (Jn.4:14), the abundant life (Jn.10:10), the fields full of plenty (Ps.23:1-2), and the feast that will satisfy (Isa.55:2)? No, there must be another explanation.

Again, we misunderstand the ways of evil. The lies we have been fed are far more effective than we think. When a Christian begins to recover the joy of the Lord and get a taste of victory, the enemy moves in with a vengeance. If he can quench that new life before it grows to maturity, the hapless Christian will then be exposed to the lie of the "short-term victory" that comes at such great cost and leaves with such ease.

Discouragement at the moment of victory is almost axiomatic. As soon as we begin to experience life more fully, we press against the kingdom of darkness. Whenever we begin seeking new avenues of growth, we usually find ourselves stretching a bit more than we are used to. If we mistake our discomfort for a wrong turn, we may draw back when we need to walk forward. If we mistake it for "coming down from the mountain" we may give up without a fight. Whatever nonsense the enemy can make out of our situation, he will try to keep us from seeing our discomfort for what it really is — a teachable moment, an opportunity to let Christ live in us more fully, an opportunity to confront the fears that keep us from moving forward through difficulty, and an opportunity to uncover the lies we have believed that make us vulnerable in that particular moment of victory.

What if we could internalize truth with the same intensity and impact with which we initially internalized the lies? What if we could see life more the way God sees it? We could then experience the life that comes from being renewed, instead of the destruction that comes from being deceived! We would be able to live more and more in the Kingdom, where our thoughts and feelings would increasingly reflect the reign of God in our heart and leave behind the thoughts and ways of the world.

Can you guess what is the single greatest barrier to this kind of life? Yes, disbelief, yet again. Many find it too hard to believe that a life of increasing victory is possible. Others have trouble believing that truth could be that much of a factor. And those two lies alone are more than enough to keep anyone out of Kingdom life, no matter what else they may try.

Chapter 7
True Belief is Hard Work

Once we get past the misconception that belief is nothing more than an intellectual agreement with certain doctrines, we are faced with a particularly difficult problem. How do we change the faulty beliefs that we have already internalized? Uncovering our underlying assumptions about life is a difficult task, because internalized beliefs can shape our perceptions so extensively that they seem to be reality itself rather than our own interpretations of it. Telling the difference requires more work than we might think.

Life in the Wake of the Exodus

In studying the history of Israel after the Exodus, it is very easy to be critical of their behavior. They complained to Moses at every turn of events and failed in their first attempt to enter the land. All of this in spite of God's constant provision, His appearance on Sinai, and the miracle of their deliverance from Egypt. But one must not be too hard on them. Do not forget that they were all severely malformed by generations of slavery. Just imagine the implicit beliefs they must have developed in their bondage and held without question right up to the moment when the Egyptians were drowned in the sea – and in some cases, longer.

- Hope is a dangerous thing.
- Non-Jews are a lot more powerful than Jews.
- We have nothing, we never will have anything.
- God must really hate us to make us live like this.
- We'll all die before any of us find peace.
- I have no will of my own, and what I want means nothing.

For an entire generation after the Exodus the lies continued to win out. God had to wait forty years for people who could believe that victory was possible and that God would do for them what they would never be able to do by themselves. Lies are powerful and destructive. They rob us of meaningful choices because those options are simply too far off the screen to even be considered. Only the healing work of truth will restore us to the place where we can follow God's leading. But that requires a teachable spirit on our part and a willingness to do the work necessary to receive.

The Work God Requires of Us

John records an interesting conversation between Jesus and the crowd after He counseled them to work for spiritual food rather than bodily food (Jn.6:26+). If it is permissible to take a bit of license, I imagine that the discussion went something like this:

> People: What sort of work does God require?
> Jesus: The work of God is this...to believe.
> People: Yes we know. But what are we supposed to *do*?
> Jesus: The work of God is to believe Him.
> People: Yes, you said that. But what are we supposed to *do*?

Jesus knew that believing can be hard work. We often tend to think we already know whatever we need to know and that our biggest problem is simply putting it into action. But that assumption contains at least two errors. First, the idea that we already know most of what we need to is about on par with a nine-year-old who thinks he has mastered mathematics after learning fractions. We really have no idea how much more there is to understand of spiritual realities. Second, the belief that our problem is primarily a lack of effort is dangerously naive, because the harder people try to live out of their mistaken beliefs, the worse off they will be.

No, the truth is that belief is hard, in part *because we don't know what we don't believe*. We truly are that out of touch with our own inner convictions. We may get a taste of it when we read an inspiring book, like *The Journey of Desire* by John Eldredge. We sense there is something we are missing, just out of reach. But we assume it could not possibly be more than some minor adjustment from where we are, if we could only grasp it. Or we conclude that perhaps we have just not wanted it badly enough.

A friend of mine wrote out the twenty-third Psalm and had been carrying it around for several weeks as an aid for reflecting on God's provisions. When he showed it to me he said something very honest and revealing. "You know where I always get stuck? The first line. 'The Lord is my Shepherd: I have everything I need.' You know why I get stuck there?

Because that is so hard for me to believe." Yes, my friend, it *is* hard. And if I am not careful, I will think it is too easy and that I already believe it (because I'm supposed to believe it) when I really do not.

Adding to this gap between what we *think* we believe and what we *really* believe is the fact that we are rarely aware of the many dark things we really *do* believe. After begging God for years to free me from some persistent sin, I may conclude that He has little concern for my spiritual bondage. Or after losing a loved one in a terrible accident I may wonder whether God cares about me at all. Many Christians harbor a deep distrust of God and are either unaware of their distrust or have no idea that they actually believe false things about Him that foster distrust. Those who *are* aware of their distrust are convinced that God is in fact not trustworthy. When we assume we already believe the right things, we add one more layer of deception and make those beliefs even more resistant to exposure and change.

Reread the list of bullet points about what the Israelites were thinking prior to the Exodus and consider the following question. How many of us have had those same thoughts?

Belief is hard work, some of the hardest work you will ever do.

The Work of Belief Can Change Your Life

One of the most promising observations about this view of reality is the way it has helped some of the most severely traumatized among us. As many Christian counselors and those working with healing and freedom in the body of Christ have reported in recent years, survivors of terrible forms of childhood abuse are finding tremendous freedom and transformation from learning how to participate with the Holy Spirit to gain a God-oriented understanding of their own lives. If this approach to transformation really works for them, how much more effective can it be to address the garden-variety lies which the enemy has woven into all of our lives? This is all very promising.

Still, among the various keys to this process there remains a very sticky issue regarding the level to which people are responsible for perpetuating their own problems. It becomes sticky because the very notion that we ourselves are in some way perpetuating our bondage and pain because of our own beliefs is intolerable to a great many people. And without a thorough understanding of grace they may be unable to resolve this particular problem because it feels demeaning and shameful. It may even sound like a "blame the victim" mentality. So it is with some apprehension and careful consideration that we turn to a rather touchy subject.

Why Does the Work of Recovery Fall to the Wounded?

One problem in particular has been a major obstacle for those who find themselves still suffering as adults from the intrusions and deprivations of childhood. Often survivors of severe trauma spend years recovering from their early wounds. During that process it is common to hear them speak of the injustice of having to deal with the pain a second time as they wrestle with their past. Some develop strong resentment about the work of recovery itself. After all, they did not do the damage, why should they bear the pain of the repair work? If the wounds came from outside, should not the healing come from outside as well? They may wonder why God takes so much time and some even give up on part or all of their recovery because it feels so overwhelming and unfair.

This brings us to a difficult question. How responsible are adult survivors of childhood trauma for their own healing process? To answer this question properly requires several steps, each of which must be understood completely before attempting the next step.

The first step is to state categorically that children are no more responsible for their *response* to trauma than they are for the trauma itself. God designed us to grow our capacity for suffering over a lifetime. Children have relatively little capacity, especially in the face of suffering at the hand of the primary caregivers to which they are deeply bonded. They are fairly easily overwhelmed beyond their ability to manage the trauma. Once overwhelmed, they do not make choices about how to cope, any more than a drowning person makes choices about what to grab onto in order to keep their head above water. There is no deliberate selection of preferences or time for application of Sunday School teaching. They simply find a way to manage their intolerable feelings of rejection, abandonment and shame.

Thankfully, God has equipped children with all sorts of mechanisms for survival, some quite creative. They may invent some erroneous meaning for the pain, take the blame to exonerate those upon whom they depend for life, blank out and forget entire events, or even dissociate from the experiences. These are all ways of getting through the trauma, which is the child's only real job at the time. All the responsibility for overwhelming a child's capacity and triggering the means of coping belongs to the person or persons who were being hurtful.

Step two in this answer is to understand that all of these coping systems are, at their root, *various ways of distorting reality*. Again, this is not the child's fault. What we are saying is that adults who should have protected the child and aided the child's development of a healthy perspective on life have instead used their power to overwhelm the child's capacity for suffering. The adults have effectively imposed on them a twisted view of relationship, identity, safety, love, God's intent for the child, and a host of other spiritual realities. This is the stuff of which evil is made. When Jesus said that the thief comes to steal, kill, and destroy, this is part of what He meant and why He was so forceful in His statements about what would happen to those who harmed children (Lk.17:2).

The third step comes in recognizing the true source of the pain that is felt by an adult survivor in the form of deep-seated self-loathing, anger at God, inability to relate well to others or form lasting love bonds, and so forth. It is very tempting to say that this pain is all caused by the trauma. But that is not fully accurate. The true source of the pain is *the distorted sense of reality* that was forced into the child's world along with the child's means of coping with evil. For although it served a temporary purpose at that time by allowing the child to survive intolerable conditions, that same distorted sense of reality repeatedly *fails* the child both then and later in adulthood. Over time those distortions prove to be shaky, even destructive, foundations for building functional concepts of self, others, and life. They also tend to distort all new information that is received about spiritual things. *Living with a poorly constructed map of life is a painful way to live!* And that is the condition of the adult survivor.

Step four is then, How do we get a workable map? The long answer to that question brings us to the whole issue of inner healing that transforms the soul. In Part 3 of the book we will cover how truth provides a powerful resource to help us in that process. The short answer is that we can in fact trade in our map for a new one. Or more precisely, we can fix the map piece by piece with the help of the Holy Spirit. The more accurately our map reflects the truth of who we are, who God is, and how He intended for us to live, the less unnecessary suffering we will endure.

Fifth, very little of this can occur in a relational vacuum. In fact, much of the responsibility for aiding one another in revising our maps falls on the community as a whole. An important element to keep in mind here is that *revising our implicit beliefs can be limited by our capacity to process stressful emotions*. Unfortunately, due to the heavy influence of individualism in our culture, we tend to be blind to the truth that this type of capacity is best developed within the context of significant relationships,[71] which means that our families and spiritual communities must take some responsibility for this process, especially with regard to our low-capacity members, even if they happen to be walking around in adult bodies (Rom.15:1).

In other words, one very important job of community is to help its wounded members grow in maturity and in the capacity to endure emotional stress, as well as the ability to engage in self-examination without condemnation. The more that people grow in these areas, the more they are able to face the destructive misbeliefs they hold without being overwhelmed and re-traumatized by the attempts to receive healing. This part of the puzzle may be a new thought to many Christians who have not understood their role, or who may have thought that all people needed was enough faith to overcome any obstacle. While the topic of emotional capacity goes beyond the scope of this work, the point I want to make here is that identifying false beliefs as the cause of our pain does not automatically imply that an adult survivor is prepared to face whatever lies they are holding onto.

This brings us to the **final step** in our answer. At some point the survivor must come to grips with the truth that the source of their pain may no longer be the original trauma or even the memory of trauma. What causes a person to feel pain years after an event is *the false interpretation of reality* which they internalized that provides meaning for that experience. Thus the problem is no longer in the past or with events outside of the

---

[71] Wilder, *The Complete Guide to Living With Men*. The role of relationship in human development is demonstrated repeatedly throughout the book.

person. The problem resides inside the survivor in the present. Healing then requires the survivor's active participation, meaning that the person cannot simply wait for life to get better, but that he or she must do the hard work necessary to uncover those things that are actually perpetuating the pain, which always includes one or more implicit beliefs that must be removed and replaced with the truth of God.

This whole context has been beautifully illustrated in a fictional story told by Dr. John Townsend in *Hiding From Love*.[72] It is the story of nine year-old Jenny who lived in a European village near a forest during World War II. When the Nazi soldiers came to the town she ran off and hid in the woods for several years. During her time in the forest she developed elaborate means to protect herself in every possible situation. Eventually the war ended without her knowledge, but she was still terrified and hid whenever anyone came looking for her. Finally, after many trips into the forest, an old friend was able to reach her heart. She had to resist tremendous feelings of fear and give up the safety of the forest in order to go home, but eventually she was able.

Now we could ask to what extent Jenny was participating in the problem that was keeping her from going home. However, it is really the wrong question. More appropriately, what does Jenny need in order to return home? The answer is a caring heart that is willing to meet her where she is and help her to discover that her reasons for fear and self-protection are no longer valid. Yes, there did come a point where she needed to challenge her own beliefs about the world. No one else could change her heart for her. But it was only when she felt the trust of a friend and the assurance that he would walk with her into a new reality that she was able to let go of the beliefs that were preventing her from going home.

Great care must be taken when trying to communicate this truth to someone who is still "in hiding." In fact if the person has not yet begun the healing process, it may be better not to bring it up at all. The more responsible solution is for the community to do the hard work of building trust and then helping the person through the first few encounters with truth. After that, it becomes possible to point to the relationship between truth and freedom and present the notion that more freedom will come

---

[72] Townsend, *Hiding From Love*, pp. 17-28.

from further self-examination and submitting to the Spirit for resolution. There is no point in hammering home the fact that the person's own beliefs are contributing to the bondage.

These Principles Apply to All of Us

It is also worth pointing out that although this discussion focused on survivors of early trauma and abuse, the principle discussed actually applies to virtually everyone. We are all in need of retraining and recovery from malformation, whether from overt abuse or just common lies that affect all of us due to life in a broken world.

Take for example a woman in her late twenties who has been rejected by several romantic interests over the years and wants desperately to find the love of her life. She may grow more fearful of relationships as time goes on and decide that in order to protect herself and still keep her options open she must try harder to manage men's impressions of her, based on a belief that the most important thing is to keep them from leaving. Another woman with a similar history may decide that she needs to lower her standards, because the most important thing is to not be alone. Yet another may give up on relationships altogether based on the belief that men are impossible. All of these represent defective strategies that arise out of value systems that have been shaped by experience. What is missing in each case is a recognition that their own internal values are interfering with their responses to life and their future, and that they need a perspective that is bigger than what they can grasp with their own resources.

We have all developed rather elaborate schemes that are filled with misperceptions of who we are, who God is, and how we are to live. To whatever extent we persist in those patterns we may actually be participating in our own undoing. That is, of course, the enemy's strategy behind using lies. And that is why we all need to seek the truth of God regarding our own life.

Part 3

Lies About Truth

"You have taken away the key to knowledge.

You yourselves have not entered,

and you have hindered those who were entering."

(Luke.11:52)

Part 3 – Lies About Truth

Chapter 8: Lies We Believe About Christian Development

Not surprisingly, the reason we have so much difficulty with the Christian life is that our dominant approach to spiritual growth is deeply flawed. It is built on faulty premises and encourages self-defeating practices for change.

Chapter 9: Truth is More Than True Information

Why is it that we can be challenged by what we read in the Bible, but find it so hard to change? A major part of the problem is our misunderstanding of the nature of truth itself.

Chapter 10: Internalizing Truth

The key to internalizing truth in ways that are life-changing is to be taught by the Spirit of God instead of relying on our own methods of intellectual inquiry. Engaging with God as our mentor, learning to hear from Him and receiving His truth deep into our soul changes everything we ever knew about how truth changes lives.

Chapter 11: Realigning Our Christian Development

Bringing all these pieces together, we can now formulate a coherent picture of where we are and what we need in order to change and grow.

Chapter 8

Lies We Believe About Christian Development

There are quite a number of reasons why spiritual growth is elusive for so many Christians. We suffer from faulty presuppositions about Christian living, a lack of intentionality, aiming at the wrong goals, fighting the wrong fights, and using the wrong means, to name a few.

But there is a single consistent thread that runs through all of these problem areas, something that lies at the very heart of transformation: *misunderstanding the nature of truth*. What it is, how to find it, how to internalize it, and how to be transformed by it, are all crucial to changing our character and growing up spiritually. In the light of our past difficulties with spiritual growth, this means that we must not only internalize the specific truths we need personally so that we can live more the way God designed us to live, we must first learn the truth about encountering truth. To help minimize the influence of common misunderstandings about spiritual growth in this discussion, we will begin by looking at some of the problems that have permeated the Christian world for the last few centuries, problems that have put growth out of reach for a great many people.

Traditional Approaches to Christian Growth

If you have been a Christian for any length of time, you have probably heard that to grow spiritually you have to do the following three things: go to church, read your Bible, and pray. There may be other items thrown in (like volunteer for some job in the church), but these are the core behaviors that are supposed to help everyone grow. If you find that these things are not working for you any more, you may face a number of obstacles in trying to obtain some real help. In some circles there are unwritten social prohibitions about admitting helplessness as a Christian. To say you need help is like saying you have leprosy. The fact that such taboos are rooted in distorted perceptions of Christianity will do very little to alleviate your second class status. But if you are brave enough to ask for help, you may well get an answer that sounds more or less like one of these:

- You need to try harder.
- You have sin in your life for which you need to repent.
- You are going too much on what you feel, just be obedient.

Unfortunately, these answers are far too easily believed because there could be some measure of truth in them if spoken at the right time to the right person. Even so, they fall far short of what is really needed. The real problem goes far deeper. Woven all throughout the way we teach our doctrines of the new birth and sanctification are powerful threads of misunderstanding and distortion that sell the gospel short and leave us wondering where all the power for life has gone.

You may have seen the infamous bumper sticker, "Christians aren't perfect, just forgiven." Every time I see that my heart sinks a bit, and I want to ask, "Is that all?" Is that what separates a Christian from a non-Christian? Not to knock forgiveness, it is one of several very amazing things that God has done for us. And the statement that Christians are not perfect is right on because we will never be perfect in this life. But if the only difference between me and a lost person is that I have been pardoned, then it seems to me that the New Testament could have been a whole lot shorter!

After the Israelites settled the land of Israel, were they nothing more than just Egyptian slaves living in a foreign land? Or were they fundamentally different? Were they not *the people of God* who happened to still carry a lot of beliefs and ways that they had learned in Egypt? Can you imagine an ox cart sticker that read, "Israelites aren't free, just escaped"? No, that is more what you might expect to find on the back of an Egyptian chariot, sported by people who were unwilling to accept that God had changed the basic identity of His people.

Of course, a bumper sticker does not define the nature of Christianity. The problem is that such sound bites are indicative of a pervasive belief that Christians are nothing more than sinners who have stumbled onto a way of getting into heaven. This is a serious distortion of both the gospel and of our God-given identity! And as we saw in the chapter on how Adam and Eve were deceived, distorted images of who we are can have disastrous consequences. Teaching Christians that bondage is normal is a terrible basis for life. It fails to do justice to the language of Scripture and robs Christians of any hope for victory.

And that is only one of many false beliefs regarding the Christian life that run through the Church. Cloud and Townsend have written a very interesting book about some things that you may have learned in church that did not come from the Bible.[73] Among the false beliefs that they debunk are:

- It is selfish to have my needs met.
- If I change my behavior, I will grow spiritually and emotionally.
- Leave the past behind (just get over it).
- If I have God, I don't need people.
- Just doing the right thing is more important than why I do it.

Cloud and Townsend take a close look at each of twelve such beliefs that are commonly heard among Christians, and show not only why they are wrong, but how those beliefs actually cripple Christians as they fight the wrong battles for years and become discouraged because their efforts do not bring the results they expect. If we are to grow up at all, we must recognize the pitfalls in our thinking that sabotage our progress. There are few things more discouraging than doing the best you know and not seeing any difference. Such experience can even bring a person to question his or her faith.

Thankfully, the Christian formation movement in recent years has not only recognized the weaknesses of traditional approaches to Christian growth and education, it has poured out vast resources to help Christians go deeper in their relationship with God, to pray better, to build stronger community, and to encounter God and His Word in ways that are life-giving. This book is itself an outgrowth of, and hopefully a contribution to, that new vein of Christian vitality that is beginning to change the way we understand the Christian life in our time. But there is much work to be done and much of the old way of thinking still permeates our teaching.

---

[73] Cloud and Townsend, *12 Christian Beliefs That Can Drive You Crazy*.

Most Theologies of Sanctification are Surprisingly Weak

One of the reasons that our traditional approaches to Christian growth have had such mediocre results is that they have been rooted in relatively poor theologies of sanctification. Sanctification is just a big word that refers to the process by which "the believer is separated from sin and becomes dedicated to God's righteousness" resulting in freedom from both the guilt and power of sin.[74] To develop a theology of sanctification means simply to correctly identify the principles that God has laid down by which we can experience growth and transformation.

Faced with the reality of a huge gap between the spiritual bondage we are all familiar with and the promises for victory in the New Testament, every Christian tradition has struggled to make sense of the internal battle and develop a cohesive doctrine of sanctification. Most agree there is a "now/not-yet" dimension to the Christian life that explains the lack of perfection. But there has to be more to it if we are to have any measure of victory over sin and its effects in this life, a hope that seems quite evident in the New Testament. Sadly, a careful reading of the prevailing views of sanctification reveals the fact that a wide variety of theological traditions find it extremely difficult to explain how this all works.[75]

Luther and Calvin both held fairly pessimistic views of human nature, both Christian and non-Christian. Consequently, the practical doctrines of sanctification handed down through those traditions have generally reflected that pessimism with regard to Christian growth. Wesley correctly identified the weaknesses of Protestant theology in this area, and offered a number of incredibly important insights regarding our need for a deeper relationship with God in order to grow spiritually. But his own proposal of sanctification as a crisis experience leading to sinless perfection is difficult to support biblically. Pentecostal theology tried to restore emphasis on the Holy Spirit's visible role in the Christian life, making spiritual power more accessible. However, their over-reliance on miraculous experiences led to the expectation that transformation would follow automatically from an infilling of the Holy Spirit. Dispensationalism created still another scenario

---

[74] Lockyer, Nelson's *Illustrated Bible Dictionary*, p. 948.

[75] Dieter, Hoekema, Hortan, McQuilkin, Walvoord, *Five Views of Sanctification.*

by postulating that Christians carry with them two separate natures: the old Adamic nature and the new one created by God at conversion. But if the old nature cannot change for the better and the new nature needs no change, how do we change? Evidently, they think our will somehow resides outside our two natures (in a third nature?) and is able to arbitrate between them. Of course, these leaves us trapped in a permanent internal war between good and bad urges with no real solution to the problem of sin.

In most of these views, the Holy Spirit is given honorable mention as the author of sanctification, but as soon as these theologians get to the part where they have to describe exactly when and how the Spirit works, or how change actually occurs, the language suddenly becomes quite vague and indirect. After quoting lots of verses, the authors tell us that sanctification is clearly a work of the Holy Spirit, something that we are to take as a matter of faith no matter how much it looks like we ourselves are the only ones making an effort.

However, since there are also a great many imperatives in Scripture directed at us with regard to sin and holiness, we are told that our part in this venture is to try as hard as we can to do the right thing. Apparently the Spirit only changes us while we are putting forth our best effort, something like a special vitamin that works its way into our soul only when we are in motion. Apart from Wesley's perspective, rarely is anything said about directly engaging with God. We find very few useful tools to help those who are stuck, and what little that is offered can be quite condescending or condemning. Frankly, it is hard to see how this approach is much different at all from "God helps those who help themselves."

It really should come as no surprise then that the Church has had great difficulty teaching its people how to combat sin or overcome their wounds. Having articulated such vague and weak foundations for spiritual development, the practical teaching we receive tends to address our struggles at the wrong point in the process, like closing the barn door after the horses are already gone.

Most discipleship training comes down to developing positive attitudes and trying harder to do the right things, a kind of behavior modification program that uses the Bible for guidance. But these approaches have limited results because we have not learned how to change the underlying engines that give rise to sin and negative attitudes in the first place. We fail to see the fruits of the new life because we have not changed our underlying beliefs about the life we have. Instead, we spend our efforts "trying to get people to do things good people are supposed to do, without changing what they really believe." [76] Quite predictably, the results are burnout, disillusionment, and outright disbelief in ongoing transformation.

> Weak theories of change will inhibit transformation.

The way many Christian organizations teach sanctification often sounds more like an apology for why change happens so slowly and why growth is so unpredictable, rather than a serious and practical plan for how to actually grow. One would think that *much of the Church has dismissed transformation as merely visionary*, and settled for relatively weak theologies of sanctification in order to make sense of the limited growth in the average Christian. This of course is just one more way in which the father of lies has robbed us of our rightful inheritance. He knows that if we define away our hope, we will not be able to live it out. We have lowered the bar so far that many Christians today are seriously skeptical about any teaching that says we can participate deliberately with the Holy Spirit in ways that transform our character.

But once we understand the nature of transformation and the role of truth in that process, all of this can change. Because when the energy behind sin and self-defeating behavior is gone, the battle becomes an entirely different sort of problem that actually has a solution.

Truth is Real, Not Relative

Although this book is written primarily to Christians who have a basic understanding of Scriptural truth, in today's climate of extreme relativism we must acknowledge the fact that many people now have a greatly diminished grasp of the nature of truth. For that reason, we cannot ignore this problem or the gravity of its consequences for our culture. At the same time, it must be said that a full review of this topic would require several volumes, a task that is beyond my ability in any case. My hope here is to at

---

[76] Willard, *The Divine Conspiracy*, pp. 307-308.

least raise some awareness of this problem before moving on to the lies about truth which have overrun much of the Christian world.

Generally speaking, this problem we have with relativism falls into two major areas. First is the fact that for over fifty years now, much of the academic world has rejected any notion of spiritual truth at all. This is an extremely serious and complex problem for which I would refer the reader to the works of Dallas Willard, a world-class philosopher who addressed this issue with incredible wisdom, regarding a potentially catastrophic failure of our culture which he referred to as "The Death of Moral Knowledge." [77]

A second problem that has accompanied this move toward relativism has to do with what happens when a culture abandons truth as an external compass which we can rely on for a basic sense of direction. The Western world has now reached a point where we are rapidly losing the distinction between *discernment* and *desire*.[78] That is, not long ago nearly everyone knew that good discernment was a skill we could develop over time with proper training along with learning from our own personal experience. Underlying this goal was the presupposition that ideas have consequences, as do behaviors. For that reason it was important to acquire the wisdom to make wise choices and to know the difference between good and evil.

However, more and more people today are simply following their gut, going almost entirely by feeling rather than reason in order to make choices. These feelings are in turn heavily influenced by their friends and idolized celebrities. This is why it is becoming ever more difficult to have intelligent conversations about moral issues in our culture. Right and wrong are terms that quickly lose their meaning when personal desire is the driving force behind what a person is choosing. What's more, people are now actually offended by the idea that their gut feeling about something might be entirely misleading. Any direct challenge to their feelings about something is even denounced as "hate speech."

One of the most blatant examples of this can be seen in how the so-called "pro-choice" activists think about abortion. What they really want is a totally unrestricted right to make whatever "choice" they "feel" like making. There is no right or wrong for them beyond what they desire. Thus they

---

[77] For a layman's approach to moral knowledge, see Willard, *Knowing Christ Today*.

[78] Again, an observation made by Dallas Willard.

feel deeply offended by any attempt to discuss an inherent right to life or to present any basic facts regarding normal fetal development. Their desire has replaced any discernment they might have had, and anything which might call that desire into question is experienced by them as a personal attack rather than a voice of reason.

Of course, the issues at hand need not be as serious as abortion. Every day we hear things like, "Your truth is different than my truth" or "What is true for you is not necessarily true for me." These statements are symptoms of a relativism whose real purpose is to eliminate any responsibility to consider a principle higher than personal desire.

Now when it comes to the physical world, no one seems to have this problem. If you get in your car and turn the key and nothing happens, your desire to go somewhere will have no impact at all! And when you wish the problem was a run-down battery rather than an expensive starter motor, again your desires are totally irrelevant to the actual mechanical defect. It is what it is. We all understand that physical reality does not bend to your gut feeling. It exists as it is regardless of what you feel. If you decide to jump off a roof because you feel like you can fly, it will make no difference. The laws of physics will continue to work in spite of what you want.

But when it comes to matters of character, spirituality or morality, many people seem perfectly willing to disregard several thousands of years of moral knowledge that has been gained from human experience (as well as God-given revelation) in favor of whatever they want when they want it. For these people, the following discussion regarding particular lies about truth would be absolutely meaningless, because they do not consider moral truth to be a meaningful category when they deal with spiritual realities. And while this trend is quite an extreme reaction to truth, we must admit that we are all capable of giving in to our emotions rather than dedicating ourselves to what is true and real from God's point of view.

Bear in mind that nothing here is meant to convert those who have given themselves over to desire as their means of navigation. They would probably not read a book like this anyway. My intent is to speak to the rest who are able to grasp the difference between discernment and desire, and to implore you to make every effort to train your children and their children how to discern what is true. Confusing desire and discernment may well be one of the most important spiritual issues of our time, because if this trend continues, the consequences will eventually be catastrophic to our way of life. And if you will forgive that short diversion, let us try to pick up again where we left off.

The First Lie About Truth:
Its Main Function is to Show Me What To Do

Returning to our earlier diagram of how our implicit beliefs impact the way we live, remember that the deeply internalized beliefs pictured in the diagram include conclusions our mind has reached from life experience, and not just the things we think are true because that's what we are *supposed* to believe. These implicit beliefs impact how we see the world, how we interpret our perceptions, and how we respond to those interpretations, both emotionally and physically.

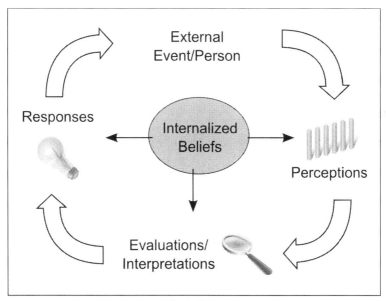

How Beliefs Drive Our Life

When reading the Bible, we discover all sorts of things that God has declared to be holy and things He has identified as sinful. The entire Old Testament law is about God's standards for purity and His demands for holiness. As we read, it becomes very clear not only that God determines what is right and wrong, but that humanity has completely failed in regard to holiness. We sin constantly, and often in complete ignorance.

Given that we seem to have some level of control over our choices and behaviors, it is very tempting to view the Christian life quite simply as a matter of choosing what is right and shunning everything that is wrong. If that is the case, then God would expect us to dedicate ourselves to the task of obedience and to try our best to do what He requires of us. In short, truth is seen primarily as a Moral Compass to guide our lives, and we ourselves are seen in terms of how obedient or disobedient we are to God's commands. The problem with this perspective is that *viewing truth primarily as a moral standard to live up to is far too shallow an understanding of truth to bring about transformation.*

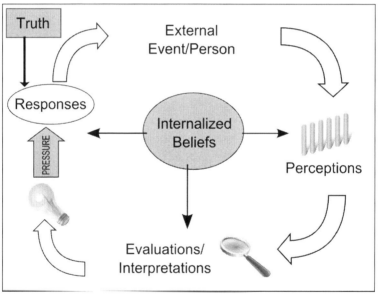

Using Truth to Focus on our Behavior

The reason why this is insufficient to promote real growth is that this places all of the focus on our *responses* to life and fails to properly address the underlying factors that *drive* our responses. The assumption is that with enough dedication, repentance, and prayer we can somehow override our inner drives by sheer willpower. The teaching around this idea is heavily laced with phrases about what we "should" do, the attitudes we "ought" to have, and the need to be "obedient" and "accountable."

Do not misunderstand. There really are things that ought to characterize the Christian. But they are primarily *descriptive* of what God wants in our life. They are not necessarily *prescriptive* of how to live.[79] It is good to know where we are going and what it might look like when we get there as we begin to move toward God's design for us. What we need to keep in mind, though, is that *it is a mistake to think that we can get there by direct effort*. It is in fact a *distortion of truth* to see its function primarily as a moral standard for us to live up to. One of the reasons we can know that it is a distortion is the fruit that it bears in burnout, disbelief, and joyless living on the one hand, and in pride and self-righteousness on the other.

If our car engine begins to cough and sputter, the answer is not to press down harder on the accelerator but to diagnose the cause of the malfunction and fix the underlying problem. In the same way, when we feel our internal "engine" hesitating or resisting God's standard in some way, the solution is not to force the right outcome by sheer willpower but to work with God to renew the part of our mind that is causing the problem. What's more, if I have to override my inner urges in order to "do the right thing," what does that say about the condition of my soul? Becoming more like Jesus surely implies something beyond repressing sin. If anything, this kind of problem tells me I still need more transformation of character.

Viewing truth primarily as a moral standard has an extremely powerful impact on our lives as Christians that is *the opposite* of what the teaching is intended to bring about! Rather than deliver us from sin, this kind of teaching most often creates an additional level of bondage, because it commits us to an internal war with the unspoken ideas and images that come from our internalized beliefs. As we can see from the diagram, our implicit beliefs drive how we perceive and interpret our circumstances. As our perceptions and interpretations become distorted, we feel pressure in our heart and mind for an internal response that is at odds with our moral standard. So we end up fighting our own character in order to respond externally in a way that lines up with our rules.

---

[79] Credit for the descriptive/prescriptive terminology goes to Dallas Willard.

For example, when someone wrongs me in some manner I may verbally "forgive" him because I know that is the right thing a good Christian should do, while internally I may harbor all sorts of contrary thoughts and attitudes toward that person. Deep down I may think that he still owes me something for his transgression, or that I really would prefer to engage in some kind of underhanded revenge, or that what he did is actually unforgivable. However, since I know it is wrong to live in a state of unforgiveness, I force myself to "forgive" him, although it would be more accurate to say that I go through the motions of forgiving.

We could go on to give dozens of such examples. This internal war is so common that it has even been legitimized. We call it the war between our old and new natures. In assigning that label, however, we have added yet another level of distortion on top of our misappropriation of truth, because it is a rather poor explanation for our struggle.

That is not to say that there is no conflict between our current state and what we are called to be. But the reason for that difference is not so much a matter of willpower as it is the result of deeply held distortions that are driving our understanding of life. The internal war is significantly intensified by the added pressure of trying to live up to a moral standard without changing how our mind continually distorts spiritual realities. This is exactly the point Paul is making when he said that the Law kills (Rom.7:9-10). Such an approach to life can only bring about condemnation.

As noted earlier, when we finally hit the brick wall that says we are failing to live up to this moral standard, we are offered a number of stock answers that are equally flawed.

- You need to try harder. You need to care more.
- You need to repent of some unconfessed sin.
- You need to be more committed.

But these explanations just add fuel to the fire, condemning us for what we are not doing right. In the end, we end up telling ourselves things like:

- There must be something wrong with me.
- I'm irredeemably flawed.
- Maybe I'm just not the kind of person who can follow God.

In reality, these faulty interpretations of our internal struggle fail to offer any means for real transformation, and consequently distort the nature of truth even more. We need a better approach for changing our character than relying on our own effort to achieve an impossible goal.

The ultimate purpose of the Law was not to set a standard for us to live up to. It was intended *to bring us to the end of our own effort* so we would discover that our only hope rests in a *relationship with God* instead of some sort of self-developed righteousness. We keep trying to exercise direct control over our character, which is something way beyond our ability. The perception that holiness is the same thing as obeying all the rules is as deeply flawed as the theory that we can get there if we simply desire it bad enough and try hard enough. It is an attempt to fix the heart by cleaning "the outside of the cup" (Mt.23:25-26) and it will not work.

Viewing truth primarily as a moral standard that we need to live up to and become obedient to is a distortion of truth that leads to failure and bondage. Quite simply, the above image is what legalism looks like in graphical form – trying to follow a written code of ethics rather than learning to engage with the Author in order to be transformed from the inside out. And that is not the only way in which we misappropriate truth.

The Second Lie About Truth:
Its Main Function is to Show What is Wrong with the World

A second way in which truth is commonly misapplied is when we assume that as Christians we already possess the truth we need (generally in the form of correct doctrine), and the problems in our lives are primarily due to circumstances and other people. "If I could just get everyone else to believe and act the way I do, everything would be all right. The main reasons why I have conflict or troublesome emotions are because of the failures of others. The best thing I can do is to try to correct the world around me."

In this approach to life, truth is seen as a blueprint that tells me how things ought to work and how people ought to behave. From a practical perspective, truth becomes a hammer or crowbar to be used to fix people and systems around me so that life works the way it should. My biggest frustration comes from the fact that other people refuse to do what is right, and my job is to call attention to the failures of others and try to motivate them to correct their ways. I am sure most of us know someone who is really good at this job.

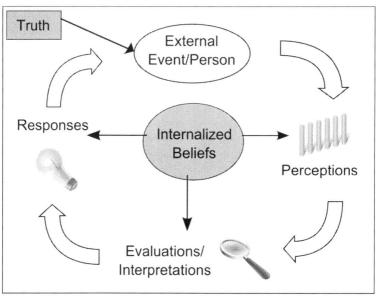

Using Truth to Focus on the World Around Us

In many ways, this is an extension of the first lie about truth. If I have a standard that I am supposed to live up to, and if I think I'm doing a pretty good job of trying, then I may become keenly aware of others who are not following the rules and not doing their part. I become justifiably judgmental and may be tempted to "speak the truth in love" to all who need correction. After all, I'm simply trying to alleviate the unnecessary suffering that comes from not following God's laws. I am the bearer of truth needed by my surrounding environment, an expert with the knowledge to fix people's lives. My mission is to speak the truth and use whatever means I can to convince others to follow my advice.

Again do not misunderstand. There are many ways in which evil has ingrained itself into the world systems around us, creating poverty, pain and oppression. Truth has much to say about those problems and how we are to be involved as bearers of the Kingdom in alleviating suffering. That is a matter for another time.

What we are addressing here are the daily concerns of our personal lives, including the people and circumstances we deal with moment by moment. To whatever extent we ignore our own need for change and instead focus on what is wrong with everyone else, we will be in danger of becoming more judgmental and contemptuous, and less conformed to the character of Jesus.

When applied from the pulpit, this hammer of truth often takes the form of subtle or not-so-subtle shame piled on all those who have failed in some way. You have not loved enough, cared enough, or tried hard enough to do what everyone knows you ought to do. You are defective, disobedient, or spiritually lazy. And the goal of both the minister and the message is to break you down to the point of repentance and recommitment to what you should be doing.

Aside from the fact that this is far more condemning than caring (despite arguments to the contrary) there is a much more relational, truly loving, and far more effective way for truth to penetrate the heart, without coercion and performance evaluations – a way that heals and restores, a way that changes a person's heart and life and births within them a desire to be more whole. When we encounter truth in this manner, it feels much more like water in the desert or a light in a dark forest.

Helping people find the treasure hidden in the field is far more effective and transforming than trying to push them into a religious lifestyle.

The Truth About Truth:
Its Main Function is to Illuminate and Change Our Heart

Given the pervasive darkness that exists in the human soul – distortions of God, self, life, and relationships – it becomes quite evident that our greatest need is for light, to see our next step, and to reveal and replace the malformed ideas we have about our own life. Shining the light on our efforts to live up to a high moral standard does not really do us much good, because we cannot get there by direct effort. And focusing the light on everyone and everything around us may make us *feel* better than others, but it does not actually *make* us better.

What we need to understand is that in order for truth to be transformative, it must be encountered as a light that illuminates our own internalized beliefs so they can be healed and replaced by God's perceptions and interpretations of our experiences.

Once that inner circle begins to change, its pressure on our internal process is altered, and everything else in our heart and mind starts to respond differently than it did before. Our *perceptions* become clearer and closer to how God sees reality. Our *interpretations* are aided by an internalized sense of how life works in the Kingdom for us, and how God is close to us and cares for us. Our *responses* begin to reflect more and more the character of Christ. As we learn how to participate with the Holy Spirit in ways that cause the light to illuminate our own soul, He can begin to work *within us* the process of renewal.

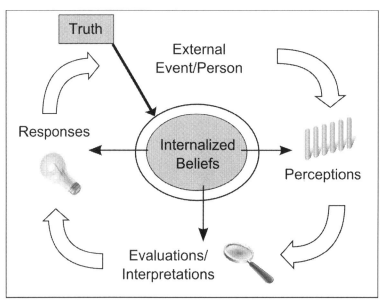

Focusing Truth on Implicit Beliefs for the Purpose of Change

This is not about confessing our sins or digging up as much dirt as we can about ourselves or seeing how terrible we are as human beings. Engaging with God for renewal is a life-giving process. Much of the time this mentoring feels as though we are being handed gifts that make our journey more possible, like finding a path to walk on instead of fighting our way through the brush day after day. Other times it has more the flavor of training, like being shown how to hold an implement so that it works better than the way we were holding it before. Of course when it's time to heal old wounds the process can be painful, just as surgery is painful. But it's like getting a tumor removed – we rejoice to see our life improve.

Most importantly, we discover how much God wants our restoration and how much He enjoys the process of renewing our life. If we are honest, most of us have wondered whether or not that has been the case. Having struggled for years with burdens and bonds that seem much stronger than we are, it is quite a surprise to discover how much God wants to remove those things from our lives and bring us to a place of deeper communion with Him.

In the next chapter we will redefine truth in relational terms so that we can recover the means necessary for this kind of engagement with God. After that we will look at the specific means available to us for internalizing truth in ways that change our deep-seated beliefs. For now, I'd like to leave you with a sobering thought.

If You Lose The Key, You Can't Open the Door

Mishandling truth and missing its true function has been the single most costly error in Christian practice since the inception of the Church. This is the primary source of all legalism and virtually all forms of spiritual abuse that have driven people away from God and given Christianity a bad name. It is also the single most significant reason why Christians feel powerless and defeated in their attempts to grow spiritually. The problem is not God, nor is it some sinful nature that is impervious to change. The problem is that we have lost touch with how to engage with truth and other resources for transformation and thereby have lost the keys to Kingdom life.

My hope is that by completely overhauling this whole process of Christian development and transformation, we will clear away enough of the old paradigm so that people will find the means they need to re-engage with God in ways that will truly change their lives.

Chapter 9

Truth is More Than True Information

Perhaps it is because of our rationalistic culture that we are tempted to reduce the Gospel stories to the principles we find at work in them. But truth is far more than correct propositions or a proper understanding of doctrine. *Truth is the very presence of God in our lives to provide continuous awareness and discernment of the unseen realities within us and around us, interpretations of life that allow us to relate to God and others as He intended.*

Unless we know how to engage with God in ways that reveal to us what He sees in our heart and in the world around us, we will be like someone trying to use a sledgehammer to repair a clock. Truth itself is one of the things that we need to understand – what it is, how it works, and how we can reliably pursue it.

In Search of Meaningful Language

In order to say more about truth without a lot of misunderstanding, it must be pointed out that one of the great difficulties in discussing the nature of truth and how it is received into our soul comes from the inherent difficulty of trying to convey experiential knowledge in words. It's a bit like trying to talk about the Grand Canyon. Descriptions of the raw data cannot possibly convey the experience of being there. One reason why so much of the Bible consists of stories of people who have wrestled with aspects of truth and deception rather than long doctrinal expositions, is because the whole thing resists being reduced to propositions, and the meaning of things is often better conveyed by example. In order to speak here more directly about truth and its related terms, we need to be very careful about our definitions so that the meaning does not get lost somewhere. *Truth, obedience, relationship, and belief* are among the more significant words that have come to mean so many things that unless we take the time to clarify what they are and are not, we run a great risk of missing the point.

Truth

There are a number of voices today that say, "truth is not enough." In most cases the proponents argue that it takes truth plus something else such as obedience, in order to grow spiritually. And while we certainly need other things in addition to truth, this particular expression of "truth plus obedience" is deeply rooted in an understanding of truth as a set of true propositions that must be followed in order to produce spiritual maturity. *This is not what the New Testament usually means by the word "truth."* When we equate "truth" with knowing the right doctrine and ethics, we necessarily misread the text and fail to hear the significance of what is being conveyed by the Biblical authors.

Most importantly, when we think of truth only in terms of knowing the right answers or the proper way to behave, we lose touch with its power to transform. Jesus' statement that the truth would set us free no longer has any real meaning for us. Knowledge of what is true may give us a better picture in our mind of what freedom would look like, but we are still left with the problem of how to live differently as a result of that truth.

Not that Christian education has no effect at all – quite the contrary. Just as a nice home in Des Moines would be a tremendous improvement over living in the streets of Calcutta, so also a general knowledge of God's view of life is vastly superior to whatever notions our culture has for the meaning of life. Because of this, it is tempting to say that more education would produce better Christians. But there are some major problems with that assumption.

Recall that in Part 2 of this book we made a point of identifying various levels of belief, and how some kinds of belief are more amenable to change than others. As it turns out, the beliefs that are most impacted by education alone are those that are fairly easily dislodged. Education can be effective in clearing up previously undefined areas of belief and in correcting obvious errors that do not hold up well under close examination. But education is often completely ineffective in addressing beliefs that we internalized under emotional distress.

So when a person is converted at the age of twenty and begins attending a church with a good education program, he may find his life completely turned around in a matter of days or weeks. Instead of going to beer parties every weekend and getting smashed, our young convert may be involved in a Bible study or simply learning how to have clean fun with new friends. Instead of seeing how many college coeds he can get into his dorm room, he may be volunteering at a local food shelf and really enjoying it. That's an amazing level of transformation from very little insight into the nature of the Christian life. And this is exactly what we would expect would happen when you hand a compass to a man who has had no direction in life.

Now fast-forward a few years. Our young man's education has become quite broad and he has a growing awareness that there are more and more discrepancies between what he knows is right and what he is able to do. He knows that he is not supposed to covet or lust, but he does not seem to be able to conquer either one of those drives. He has burned out working at the food shelf and his devotional time has all but disappeared. Due to his hair-trigger temper, "love your enemy" does not even come up on the radar. He wants to change, but no matter how hard he tries, his heart will not cooperate.

What happened? After our friend's initial growth spurt, his spiritual development ground down to a snail's pace. This is where the whole paradigm begins to break down. But rather than question the process, most people try to find ways to prop up these mistaken ideas about truth. Consequently, the wrong answers are given to Christians who genuinely want to do better.

Since education about true things seems to bring about change some of the time, people often assume that this is all the Bible means in regard to the truth setting us free. So they keep repeating the same truths about what good Christians are supposed to do and expect that if you really care about your life, you will be able to make the necessary changes.

An astute teacher might look at this scenario and conclude correctly that education has its limits and that more teaching will not make us better Christians in the long run. They find verses that say we need to be obedient to the truth and hammer home the need to do the right things even if our heart does not change. But over time that also takes a toll and eventually we lower our expectations and stop believing that transformation can ever be an ongoing reality. We settle for a life based on forced obedience and a continual inner battle against the parts of our soul that refuse to change.

Unfortunately, many of our Christian organizations are stuck at this point. Having run out of ideas about how to foster development, they either adopt a theology of low expectations or else attempt to motivate people by fear and shame into behaving better or praying harder or whatever they think it takes to become a better Christian. But the end result of all this prodding is often an even deeper disillusionment.

The real problem is that we have trivialized truth itself. Christian growth is not simply a matter of knowing the right things, nor is it just a matter of doing what we know is right. Growth happens when we internalize something of the Kingdom that we did not have before. New converts often experience a flood of new truths that displace the weak grasp they had on life before their conversion, with the result that their lives may change dramatically in a very short time. The reason that growth slows down is because the distortions of life which they still have embedded in their soul are more deeply entrenched, and internalizing change is no longer as simple as hearing true ideas presented in a classroom. Adding obedience to truth does very little to promote change. What is needed is a more profound understanding of the nature of truth and a more substantive way of receiving it into the depths of our soul.

We must not lose sight of the fact that, as God Himself tells us, *truth is absolutely essential to life*! One of the biggest reasons people feel trapped is because they are living out the implications of lies they believe. When they fully internalize the truth of a matter and its significance, they are liberated to *be* obedient and live more in line with how God intended, without an internal war opposing them at every turn.

If we tell people that we need to add obedience to what we know is true, we run the risk of advocating the same kind of "see and do" religion that has plagued the Church since the gospel was first preached. The Pharisees were experts at combining education and obedience, but they missed the very heart of the covenant they were trying so hard to keep!

Yes, there is such a thing as "dead faith," hearing and agreeing with true statements without ever experiencing any change in the soul beyond a mild tug of emotion or an appreciation for knowing the facts. Our churches are full of this. However, the solution is not found by linking education and obedience, because that perpetuates the misunderstanding that truth is nothing more than propositions with which one might agree or disagree, like the rules for a proper diet. *Instead of trying to add something to education to make it more effective, we need to move beyond this understanding as one that is rooted in self-effort, and adopt a more profound vision of truth as that which speaks to the soul, not just the mind.* Truth is that which declares to our heart the full significance of who God is, who we are, and what our relationship with Him actually consists of. That is why Paul continuously prayed for his churches to truly come to know this God whom they professed.

> Truth is more than true information
> just as righteousness is more than doing what is right.

Jesus *is* the Truth and Way and Life that we need. This is no mere metaphor, it is the very meaning of truth. Truth is alive and incarnational. Truth is personal, relational, and communal.[80]

Perhaps we need to think of truth more like a way of life than as propositional statements, more of a verb than a noun.[81] Just as the phrase "being a true friend" implies a whole array of values and choices that reflect integrity and the deep desire to stand by a friend even when it is costly, so also *encountering truth involves our surrendering to honest self-examination, rooting out the old beliefs, receiving light to see things the way God sees them, and doing the work of engaging with the Holy Spirit so that He can anchor truth in our soul.* That is the meaning of truth in the way that Jesus uses the term. The propositions of doctrine and dogma are at best a small aspect of truth, and should not be confused with the totality of the term.

When the Bible speaks of "knowing" the truth, the image the author has in mind is not like that of knowing which species and genus a particular lizard belongs to. Rather, it is that of an intimate relationship, the way a mother *knows* her baby. The object of our knowing is taken into our soul and savored, held, examined, and seen from every angle, felt in the deepest part of our being and received with impact. Above all, it is *experienced*. Internalized truth is far more than memorized principles or one option we

---

[80] Palmer, *To Know As We Are Known*, pp. 47-68.

[81] "For the word of God is living and active...it penetrates...it judges the thoughts and attitudes of the heart" (Heb.4:12).

hold among many. It is a way of being that responds to people and life events with God's perspective and a Christ-like demeanor.

If we zoom out and look at the big picture, *truth is all of reality (seen and unseen by us) as it is seen and known by God.* In reference to my own life, it includes all of who I am presently with all of my history (good and bad), as well as the person God created me to be, and all the process by which He intends to move me from my identity of past experience (successes, failures, and losses) to my identity of promise (who He has created me to be). But my own perceptions of that reality are extremely limited and even distorted, regardless of the extent of my knowledge of Christian doctrine. More education may provide me with some clues to life, but it can never provide the clarity that God has in that regard. Only by engaging with the Holy Spirit directly and hearing His perspective can I begin to see what God sees and understand my own life in ways that are more in line with the truth.

For example, Jack was a man who was haunted by past mistakes that had grown into debilitating regrets. He was racked with shame and grief about his career choices, mistakes in his marriage, how he raised his children, and so on. Although he had been a Christian for over forty years and knew that he had been forgiven for whatever he had done, the cost of those mistakes was still with him and often prevented him from making decisions due to the fear of making yet another mistake. When he finally took the whole issue of *regret* to God, he encountered an entirely new experience of God's grace, the reality of his own limitations, and the truth that his hope rested in God's character, not his own track record. As the significance of these things began to sink into Jack's soul, the pain of all those poor choices began to lift and he found a new peace that he had never known.

Only when we see life through the eyes of heaven can we know who we really are and who God is and how life works. Truth is a way of seeing and knowing that goes way beyond having the right answers.

Obedience

While it is clear from Scripture that obedience is an essential element of following Christ, we must be very careful with what we mean by that term. If by obedience we mean doing something that we think we are supposed to do in order to be good Christians then we are in danger of following a

Pharisaical imitation of the gospel instead of the real thing. If by obedience we mean doing things even though we find them wearisome and draining of life, then we run the risk of placing unbearable burdens on the backs of people instead of learning what it means to take on the easy yoke of Christ.

On the other hand, Christians are not supposed to simply wait until they feel like doing something before acting. With that approach, emotions quickly become our master.[82] *The question is not whether or not obedience is important, but what form that obedience must take*. However competent we may think we are, we are not truly capable of attempting what Jesus did unless we first take on His character. As we become more like Him, we are better able to relate to others the way He did, do more of the things that He did, and more in the way that He would do them.

This implies that the first order of obedience is our submission to the role of an apprentice, so that we can become more like Jesus. As an apprentice, our task is to learn how to participate with the Holy Spirit, which is *within our ability*, so that He can change our heart into one that is inclined to do things we could not have done by our own direct effort.[83]

The word "obedience" usually conjures up images of hard work, long hours, and white-knuckled insistence on doing the right thing at all costs. I know that hate is a bad thing, so I do my best not to act in hateful ways or let myself *feel* hatred toward a person I actually hate, and perhaps even congratulate myself for not hating. This kind of behavior reduces obedience to legalistic dimensions that truly violate the intentions of Jesus' commands, because God wants much more from us than mere compliance.

In order to move in the right direction, we need to think of obedience less in terms of what we do and more in terms of a relationship that helps us to know who we are and *whose* we are. That is, obedience to a demanding employer is an experience entirely different from obedience to a beloved mentor. God uses the term "obedience" because it lends substance to the meaning of our apprenticeship, letting us know that training is not

---

[82] One of the greatest dangers we face in our day is the fact that people are losing the distinction between desire and discernment. Making life choices primarily on the basis of desire will inevitably lead to disaster.

[83] Willard, *The Divine Conspiracy*, p. 353. This is roughly Dallas Willard's definition of a spiritual discipline.

optional, that it requires our attention and persistence, and that He is in charge of the training, not us.

The word obedience also tells us our training is not merely cognitive, but requires activity involving our whole body over time.[84] Obedience sets some of the parameters for our relationship to the Master from whom we are learning what it means to be an heir to the Kingdom. But under the New Covenant it was never intended to mean that we could become Christ-like merely by trying to do the right things.

> God wants more than our compliance.

Obedience in the New Testament is first and foremost a *relational* term, not an obligation. Rather than view it as "that which I'm supposed to do" we can rediscover obedience as a *relationship based on faith and trust in God, that His way is best, that He holds me in His heart, and that He knows my place in the Kingdom better than I do*. I rejoice in the possibility of joining Him in what He is doing and in whatever He says will be beneficial for my training, in order that I might be closer to Him and become more like Him. It is a way of *abiding* with Christ and living in the sphere of His way of life.

When I was a young boy I simply could not wait to learn how to play the piano like my dad, who was an excellent pianist. I loved to hear him play and dreamed of the day I could make a piano sound like that. Imagine my excitement when I finally got to take piano lessons! No matter that the first assignments sounded nothing like Chopin. I gladly followed the teacher's every direction to the letter...ad nauseam, and routinely practiced until my siblings begged my mother to make me stop. You could say I was an "obedient" student, but that hardly captures the spirit of my experience. I did everything she said, not just because it was right or because I was grateful for the lessons, but because I could not wait to be more like my dad. That is what obedience to Jesus is meant to be like. Not overriding your inner desire to do something else, but wanting what He has for you enough to do whatever it takes to participate with Him.

---

[84] Willard, *The Divine Conspiracy*, pp. 75-94, provides excellent insight into how our whole body is involved in formation.

God sometimes uses the term obedience not because He has to rope us into doing a lot of really hard things, but because most of the work is so basic that we are likely to dismiss it as too trivial or demeaning for us to engage in! The problem is not the difficulty of the tasks, but our unwillingness to submit to and be inconvenienced by such menial labor. That is one of the reasons why Jesus got down on His knees and washed the dirty feet of His disciples. He modeled for them what He meant by service, which is a form of obedience. Peter, for one, was horrified by the spectacle of a person of honor acting in so humble a manner. So Jesus made it abundantly clear that we cannot dismiss the work before us on the basis of its apparent "downward mobility."

This is where obedience does much of its work, revealing the resistance in our heart which is almost always rooted in various misperceptions. When we consider the possibility of spending a day in solitude with God, we could imagine what that might be like and quickly find reasons why such an act would be unnecessary or even counterproductive. Sure the quiet would be good for us, but we have lots to do and putting that stuff on hold will just make the next day more hectic. So what good is the timeout? Or we may envision ourselves becoming bored after half an hour and therefore a bit anxious about spending a whole day alone in prayer.

Having encountered internal resistance to the possibility of solitude, one of the worst things we can do is run roughshod over our emotions in an effort to be "obedient." What we need to do is take our resistance to God and ask Him to reveal the real underlying issues so that we can receive His desire for us in regard to our need for time away with Him.

Notice that this is not at act of giving in to our emotion. I am not suggesting that we let emotions rule our life. But those feelings of resistance are incredibly important – important enough to take the time to ask God to heal our internal map of life so that we are more naturally inclined to desire a day with Him rather than to avoid it. Then we can be "obedient" because of who we are and not in an effort to override who we are.

One area in particular where we often see internal resistance is in asking God what He wants us to do. This can be a scary proposition for many Christians because we are afraid He will tell us to do something way too hard that we would rather not do. Not knowing what He wants could even be preferable, so as to not have to face the question of obedience at all.

But shift the focus away from the thing He might have us do and instead put the spotlight on the fear and resistance in our heart, and doors begin to open to healing and renewed trust in our relationship to God. In that way, the issue of obedience becomes an avenue for our transformation rather than a test for us to pass or fail.

We could go on. The point is that obedience is one of many ways in which our faulty foundations and underlying beliefs are exposed. Jesus calls us to many things that we resist in our heart. Often we resist not because they are difficult tasks, but because they challenge our personal autonomy and our desire to rule our own lives. The answer is found neither in disobedience nor in forcing ourselves to do the "right" things, but in rooting out the underlying causes for our resistance that may be deeply embedded in our heart.

The essence of obedience is surrender, and that is precisely what we cannot tolerate. By paying attention as good apprentices and noticing the ways that we react to this work of obedience, we will discover a lot of truth about how we are malformed. God wants our obedience not only because He cares about a lot of things in the world and wants us to be part of what He is doing, but also because He wants to do more work *in us*. Wrestling with obedience will do much to bring this truth of our character to the light. Blind obedience that strives to repress that awareness will deprive us of many ideal teachable moments.

In the end, obedience is not an act of compliance but an act of faith – that what God wants us to engage in is actually better for us and for others than whatever we might have come up with. Obedience is just one more aspect of our connection to God, and it is the *relationship* that is central to our life, not our *behavior*.

Relationship

Another term that has in many ways lost its meaning, especially in regard to God, is the word *relationship*. Christians often speak of having a personal relationship with Jesus, by which they mean that they have accepted Jesus as their "personal savior" and they are trying to live according to the Bible.

But the truth is that making a profession of faith or changing our lifestyle does not really constitute much of a functional relationship.

Although relationship was truly what God had in mind when He went about the whole mission of restoring humanity to Himself, what many Christians call a relationship bears little or no resemblance to anything we might call a significant relationship between human beings. It is much more of an *arrangement*. If I feel badly about things I have done wrong and accept a certain set of beliefs about sin and atonement and my need for a savior, then in return God will allow me to go to heaven when I die. And in gratitude for that offer on God's part I will try to live better and be a good person. That's hardly a relationship. Most of us have closer connections with our employers than that.

Having a genuine relationship implies ongoing interaction, a tangible connection, and shared life experience. I *know* my wife, Jan, better than anyone else does, and she *knows* me. There are a lot of people who know stuff *about* us, and some people know us in part. But I know her heart, her inclinations, her mannerisms, preferences and hopes. I can taste a new food and tell you whether or not she will like it, or hear a song and tell whether she would enjoy it. I know when she is truly joyful and how that differs from when she is just trying to be pleasant while feeling something else. Our relationship has substance and shared history. We enjoy simply being together and sharing our time with each other.

That relationship is qualitatively different from one that I might have with, say, a paramedic who rescued me from a burning house or the relationship I think I have with an author who said a lot of good things I agree with. I may have some affinity for those people, but that hardly constitutes a relationship.

This understanding of relationship is critical, because truth and relationship with God are inseparable. Truth has a deep relational aspect to it that can only be known within the context of a life-giving, on-going relationship of experience and substance. *If that relationship remains mostly an abstraction, then truth has great difficulty getting beyond a merely cognitive level of understanding.*

One of the reasons that "Love God" and "Love One Another" are the greatest commandments is because relationships rooted in love will literally change who we are, as well as our understanding of life. The stronger our bond with God and the more secure our real experiential connection with Him, the more we will see life through the eyes of heaven. Our discernment will come to life as we learn to know what God's heart is really like, what He wants in our life and in our relationship with Him, and how He responds to the ups and downs of a broken world and the imperfect people we encounter.

To sum it all up, we could say that truth is fundamentally relational in nature. Life-giving truth comes to us via relationship, impacts our relationships, and changes how we relate to the world around us. And this aspect of spiritual truth is every bit as important as its ability to describe for us the unseen realities of the spiritual world.

Belief

Although belief was covered extensively in Part 2, it is important to revisit it here briefly before moving deeper into the nature of truth. As should be clear by now, belief in this context refers not to religious doctrines or a moral standard, but to deeply held internal assumptions about how the world works, conclusions that we have come to over time from our relationships and life experience. A surprising amount of what we believe at this level turns out to be severely warped by the darkness in which it was formed, more so than we are prone to acknowledge. Only when we begin to encounter the kind of truth that challenges our inner world do we begin to see how malformed our souls have become.

To believe something means to be prepared to act as if it were true. If in my past experience I have come to see that evil is often more powerful than good, then I may be prepared to cave at the first sign of any harmful conflict. That might be the only way to respond to evil that fits my worldview. Or if I am not all that convinced that God will take care of my needs, then I will be quick to worry and become anxious over anything that appears even remotely threatening, such as an unexpected bill or trouble with the car. My underlying beliefs predispose me to act in certain ways.

Beliefs of this type generally cannot be changed by an act of the will and those that run deep do not respond much to Christian education. These implicit beliefs will drive our feelings, attitudes and behaviors, and filter our observations in ways that tend to keep us from reevaluating the beliefs themselves, which makes them quite self-sustaining. That is why only certain kinds of encounters with truth are able to penetrate our defenses and expose our underlying beliefs, and also why we can hear truth preached week after week without being changed much at all.

Stories of Transformation by Truth

When we speak of truth as it pertains to transformation, we are referring primarily to those truths that give meaning to life experience and tell us who we are and who God is. Much of this has to do with revealing the true nature of where we are at the present moment. Very little restoration of the soul is possible until we see clearly what sort of damage is present in our own heart and mind – the extent of malformation and deception, our capacity for self-deception, and the simple fact that we do not know nearly as much about spiritual living as we would like to think we do.

Of course, an in-depth inventory of our flaws will never reveal more than a small part. We have neither the eyes to see it all nor the fortitude to withstand all there is to see. Graciously, God limits our access for the most part to that which we can tolerate and deal with. Then with our participation, He brings us into the presence of the light that can expose the nature of the lies and give us the truth we need to replace them. Thus this truth is expressly personal in nature, tailored to what we need to change.

As an example of this, Bob woke up one morning after a rather vivid dream in which he saw his son trying to run with a leg brace on one leg. In the dream Bob was racked with grief and self-recriminating hate because he knew that he was somehow responsible for his son's disability. After waking up, Bob continued to feel that intense pain, knowing that he had injured his son emotionally in ways that never should have happened.

When Bob began to ask God how he could possibly be free of this terrible guilt, the first thing God showed him was that he had been actively resisting God's forgiveness in this matter for years. Bob believed deep in his heart that the ways he had failed his son were truly unforgivable. He had sworn before his son was born that he would not do to his children what his parents had done to him. Yet here he was looking at his own track record, and all he could do was lament his failures.

So Bob asked God how such a thing could be forgiven, when it seemed to him to be too horrible to let go of. God reminded him that the whole reason why Jesus came to earth was to rescue people like Bob from condemnation, and that his feelings of self-hate were an active rejection of God's grace toward him. The message sunk all the way in, and Bob felt a peace and a quiet in his soul that he had not felt in a long time. All Bob could say was, "You are truly an awesome God." Although he continued to feel sadness for the pain he had caused his son, he could also sense God's warmth and forgiveness, however undeserved.

Bob's story is a common one. From a purely theological perspective, Bob had already known that God could forgive anything. But at a personal level his failures as a parent had grown into a pervasive self-hate that condemned him mercilessly. Only when God spoke into this specific situation was there any relief from the hateful things he told himself. In the long term, God's mercy toward Bob drew him closer to God and increased his desire to be more loving and more engaged with his adult son. Without this personal encounter with God, Bob would have continued to condemn himself and to nurse the pain that made it difficult to face his son.

Sometimes our hidden distortions of life can be triggered by what might otherwise be rather benign events. A few years ago while attending seminary, I received a grade of 75% on what I had thought was an insightful book review. The initial shock felt like a blow to my whole identity. Unable to let it go, that grade haunted me all the rest of the day. I was quite overwhelmed by feelings I had difficulty naming, and at the same time somewhat perplexed by the intensity of my reaction which seemed so out of proportion. When I finally had a chance to pray about it, the words I began to write were brutal: "I am such a failure! If I can't even get a decent grade on a stupid report, how am I ever going to offer anything to people in need!" and so on. Still, I found the intensity of my reaction baffling.

Finally, in the midst of my ranting God brought me to the point that had triggered my reaction. A *professor* had disapproved of my work. Suddenly it dawned on me that I had a life-long pattern of trying to impress pastors and teachers. Apparently I needed their approval to compensate for my own belief that I might not have anything to offer. Seeing that so clearly for the first time in my life broke much of its power in that moment. I saw my dependence on God more completely than I had ever known before, and asked Him to be my source of meaning – to know that if I mattered to Him then my life had value. What began as a devastating hit on my self-worth became another flash point in my relationship with God.

Sometimes these transformations move us from something destructive to something very life-giving as in the prior two examples. Other times the process is more of a dawning that anchors a previously known truth deep into our soul. Once I was reflecting on that poetic segment of Philippians Chapter Two where Jesus emptied Himself before coming to earth. As I thought about what it might have meant for Jesus to empty, a thought came to me with all the power of a stage light suddenly being turned on in a small room. *Jesus emptied Himself until all He had left was His relationship to Abba .... and it was enough to change the world*! For quite some time the implications of that continued to wash over me like an incoming tide. How incredibly important, our relationship to God! What amazing things come from being with Him, receiving what He has for us! I want that kind of relationship!

Transformation comes from engaging with God. Even our worst moments can be doorways to life, if only we would let God show us what He sees in the situation. Our own ways of interpreting life are so deeply flawed, we do not know how to find our way out. Hearing truth spoken in the classroom can roll off us with no effect at all. But hearing truth spoken by God deep into our spirit is like feasting on the best of foods or drinking from the water of life.

Only God Can Tell Us Our Story

All of us are living within a story that contains many characters, interwoven plots, and innumerable events and messages that hold meaning for us. How do we make sense of all of the data? How are we, as the main character in our own story, related to God? What does the story teach us of hope and life? The key to the mystery lies in *our interpretation of the story line*. Curtis and Eldredge tell us that part of Satan's grand strategy involves interpreting our own story for us in terms of chaos and destruction and hopelessness.[85] With those misconceptions and outright deceptions, he insures that the lead character is repeatedly led astray. Only when truth breaks into the scene and reinterprets our story can the frustration and bondage be altered, and the story take on a new dimension of hope and redemption. Only God has the wisdom to tell our story well.

Truth As a Means of Transformation

Having looked closely at a few examples of the direct contrast between deception and truth and how much our lives depend on our underlying beliefs, we can better appreciate the way in which the Bible speaks of truth. We will now examine a few of the more prominent passages in Scripture from which we can draw out some of the implications about how to participate better with the Holy Spirit.

Biblical View of Truth

Much more than simply a matter of correct doctrine, the Bible consistently portrays truth as an important means by which we are guided to righteousness and made holy. To make its point clear, Scripture approaches the matter of truth from multiple angles, all of which are framed in very experiential language. One of the most common pictures is that of being set at liberty from some form of bondage.

> *The truth will set you free (Jn.8:32)*

Of course, we must bear in mind that Jesus is talking here primarily about experiential truth. He is not suggesting that we can educate ourselves into the freedom we need, but that truth, properly engaged, will free our soul. That is quite literally the premise of this entire book.

Another common picture of truth in Scripture is that of bringing light into our soul and the related vision or guidance that comes from that light.

> *And you will do well to pay attention to it, as to a light shining in a dark place. (2Pet.1:19)*

> *Send forth your light and your truth, let them guide me; let them bring me to your holy mountain, to the place where you dwell. (Ps 43:3)*

---

[85] Curtis and Eldredge, *The Sacred Romance*, pp. 107-110.

Going beyond the metaphorical, the Bible speaks of truth as an important means by which change and transformation occur.[86]

Sanctify them by the truth; your word is truth. (Jn.17:17)

Be transformed by the renewing of your mind. (Rom.12:2)

Finally, there are several powerful passages that combine these elements and clearly exemplify the inherent relationship that exists between truth, freedom, and holiness:

To open their eyes so that they may turn from darkness to light and from the dominion of Satan to God. (Acts.26:18, NASB)

Walk no longer just as the Gentiles also walk, in the futility of their mind, being darkened in their understanding, excluded from the life of God, because of the ignorance that is in them...But you did not learn Christ in this way, if indeed you have heard Him and have been taught in Him, just as truth is in Jesus. (Eph.4:17-21 NASB)

Notice how many terms in that last passage relate to truth and spiritual understanding. Paul is contrasting the mind of a lost person with the mind of a growing Christian. Spiritually mature people think different thoughts and in different ways. That is why they "walk" in a different manner. Having our mind renewed is an integral part of what it means to participate in the "life of God."

Taken together, the above portions of Scripture speak strongly about the causal (not casual!) relationships between truth and freedom from the power of Satan, between truth and transformation of the soul, and between truth and holiness. God's truth is very experiential in nature. It changes the way we live. It is so foundational to life in the Kingdom of God that Jesus identified "truth" as one of the primary reasons for His own Incarnation.[87] And in the face of the pervasiveness of deception and its ability to cripple and destroy the human soul, this emphasis on the power of truth makes perfect sense. God alone is the author of truth that leads to life. Everything hinges on our real connection to Him and whether or not our eyes are open to the truth we need.

---

[86] See also Eph.1:17-18 on the importance of true knowledge.

[87] "For this I came into the world, to testify to the truth" (Jn.18:37).

Seeing Every-Day Life and Others Through the Eyes of Heaven

When we understand our human limitations and the extent to which our vision has been distorted by life experience, we can then begin to appreciate how much help we need in order to encounter truth in ways that renew our heart and mind. Only God can see clearly. And only when we seek to see what He sees do we have any possibility of knowing anything as it truly is, including its significance, its impact on those involved, and what might constitute a meaningful response.

Brad talked to his friend Tom about God for years without ever making a dent in Tom's agnosticism. The discussions were friendly enough, but Tom was hard to convince. He was a very intelligent and well-educated skeptic who wanted hard evidence of God's existence and the truth of Christianity before he would believe. Brad had used every sophisticated argument he could find and all the good books on apologetics for laypersons, to no avail. In desperation, Brad finally called out to God for help in reaching his friend. Very clearly he heard, "Tell him your story." In his mind, Brad objected to the idea because he was sure Tom would think that such "subjective" evidence was foolish at best. But Brad continued to hear God urge him to tell his story and he finally agreed.

When the opportunity arose, Brad carefully relayed to Tom the story of how he had experienced God over the years. There were times God had pursued him when he didn't want anything to do with God, there were emotional scars God had healed, there was a Spirit-led revival that he had witnessed, and many other encounters with God as well. It was actually quite a remarkable story, as God had been very active in Brad's life.

When he finished talking, Tom just stared in amazement. "I had no idea," he said. That conversation became a major turning point in Tom's spiritual journey toward God. Even though Brad was doing all the "right" things to reach Tom's heart, only God knew what Tom needed. When Brad finally grasped God's perspective, he was better able to participate in what God was doing in Tom's life, as well as grow closer to both Tom and God.

Even when we think we are doing our best to live and proclaim the truth, with all of our Christian education to support our understanding, we still lack the capacity within ourselves to see things the way God sees them. Overconfidence in our ability to discern what is best can actually get in the way of our connection to God. His wisdom far exceeds ours in both uncovering truth and applying it to real life events and relationships. Truth illuminates in dynamic ways that we cannot imagine on our own. Only when we rely on the Originator of truth to show us how things look through the eyes of heaven can we hope to perceive anything close to what is true. That is why truth is so much more than just a compilation of correct doctrine or true propositions. It is light to move and live by, in ways that are beyond our natural powers of reason.

Truth as a Gift

One of the things that puzzled Donna for many years was the way in which people could hear the truth regarding something and completely ignore it in favor of their own opinion. In most areas of life, she usually felt very drawn to the truth as she understood it, whereas she often witnessed tremendous resistance in others to those same truths. When she was confronted with truth, she usually changed in order to be more in line with what she understood to be right and good. But when she confronted others with truth, they often retaliated or blew up at her. She was continually amazed at how routinely the truth seemed to have no power at all to bring about change in people.

What finally occurred to Donna was that truth is completely non-coercive in nature. It can only be offered as a gift and does not force anyone to change. Only when received by the person who needs and wants it can truth can have the force of life, because when light and darkness fully meet, the darkness is dispelled. Truth does not alter hearts and minds apart from the participation of people. Whether one passively encounters truth or actively resists it, expecting truth to do some magic without any effort on the part of the person is unrealistic. Only one who is actively seeking and responding to truth can expect to encounter it in life-changing ways.

That brings up the matter of grace and its relationship to human effort. First, grace is often thought about only in terms "the forgiveness of sin." Such a viewpoint is far too limited. Grace is everything we need God to accomplish in our life that we cannot do on our own.[88] That includes forgiveness of sin, but extends far into the Christian life to all areas that

---

[88] Dallas Willard, *Knowing Christ Today*, p. 159.

require the work of the Spirit. On that basis, as we get closer to God we need more grace, not less.

At the same time, we must understand how God actually works with people in order to know what part of the relationship is up to Him and what part is our responsibility. Historically, much of the Church has taught that grace is an event in which God does everything and we can do nothing. This is a tragic distortion of the nature of grace, making it into some kind of abstraction that we hardly experience at all.

Grace is simply God's part in an event, the part I cannot do. So grace is really not opposed to effort, it is only opposed to earning our own way and attempting to do what only God can do.[89] Most of the time, the effort we contribute is the work of trusting and believing[90] and being persistent about making a space to engage with God. But that is still effort.

In terms of receiving and internalizing truth, we are intimately involved at every step. We must surrender to examination of our own implicit beliefs, open ourselves up to the work of the Holy Spirit, remain teachable at the deepest part of our soul, and determine to follow the Spirit over and over as He repeats this process in our life. There is tremendous grace in the giving of truth to us because we cannot find it apart from God revealing it to us personally in ways that penetrate our deepest beliefs. Yet people turn aside from grace all the time either because they do not know how to receive it or because they will not do what is necessary to receive. This is a major reason why the gifts of truth and grace take root in some hearts and not in others, and also why we may need to encounter the same truth multiple times before we see it for what it is and receive it into our heart.

The Goal of Truth

Having said all of these things about the nature of truth, there remains one extremely vital "truth about truth." The goal of truth is never revelation for its own sake, so that when all is said and done we are simply wiser than before. Truth always has as its aim the transformation of our character, our relationship to God, and our relationships with others.

---

[89] Willard, *The Divine Conspiracy*, pp. 25, 38-40.

[90] "The work of God is this: to believe in the one He has sent" (Jn. 6:28-29).

Truth illuminates both where we are and where we are heading, it reveals who this God is with whom we are designed to relate, and it lays bare our own heart and mind in regard to our relationships with God and others. Without that light we have no way of knowing how to begin, how to relate, who we are relating to, or what those relationships will look like when they are working well. Truth then becomes a means to a greater end: our relationship to the God of truth, to His people, and to the world at large. The single most important thing we need to know is that *we were designed to experience life in the presence of and in relation to the one true God.*

In the end, life-giving truth and relationship to God are inseparable. Relationship with God is the source of life-giving truth, and truth reveals to us this life-giving God and what it means to have a relationship with Him. That is why both truth and engaging with God are so transformative in nature, and why they so often lead us back to the twin themes of healing and growth. Because in our malformed state we understand neither truth nor what it means to have a connection with God. We need to be healed in the broken places of our life from those things that have taken their toll on our soul and from the damage done by our own malformed choices. And we also need to grow up in new ways that were previously unknown to us, the ways of God.

Hopefully, it has become clear by now what sort of truth we are talking about, *truth as a penetrating light that exposes our heart and mind, revealing the inner workings of our malformed soul in ways that allow the Spirit of God to re-form our implicit beliefs about who He is, who we are, and what we need in order to live as we were designed.* What remains are the actual means of encountering and internalizing truth, and the implications of engaging with God in this way.

How Truth Causes Transformation

If we have indeed been born spiritually blind into a world buried in darkness, and raised and trained by others who themselves have been wounded and malformed by their experiences, how could our restoration to wholeness *not* involve the light of truth? We have already seen that we are heavily driven and formed by our internalized beliefs, and that much of what disables us spiritually is a complex web of deception that is made up of lies, mistaken assumptions, faulty explanations, and ignorance of spiritual realities. But just as deception is causal in nature, so also is truth. And to whatever extent truth is taken into our soul deep enough to realign us with the spiritual realities of the Kingdom, we will be liberated to live as we were designed to live and our character will become more Christ-like in nature. Light truly does obliterate darkness, and the more truth we incorporate into our life the more we will live in harmony with the principles that make for joy and love and reconciliation to God and others.

The real question before us is not whether truth is able to bring about change. As documented throughout this work, that is an absolute fact that is repeatedly demonstrated in Scripture in stories and parables, in explicit teachings, and in the underlying assumptions of the authors.[91] The thing we have trouble with is *how to engage the truth in ways that bring about transformation*. We already know that traditional Christian education has minimal impact on character, and the experience of the Pharisees tells us that true ideas can in fact be misused in ways that actually bring about religious bondage above and beyond the problems we already face. Yet it is abundantly clear that truth has to be a major component of our experiential liberation from the power of darkness. So the question is how do we engage the truth in ways that matter to our soul.

---

[91] For example: "Otherwise they might see with their eyes, hear with their ears, understand with their hearts and turn, and I would heal them" (Mt.13:15). "The knowledge of the truth that leads to godliness" (Titus.1:1).

Chapter 10
Internalizing Truth

We now come to the actual means at our disposal for encountering and internalizing truth. The first step is to redefine our resources, which is necessary because so many Christians have been trained to think of these resources in ways that are inconsistent with a transformational model of growth. The next step will be to look at our role as an apprentice who is making use of these resources, and finally we will describe in detail what it looks like to engage with God in ways that can change the way we experience life.

Redefining Our Resources to Help Internalize Truth

As the preceding chapters have shown, much of the Christian world today relies on faulty approaches for spiritual development. In misunderstanding the nature of truth and the problem of deception, we have been practicing a religion of ethics and behavior modification that depends almost entirely on willpower and human effort. Consequently, the fundamental resources available to us for transformation have been largely misappropriated and Christians have been poorly trained in the proper use of those resources. So our first step will be to cast a new vision of the provisions God has made for our restoration.

A New Role for Prayer

One very well known model for prayer is called ACTS. The four letters stand for Adoration, Confession, Thanksgiving, and Supplication. As important as these basic forms of prayer are for us, and as helpful as that model has been for many people, it is in some ways both misleading and devastatingly deficient. Misleading, because of the implication that this is in fact complete, and deficient because it leaves out those elements of prayer that are by far the most life-giving. Besides an opportunity to tell God all the things we can think to say about Him and ourselves and our needs, prayer is an avenue for receiving from, listening to, and interacting with the Spirit of God. Without those life-giving elements, prayer loses much of its potential to aid our spiritual growth and runs a very real risk of being reduced to "something we are supposed to do" rather than a way to interact with God.

Most of us have been taught a form of prayer that resembles a one-way monologue. We write postcards to God, toss them over the wall, and then look around to see if anything changes. We may even attempt to interpret the signs of everyday life to see if we can figure out what God is trying to tell us, which is really a rather strange process when you think about all that the Bible has to say about being led by the Spirit of God. It is far too much like watching a movie in which the characters are trying to decipher ambiguous clues from the events surrounding them. Nearly everything in life can be interpreted in multiple ways. Relying on our powers of analysis to navigate spiritually is a sure-fire recipe for misunderstanding and failure. Surely God had something else in mind for our connection to Him as Teacher and Guide.

With such a one-sided view of prayer we fail to see that *having real conversations with God is absolutely foundational to having a functional relationship with Him.* While this should be obvious it needs to be explicitly stated because until recently, few Christian organizations made much of an effort to teach their people how to *hear* the voice of God. Many even *discourage* people from trying to hear God because they are afraid of the inherent dangers that go along with it. Granted, most of us have witnessed people who claim to hear from God while acting crazy or terribly delusional. But the answer is not to give up on hearing God. Instead, we need to address our fears and take on the messy work of helping people discern His voice.[92]

When Jesus described His relationship to us as that of a Good Shepherd He said, "His sheep follow Him because *they know His voice.* But they will never follow a stranger...because they do not recognize a stranger's voice" (Jn.10:3-5). Now if Jesus' expectations were at all realistic, it follows that we should be able to hear the voice of God and to separate it from the other

---

[92] See Takle, *Whispers of My Abba* for more on listening to God.

voices in our head. For many Christians this may be a radical idea, but it is absolutely necessary to finding our way. What else would God mean when He says the Spirit will lead us?

If He meant that the Spirit would drop subtle hints around that we are supposed to pick up on and interpret, then we have no real way to participate in His leading. For all practical purposes, we are then back to relying on our own resources for figuring out what to do and nothing has changed. The New Covenant ends up being not much better than the Old One. Perhaps that is why John was so careful to make sure we knew Jesus had far greater expectations.

> *It is written in the Prophets, "They will all be taught by God." Everyone who listens to the Father and learns from Him comes to me.* (Jn.6:45)

Dialogue with God is not only possible, it is essential. Ability to hear our Teacher is a necessary part of being one of His disciples. Once we break through that barrier a whole new world of possibilities opens up to us. First and foremost, we gain a relationship that we have never been able to experience before. There is great joy in discovering experientially that God really wants to be with us and talk with us. This in turn begins to heal our broken images of God as distant or unconcerned with our lives. From this we gain an entirely new understanding of how the Holy Spirit works in us. He is no longer an abstraction or a hidden force who works behind the scenes, but an active advocate of our restoration with whom we can have conscious interaction. We discover that within us there lives a personal mentor who longs to train us in the art of life in the Kingdom.

> Dialogue with God is essential to life.

As we learn how to talk to God and listen to His voice, we experience Him in ways that would otherwise be impossible. Our relationship with Him becomes truly interactive, our perceptions of God are radically altered at a very deep level, our trust becomes more certain and relational, and our desire to spend time with Him finds new incentive from the sheer joy of being close to Him. Jesus' words are then fulfilled because doing what He says results in an experience with truth that sets us free from our previous limitations (Jn.8:31-32).

A New Role for the Holy Spirit

Jesus describes the mission of the Holy Spirit as one who sanctifies us by leading us into truth. He does this by teaching, by bringing to mind things that we have already been taught, and by revealing to us what needs to change (Jn.14:26). Crucial to understanding His mission is to clearly recognize the means by which He does these things. "He will speak...taking from what is mine and making it known to you" (Jn.16:13,14). The Holy Spirit does indeed speak, and when we learn to hear His voice we can become actively involved with Him as His apprentices.

Far from being some intangible force working imperceptibly in the background of our mind, the Holy Spirit is a *mentor and teacher*. He loves to teach, and He did not stop teaching after the books of the New Testament were written down. Rather, He is the personal mentor of every Christian, given to us both individually and corporately to lead us into the truth we need in order to become what God wants to make of us. And like any other teacher, He actually talks to us. As apprentices of Jesus, we have every reason to believe that we should be able to recognize the voice of God so we can learn from Him.

As it turns out, His teaching style is a lot like that of an ancient rabbi.[93] If we are paying attention, He takes whatever experiences we are currently involved in and uses them as a platform for relating truth to our life. Sometimes the learning involves portions of Scripture, other times He uses whatever circumstances we are engaged in, and still other times He just surprises us with new light at an opportune moment. In any case, the messages are conveyed by the Holy Spirit speaking to our heart and mind.

The real question is whether or not we can hear what He is saying and receive what He has for us. Without this kind of personal experience of God, our natural tendency is to assume we can figure out the lessons of life on our own with the help of some doctrinal guidelines. In the process, we greatly overestimate our ability to live well by our own effort and trivialize the work of the Holy Spirit as well as the work it takes to receive and

---

[93] Willard, *The Divine Conspiracy*, pp. 107-114.

wrestle with His words. But He is extremely active in His role as teacher, and longs to engage us as active students of His work.

When we stop and think about it, the idea that God would stop speaking just because the Bible has been assembled makes very little sense. First, because throughout most of history and in most of the world, the Bible has not been accessible to the vast majority of Christians. It is also unrealistic to think most people had the means to commit major portions to memory. Those who could read were fortunate if they had access to even a small segment of the Bible. If God does not speak directly to His people, then we have to say that He put His life-giving Word out of the reach of most Christians for most of history.

Second, apart from real communication with us, the ministry of the Holy Spirit as our teacher becomes a completely unintelligible abstraction. We are quite literally relying on our own understanding of Scripture to provide us with the wisdom we need for life.

Finally, most of the New Testament assumes that the original readers and hearers had the kind of Spirit-directed life we are speaking of here. There is precious little information in the Bible on how to live the Christian life *without* the Holy Spirit guiding our everyday existence. In fact, if we postulate that God stopped speaking to His people directly, then most of the New Testament becomes very difficult to incorporate into our lives because it was written for an audience that relied on the Holy Spirit's direction.

By teaching that God does not speak to us, we openly quench the Holy Spirit, dramatically restrict our relationship with Him, and cut ourselves off from our most important source of life-giving truth. As difficult as it may seem, we must do the hard work of learning how to engage with the Holy Spirit as a mentor who communicates directly with His people.

A New Role for Scripture

Like prayer, everyone knows that proper discipleship involves reading the Word. Unfortunately, many Christians find Bible reading to be at least as boring or distasteful as praying. They complain that the Scriptures are dry and that reading the Bible feels more like doing homework than feeding their soul. Some even justify their time away from the Word by saying that they did not want their Quiet Time to become legalistic, meaning that they were waiting for the desire to read to come back.

Much of this problem stems from how we read the Bible, and to what purpose. We have been taught, implicitly or explicitly, to treat the Bible as if it were some sort of textbook that we could approach like any other subject matter. We read the words on the page, try to distill the meaning from the text, and then imagine ways that we might be able to apply those principles in our life. Putting this more concisely, we attempt to master the text through our God-given ability to be rational, thinking creatures.

Admittedly, this approach to Bible reading can provide an excellent education on some very important matters, and occasionally the truths we study can have profound impact in certain areas of our life. But by and large, this way of reading Scripture rarely fosters transformation for those who already know something about the Bible. It may, in fact, inhibit spiritual growth because we are aligning with the wrong principles.

First, we make the Bible into a book of directives to analyze with our powers of reason and then obey by an act of will, when the real purpose of the Bible is to point us back toward the God with whom we must engage in order to live well.[94] It gives us sufficient guidelines to help us know what sort of God we are engaging with, but it is wrong to mistake the map for the ultimate source. Second, we assume too much about ourselves by believing that we possess the faculties necessary to comprehend God's Word apart from revelation by the Spirit of God. In so doing we relegate the Holy Spirit to the remedial task of empowering our own ability and desire to be self-taught.

Rather than attempt to master the book, we must seek to be mastered by it, to submit to it, and to let it speak to us.[95] To take the Bible seriously as the Word of God, we must first come to grips with the fact that holiness, righteousness, and life-changing truth are far too wondrous to be captured on the written page alone or mastered by human intellect. These things can

---

[94] "You diligently study the Scriptures because you think by them you possess eternal life. These are the Scriptures that testify about me, yet you refuse to come to me to have life" (Jn.5:39-40).

[95] Mulholland, *Shaped By The Word*. The basic premise of the entire book is submitting to the Word instead of attempting to master it.

only be communicated to us by God. The Holy Spirit is not a hidden force in the background of our mind, aiding us in our interpretive efforts. Rather, He is the very one with whom we must engage directly, so that He can reveal to us what we truly need to see in the text.

For example, take a passage like Isaiah 55 with its invitation to "come to the water...come, buy and eat...and delight yourselves in rich food." We can logically analyze what the prophet intends to convey by each of the metaphors and talk about what it means to buy without money, and so on. Or we can allow the Holy Spirit to use the passage to reveal our heart, where we may discover ways that we have spent our labor elsewhere or even times when we feel as if that real food is out of reach. Presenting these awarenesses back to God and asking Him to minister to our needs can open the door to still more that the text might offer us, such as allowing the wonder of God's gracious invitation to capture our soul and stir our longings for the food that truly satisfies.

This process is very different from relying on our human ability to comprehend the Word. It is about participating in an opportunity to be taught by the Spirit, in which the Word becomes part of the learning process. The aim of the Holy Spirit in all of this is not just to make the Word intelligible to us, but *to reveal both our heart and God's heart at the same time on the same issue so that we can see with new eyes what He has for us*. If we are willing to engage with Him completely in this way, we can submit to His work in our heart and mind and fully incorporate truth into our life. He may do this through direct healing, by opening our mind to a new understanding, by leading us into some area of confession or repentance, or by giving us some gem to mull over for a few days so that we can come to see its relevance. In any case, *Scripture reading must go beyond an exercise of our rational powers and become an encounter with the Spirit of God*.

The failure of Christian education to transform lives over the long haul has led many to conclude that knowledge of the truth has minimal value or is only coincidental to other factors such as acts of service, obedience, repentance, and so on. But the real problem has been our limited understanding of truth and our self-directed attempts to appropriate the Word of God in our own strength, all of our prayers for the Spirit's assistance notwithstanding.[96] The Holy Spirit generally will not override our desire to teach ourselves, and frankly we are not that good at it, as history demonstrates. May God give us new eyes to see the true value of the Word, and to rely more intentionally on the Holy Spirit to reveal its treasures.

A New Role for Community

God did not design us to live in relative isolation, but in relationship with other people. We need strong bonds with others in order to grow up and thrive as human beings. Much of this reality has been lost in Western culture due to our pervasive individualism, and the result has been nothing short of devastating. The actual role of community in human development and mental health is very complex, and the reader is encouraged to check out the resources listed in the appendix for more information. But there are a few aspects of community that are particularly important to our understanding of truth.

To begin with, many authors and researchers have shown that we can only truly know ourselves in relationship to others. My sense of identity is formed largely by the reflection I see in the way others respond to me and by the way in which I interact with them and impact them. A healthy self-concept involves not only my true identity in Christ, but also a sense of who my people are and what we are like in various situations, whether experiencing joy or intense emotional stress.[97]

Another value of community is that it offers significant possibilities for growth that come from shared experience. As we walk through life in relationship with others, we are exposed to a wide array of responses to any given experience and learn from watching how others grapple with the emotions and consequences of their choices. This is largely how children learn values in their families, and it continues to be a major source of learning throughout life. By comparing stories and ways of dealing with life events, we discover what fits with the way God designed us and arrive at working beliefs about people, suffering, and a wide range of other values.

---

[96] Palmer, *To Know As We Are Known*, p. 27. Palmer explains why this approach to truth fails to do justice to the nature of both truth and human beings.

[97] Curt Thompson, *Anatomy of the Soul*.

This may in fact be why much of the Bible was written in a narrative style, allowing us to learn from the stories of others.

We also discover our own deficits and weaknesses by interacting with others. For example, it is easy to imagine that I am a strong person if I never get close enough to anyone to experience conflict. However, when placed in a stressful situation where I experience shame, fear, anger, powerlessness, or other intense emotions, any unhealed triggers or holes that exist in my human development will show up rather quickly. Dealing with those problems may require seeking help or spending a lot of time with others who manage those issues better than I do. But seeing the truth of where I need to grow is an essential first element of change. And this is one of the benefits of close community.

Another significant aspect of community is the tremendous value of one person identifying the work of God in another person and calling attention to it.[98] We need others to remind us of what God has already done and to point out what He is currently doing in our life. Interacting with each other in this way brings great hope, lifts up one another, and lends significance to our daily struggles. It teaches us to be mindful of God's work in others, to hold them in high esteem even when they are failing, and to view them as God sees them through the eyes of heaven, seeing people as they are designed to live and being an aid to their growth and recovery.

We also need community because individually we do not possess the whole spectrum of God's gifts to the Church. As each of us brings to the assembly those gifts that God has given us, our interdependence becomes apparent as we are edified by giving and receiving life between us. As we submit to one another, we can be mentored in spiritual things such as hearing the Holy Spirit and discerning His movement within our lives.

Finally, spiritual formation has an interdependent relationship with certain aspects of human development.[99] And the skills necessary for that development are only acquired within a healthy, working community. For example, much of the ability to suffer well is dependent upon the emotional capacity we have for carrying stressful emotions (anger, fear, sadness,

---

[98] Crabb, *Connecting* and *The Safest Place on Earth*. Calling attention to the work of God in others is the basic theme of both books.

[99] See Takle, *Forming: A Work of Grace*, Chapter 11.

shame, etc.), which in turn is largely built from hundreds of interactions with others who have gone before us and already built that capacity. So while emotional and relational growth are mostly achieved through hard work and practice within the context of community, spiritual growth is largely received through direct engagement with God. This means that to whatever extent we misunderstand these two aspects of development, we will confuse what part is our responsibility with what part is God's responsibility in growing us up, and consequently seek to apply the wrong tools to the task at hand. We need both avenues of growth in order to become the person God created us to be.

A New Role for the Individual – Participation with God

At the very heart of Christian spiritual formation is an important point of contact between God and us, a way of relating that is best described as *participation*. That is, knowing what part of spiritual growth is *God's* job, and what part is *ours*. Nearly all aspects of Christian formation depend on a proper understanding and practice of participation, and nearly all mistakes in discipleship programs relate to misunderstanding participation.

Probably the single most glaring example of this is the legacy of legalism which has plagued the Church throughout history. Legalism is in part an attempt to perform righteously as a result of studying and following moral principles (often calling on the Holy Spirit to bless the effort). As good as that may sound to some people, it is an inadequate approach to participating with God, and it will not succeed. At the other end of the spectrum, there are Christians who are passively waiting for God to take over their bodies and make them do exactly what He wants them to do. This too, is a failure to participate appropriately. The above discussions of various approaches to prayer and Bible study that do not feed the soul are also examples of mistaken ways of participating with God.

The first step in participation is grasping the true meaning of grace. As was stated earlier, grace is God's action in our life to accomplish what we cannot do on our own. What kind of action? We must be very careful to not reduce our view of God's action to that of simply assisting what effort we supply. Much of the prevailing wisdom teaches that if you do whatever you can out of obedience, then God will supply both the energy and the will to follow through with what you have begun. And while this may be the experience of some people in certain instances, such an approach to Christian service is quite literally a formula for self-righteousness or total burnout. Grace is not a daily supplement that charges us up to do the work we have set our hands to. Grace is a work of God on our heart and mind to change things in us that we have no other access to. Grace is not about us and our effort, but about God and His work. Our part then is not to try to do something with God's help, rather it is to surrender to the work that God is doing in us and through us, in a way of speaking, in spite of us.[100]

> Improper participation with God will not produce change
> no matter how hard we work at it.

Suppose I go and volunteer at a soup kitchen because I think that would be a good way to serve God. Week after week I spend Saturday morning helping to prepare massive lunches and serve them to the people who come in. I find it somewhat tiring and secretly have some difficulty getting myself motivated and out of bed on Saturdays, but I do it because it seems like the right thing to do. And when I tell other people what I am involved in, I always include the note that God must be helping me because otherwise I would not be able to do this every week. After all, if it were just up to my flesh, I would choose to spend my Saturdays another way.

This all sounds nice, but true participation with God is much more than doing good things. While it is good that I am not letting my emotions dictate my Saturday, I may be completely missing what God wants to do in my heart. I think that because I am being "obedient" to the task before me, I must be growing and serving God.

In reality, I am *avoiding* the growth I need, which would include God changing my heart about service. He does not want me to just go through the motions of service, He wants me to have a servant's heart.[101] His desire for me is that I would become the kind of person who cannot wait to get down to the soup kitchen on Saturday morning! He wants to change my heart into one that honestly looks forward to Saturday each week. Proper

---

[100] Takle, *Forming: A Work of Grace*.

[101] Hos.6:6; Mt.23.

participation with God would be the act of surrender to His gentle probing and exposing of every facet of my resentment about giving up my time, my resistance to serving in that kitchen, as well as my disgust at the people who come in the door.

Once my heart has changed from drudgery to delight, He can then proceed to impact the people at the soup kitchen in ways that I could never do, to draw them to Himself and give them hope. Again, my job would depend more on what God is doing with them through me than on my evangelism training classes and my communication skills to reach the people I serve.

Serving at the soup kitchen is not just about the great thing I can do for those people. God wants so much more out of that experience. At the very least, it could become an opportunity for the Spirit to expose parts of my heart that had been previously left undisturbed, so we could dialogue about those things and I could receive healing for the underlying beliefs that drive my negative reactions. Then He might want me to learn how to pray for or pray with the people at the kitchen as well as learn how to engage with them. He may want me to become part of the good things He desires for the people He loves there. But in every instance, participation with the Holy Spirit means surrendering to His initiative, rather than acting on my own behalf.

The grace that I experience in that service is not the power to do a task that I would rather not do, but God's work in my heart to do something in me that I could never do. He can bring me to love those people, to a place where serving them is not an imposition on my time but an honor bestowed upon me by my Father. I am always the apprentice, always learning, always receiving more of what the Spirit wants to do in me no matter what experience I am part of. Participation is what an apprentice does because He is in training with the Master who wants to instill in His students not only the tools for their work, but the heart and desire for it as well. And because the Master has many things for us to learn, participation takes on a great many forms.

Becoming Apprentices of Kingdom Life

Participation with God as laid out in the New Testament means becoming a disciple, a student of the rabbi, Jesus. When Jesus gave His final commission to His closest followers, He told them to go and *make disciples* (Mt.28:19). That is, He wanted all of His children to be trained in how to live well. We are first and foremost students of the Kingdom, learning how to live under the reign of God. The problem is that for many Christians today, the word disciple has largely lost its meaning, so I prefer the word *apprentice*, which has far richer connotations for this present work.[102]

For one thing, *apprentice* establishes our identity and role in relation to the Holy Spirit. We are *perpetual learners*, and that part of our identity is crucial. Too often the Christian experience gets reduced to some trite formula like, "convert, grow, and go" which implies that our growth and training are some sort of transitional phase, after which you are ready to join the ranks of the recruiters and trainers. Such a truncated view of discipleship is extremely short-sighted, as if all the major work God needs to do in us can be accomplished in a finite period of time, and then we graduate. Even when augmented with a kind of "continuing education" program, this view assumes that the bulk of our Christian learning is relatively containable and that we are all either leaders or followers.

The reality of the Christian life is quite different. When Paul heard of the great reputation of the Ephesians' faith and love he responded by praying that they might *know God better* and that their *eyes would be opened* to all that He had for them (Eph.1:15-23). He had a similar reaction to the Colossians (Col.1:9-12). Apparently, Paul was under the impression that they had a wonderful foundation, but they were just getting started in their relationship with God. Our apprenticeship is a life-long process that in many ways intensifies as we grow, it does not plateau or even begin to approach completion. Our primary task as a learner and disciple is to remain teachable and moldable so that the Master can continue His training.

A corollary to remaining teachable is to surrender our self-protection. Much of what the Holy Spirit needs to do in order to retrain us in our new life is to reveal the substance of what remains in our heart and mind from

---

[102] On the term *apprentice* see Dallas Willard, *The Divine Conspiracy*, pp. 271-310.

our malformation. If we have a low tolerance for self-examination or the emotional pain of spiritual confrontation, we may well avoid the very lessons we need most. When experiencing even minor shame, many people have a tendency to hide from anyone who might see, including God. Part of participating in grace is to surrender to the security of God's great love for us, so that we can risk coming closer to Him with our weakness instead of running away. The Master does not expose the shortcomings of His apprentices in order to condemn us, He does it in order to refine us. He cares deeply for our development as learners. If we resist the work of our mentor, the lessons will be lost and we will be the poorer for it.

One of the great tragedies of the modern era is that there are so few opportunities to apprentice that we no longer think of learning in this way. Our culture has accepted a rationalistic worldview that sees learning mostly in cognitive terms that are quite independent of personal development. Dallas Willard illustrates this beautifully in a true story that he tells about a young woman student at Harvard.[103] One of her classmates consistently pulled top grades in an ethics class they shared together, yet repeatedly propositioned her whenever the opportunity arose. So she challenged her professor with, "What good does it do to teach people how to *think about* being good, if in the end they still do not know how to *be* good?"

This is the basic weakness in our approach to learning. We *teach* people good things to think about, but we do not *train* them how to actually be good people. Today, most of our churches have adopted educational models that are devoted almost entirely to the mastery of subject matter, whereas the main purpose of apprenticeship is to submit to being trained by the Master experientially. This is how we must think of *participation* in the Christian life.

Ways to Participate With the Holy Spirit to Internalize Truth

When it comes to our training in real time, there are several critical factors we should take into account. For those who have been relying on education to produce change, one thing in particular can be very hard to believe and adopt as a basis for retraining. When it comes to spiritual development, the

---

[103] Willard, *The Divine Conspiracy*, p. 4.

process of learning is every bit as important as the *content* of what we are learning. We must focus every bit as much attention on how we engage with our mentor as we do on what we are learning. This is crucial, because *how* we take in what we are learning dramatically alters its impact.

Imagine that you have decided to learn how to play tennis. You could read about it in a book, but watching a video would probably be more helpful, and having an expert to mentor you would be even better. The means by which you go about learning or engaging something directly impacts the quality of your experience.

Learning how to listen to the Holy Spirit is as important as the content of what He wants to show us, because the deeper His voice penetrates, the more our soul is fed by His words. Learning how to receive from God is more important than figuring out what He wants to give us, because receiving even a small gift deep into our soul will change us more than comprehending a great gift with our mind. Compare, for example, the difference between hearing a lecture on the implications of God's love (understanding a gift) and having a sweet moment during a worship song where you experience God's love (receiving a gift).

Learning *how to see* changes *what we see* which then changes our heart or how we respond, like when we look at a small child one minute and see a responsibility that is wearing us out, but look at them asleep a short while later and see a miracle of life that we are privileged to care for. Relearning how to participate with the Holy Spirit for healing the broken places in our life will transform us far more than taking a class on the subject of brokenness. From every angle that we can assess spiritual development, the way we encounter truth is as important as truth itself.

The Importance of Teachable Moments

One of the most significant elements in this process of renewing our mind is our own receptivity and readiness to internalize truth. Deeply held beliefs learned from life experience are generally only open to change during *teachable moments*. A teachable moment is a window of time where the main elements necessary for transformation are all present, and the person involved is aware of certain factors. In most cases, this will include the following conditions:

- Something the person is reacting to. Often it is a present event such as an unexpected problem, or a statement or action by another person. It can also be a memory of an event or an anticipated future event.
- Some measure of distress felt by the individual, such as the emotional pain of anxiety, fear, anger, shame, hopelessness, or some variation of these negative emotions. These distressful feelings could also take the form of a longing or desire for something we do not have.
- Access to and receptivity to a significant source of truth that will shed light on the person's perceptions, interpretations, and implicit beliefs.

Notice that the first two elements are sufficient by themselves to cause the person to internalize new beliefs or reinforce existing beliefs, because stressful events tend to leave their mark on our mind. If the content of what we internalize is something other than God's perspective, then it will add to the distortions we hold and make life more painful and difficult. In order to recover from previously internalized distortions of life, we need the third element, a source of truth and an open spirit to receive it.

Life itself provides a great many teachable moments through adversity and emotionally charged events, during which a person gains some insight that has all the force of a personal revelation. It may be a genuinely new thought or simply a new understanding of the significance of something that the person had previously known only cognitively.

I knew a man, Carl, who spent much of his life closed off from others due to the emotional abuse he suffered in childhood. At the age of thirty-four he joined a support group in order to deal with the grief and loss of one of the few relationships he had tried to sustain. To his surprise, what he discovered there among those supportive friends was the truth that strong relationships with other people could actually enrich his life. While that might seem obvious to most people, for Carl this truly was a new way of thinking about what it might mean to have other people in his life.

Interestingly, he could recall many times when he had been blessed by the kindness of others, yet without any impact on his own faulty belief that his life was better as a loner. But at that moment in time Carl was in far more need than he had ever been in his adult life, and far more receptive. The intensity of his pain and the quality of the care he received from the group on one particular evening touched a part of him that longed to be known and connected to others, a part of himself that he had long since lost conscious awareness of. The new awareness (truth) he needed was provided by his experience of care at the right time. Carl felt the impact of that truth as an insight into the nature of his own heart.

For Carl, this experience was so novel that the transformational truth was self-evident. Much of the time, however, these teachable moments serve primarily to nudge us in the right direction, and we have to engage with God in order to receive the truth we need.

A previous chapter related a story about a man named Jack who had accumulated a lot of regrets over the course of his life. What caused Jack to confront those regrets was a movie about an old woman who had only a short while left to live and was in terrible agony about some of the choices she had made along the way. The movie touched a nerve in Jack, so he sat down and spent a couple of hours with God going over his life, asking for insight on what to do with all the mess he had left behind. As God spoke into that pain and reshaped Jack's understanding of grace, forgiveness and redeeming poor choices, Jack was released from the grief of his mistakes and went on to live a much less burdened life. In this case, the teachable moment was triggered by a movie, but Jack needed to pursue his healing with God in order to see and internalize the truth he needed.

Once we learn how to notice these teachable moments, we will discover that they occur quite often. Stress at work, irritating co-workers, problematic family members, an untimely illness and so on, all provide ample opportunity to challenge our existing ideas of life. Knowing how to engage with God about these events can result in frequent encounters with life-changing truth. Still more hopeful is the fact that we can learn how to engage truth in ways that are life-changing even in the absence of any present reaction or stressful emotions. We can do that by creating intentional teachable moments.

Intentional Teachable Moments

In addition to learning how to pay attention to the teachable moments which life brings, there is another way to pursue life-changing truth that is even more accessible and more proactive – a collection of practices that we can employ by choice that open us up to participation with the Holy Spirit.

And once we learn how to make use of these tools for growth and transformation, we will be even better equipped to engage with God in the ad hoc teachable moments of life discussed above.

Spiritual disciplines have been a very important part of Christian development since the early days of the Church. The main reason why they do not have the place of honor they once held is because they tend to be very dry and lifeless when approached with the current mindset of "try harder" Christianity. What many people seem to miss when attempting to engage in these practices is the simple fact that *the effort of engaging in spiritual disciplines does not make anyone a better Christian*. Expecting them to give life simply by practicing them will destroy their effectiveness and discourage those who try.

Some of the main goals of spiritual disciplines are to create various ways for us to engage with God and expose our heart at the same time, so He can reveal what we need and minister to our heart.[104] Transformation comes from being with God, not from "doing" spiritual disciplines. Connecting with God on a regular basis for the purpose of being mentored by Him creates teachable moments in which God shows us the truth about what is in our heart and how that effects our life, as well as the truth we need for healing and change. Following God's lead in the process will bring us healing from past hurts, deliverance from current struggles, and propel us forward in growth and spiritual maturity. Best of all, we will develop a genuine relationship with God that is rooted in our *experience* of Him, not just our theology *about* Him.

What follows here is a description of three core disciplines that can make space for direct engagement with God, which in turn will allow you to internalize truth at deep levels in your soul.

Practice #1 – Spiritual Reflection

Spiritual meditation was a common practice among Jewish believers under the Old Covenant, and there are many references to it in the Bible.[105] However, due to disuse and various forms of misuse, this practice has largely been lost in the West and is even actively rejected by some of our

---

[104] Willard, *The Divine Conspiracy*. Effective use of disciplines is a major theme.

[105] e.g. "If anything is excellent or praiseworthy – think about such things" (Ph.4:8).

churches as too "New Age." But once again, the fact that the enemy has manufactured a counterfeit does not mean we should abandon the real thing. We need time for focused reflection because it provides a powerful means of internalizing the truth of God.

The point of spiritual reflection is to ruminate on a single thought for an extended time for the purpose of better appreciating its value or to receive further insight into its meaning. This can include anything from admiring the beauty of God's creation, to recalling our morning devotional time with God, to simply enjoying His presence.

People are sometimes surprised to discover they already know how to meditate and just need to learn how to refocus that ability on spiritual matters. Anyone who has talked about a stressful experience multiple times or carried on fictional conversations in their mind with another person has engaged in meditation. All that is required is a single, specific thought that holds enough interest for you to spend time thinking about it. You then work it over in your mind, put it in different contexts, ask questions of it, and turn it over and over until the Holy Spirit shows you new ways of seeing and making sense of things.

For example, think about reflecting on the verse, "Whoever drinks the water I give him will never thirst" (Jn.4:14). What water is He talking about? Why do I feel spiritually thirsty all the time? Do I already have that water or do I need to ask for it? What would it be like to drink that water deeply? What does that mean?

Spiritual reflection need not be complicated – it can be as simple as consciously holding in our mind and heart the wonder of God's presence with us. For example, Psalm 139 is a beautiful piece of poetry reflecting the writer's deep conviction that he is fully known and fully loved at the same time.[106] Many people fear being known and harbor the belief that being fully known would necessarily result in being rejected. But the truth is we need to be totally known and loved at the same time by the same person.[107] God

---

[106] Sadly, this Psalm has been badly distorted into a source of condemnation for many Christians who have been told this means "God is watching you." But the psalmist is actually talking about how *glad* he is that God knows him.

[107] See Curt Thompson, *Anatomy of the Soul*, for an excellent comprehensive study on what it means to be known.

knows us better than anyone and still wants to be with us. That is a profoundly life-changing truth that we can internalize very deeply by spending time reflecting and letting that reality sink down into our soul. Reflecting at length about such things can have a powerful impact on our heart and mind.

Almost any Scripture verse or phrase that touches our heart can be used as a starting point for spiritual reflection. Key phrases that come out of Listening to the Word (Practice #3) often make great points of focused contemplation for days at a time. Carrying a small card with the word or phrase can be a helpful reminder to think about the specific idea, and is a handy place to write additional thoughts that come to mind that seem particularly significant. Learning to focus our mind in this way helps to fill our consciousness with thoughts of God and His truth about the unseen realities around us, and trains us to think in holy ways about life and events, rather than in the ways of the world.

Practice #2 – Dialoguing with God

By way of review, the ability to discern the voice of God is an essential part of participating in relationship with Him, just as communication is an important part of any human relationship. The Holy Spirit is the quintessential teacher and mentor. And since teaching requires the transfer of thoughts from one person to another – whether by words, images, or an overall sense of meaning – we need to have conversations with God in order to participate well as a student.

If we think for a minute about how a mentor teaches, we will understand something of what a conversation with God might be like. A good mentor does not simply spoon-feed you answers to life. He asks questions you have not thought of yet, he challenges you to think in new ways, he drops enough gems to capture your imagination, and he allows you to try on a few ideas before guiding you to the true nature of the issue at hand. By the time you arrive at a new understanding, you may have difficulty sorting out who said what and how you got to where you are. All you know is that your mentor's wisdom was indispensable in getting you to this new insight, and that you could not have had any confidence in the process without him.

So it is when talking with God much of the time. You can be drawn along a path of revelation guided by the Holy Spirit, while at the same time so actively involved that you can hardly tell where God's thoughts leave off and your intuitive leaps begin. All you know is that you have spent time with your mentor and life looks different than it did before. Knowing this is how the process works much of the time frees us from trying to quote God or hear an audible voice, or worrying too much about getting some wacky revelation like "go sit on the roof of your house and wait for the rapture." The goal is mainly to engage with Him.

There are four main aspects to conversational prayer, all of which are important and heavily interdependent.

Quieting and Focusing. In order to pay attention and listen well, it is important to prepare your heart and mind to be receptive. For those who can rest easily, simply quiet down, take a few deep breaths, and let go of all inside and outside noise. For those who have difficulty with this, it may help to walk around in some peaceful area where there are relatively few distractions, to help drain off any nervous energy so you can focus better.

Note that this is not a New Age exercise of connecting with whatever is in the unseen world around you, but a way of allowing God to fill your mind with His presence and reduce the amount of "static" that keeps you from paying attention to your deepest thoughts.

Invite Jesus to come closer to you and to open your heart and mind to His presence and His voice. Ask Him to protect your conversation and begin by faith to engage with the Holy Spirit. If at any point during your interaction you find yourself getting distracted, take a few minutes to refocus and reconnect with the Spirit of God.

Listening. God's voice most often comes to us in the form of spontaneous thoughts and impressions. Prepare yourself to pay attention to your body, your emotional reactions, the Spirit of God, and any spontaneous thoughts or impressions. This is mostly about receiving or being led through a process, rather than analyzing a text or relying on your powers of reason to solve a problem. Begin your discussion with God, and ask Him about a word or phrase you have read in Scripture that caught your attention, or ask Him any question for which you would like His mentoring and teaching.

For example, "God, what do I need to know today about my relationship with You?" or "God, what can you tell me about the way I overreact every time I am around that particular person?"

Either write out or carry on the conversation vocally, writing or speaking whatever comes to you. If your sense is more of a dialogue than just thoughts, write or speak both sides of the conversation. Do not worry too much about whether the thoughts originate with you or God, since working with a good mentor can be quite collaborative in nature, and spiritual reflection is good for your soul in any case.. *The goal is not to be able to quote God but to engage with Him.* Feel free to ask further clarifying questions and to say what you currently believe about the issue at hand. Be honest about your reactions, and be open to spontaneous thoughts that reveal the issue differently than what you might have predicted or thought "correct."

Discerning. Not everything that goes through your mind during this time originates with God. By itself, that's not really a problem. We are encouraged to remember and think on the things of God, and those thoughts come from our own memory and internal process. We just need to be aware of the difference between the thoughts that originate with us and those that seem more prompted by Spirit. If your mind begins to drift off topic, it is often helpful to go back to earlier points in the discussion to get back on track, or to ask some of the same questions over again.

After the flow quiets down, go over your conversation and ask God to draw you to whatever it is that He wants you to learn from your time together. It is not always necessary to identify who said what. Rather, tune in to whatever God wants you to take away from the conversation. Be open to asking a trusted friend or your community for help discerning whether or not what you received came from God.

Responding. At some point in the conversation you may feel led to a prayer of thanksgiving, of forgiveness, of repentance, for encouragement, for strength, for resolve, or to take action in some area of your life. If you received some enlightening truth or a phrase that is rich with meaning, consider writing it on a sticky note and putting it up somewhere to remind you in the coming days.[108]

---

[108] "Write them on the door frames of your houses and on your gates" (Deut.6:9).

We can engage in conversational prayer to talk to God about almost anything. And while it can be tempting to seek direction from God by asking yes/no type questions, it is usually more productive to ask Him to help you see the bigger picture so that you can learn the wisdom in how to choose.[109] So rather than ask things like, "Should I marry this person?" try more open-ended things like, "What do I need to know or pay attention to regarding my desire to marry this person?" Once this becomes a regular part of your conversational prayer time with God, it opens up an entirely new world of possibilities for growth and transformation.

There is much more that could be said about these four aspects of conversational prayer. For that I will refer the reader to the book, *Whispers of My Abba*.[110] One thing to keep in mind is that conversational prayer is a learned process, like developing balance or acquiring language skills. That is, we learn over time how to listen better, how to ask better questions, to discern better, and so on. If at all possible, find someone else who knows how to do this and ask them to mentor you in how to have trustworthy and fruitful conversations with God.

The value of this kind of prayer cannot be overstated. Learning how to listen to the Holy Spirit is the single most important thing you can do for your own spiritual development.

Practice #3 – Listening to the Word

This ancient spiritual practice combines dialoguing and Scripture reading into an interactive time of learning from the Spirit. In many ways this is similar to dialoguing with God, except that we use the Bible as the starting point for inspiration. Unlike traditional Bible studies, however, the focus is not on mastering the text intellectually. Rather, the point is to listen to whatever God might say through the text and allow Him to connect the text to our life. Often a phrase or verse will grab our attention, and through reflecting and listening, God will use the text to teach us about life or expose things in our heart or simply comfort and encourage us. This discipline has a very rich history and has been long regarded as a powerful means of engaging with God for transformation.

---

[109] One prime example is "Is it right to pay taxes to Caesar or not?" (Mt.22:17).

[110] Takle, *Whispers of My Abba*.

It is best to learn this practice by using passages that concentrate on our relationship to God, our identity in Christ, or God's provisions for us. Here are a few of my favorites:

- Isaiah 55
- Ephesians 1-4
- Colossians 1-3
- Psalms 27, 63, 84, 139
- John 14-17
- Romans 8

Begin by quieting down and inviting the Holy Spirit to minister to you and open your heart to receive. Read your previous journal entry to set the context for your time together. Then go to the Biblical text where you left off the previous day and begin reading slowly, taking care to listen for any promptings by the Spirit. Also listen to your own mind and body for any reactions to the text, because any surprise or resistance that rises up in you may be fertile ground for learning. When something catches your attention, stop and write the phrase in your journal. Then begin listening to whatever is going on in your heart and continue writing. Be free to ask questions, state your objections, and go off on tangents that feel important. When the conversation seems to slow down, go back over what you have written and ask God for direction and discernment in what needs to happen that day regarding what you have discussed.

Allow the Holy Spirit to guide your time. If something in your previous journal entry catches your attention, be open to letting Him teach you more about that rather than moving on to the next few verses. There is no need to get through any amount of text. In fact the slower you go through a passage the richer it tends to be. It is not unusual to take several weeks to get through a single chapter this way.

Learning how to be fed the Word by the Spirit of God is an incredibly powerful means of renewing your mind. As the Word comes alive and takes root in your heart, life will take on new meaning, anxieties will diminish in their strength, trust in God's care will deepen, and the sense of His presence with you will strengthen in ways that you never thought possible.

Making Use of All Three Ways of Engaging

You may have noticed that a great deal of overlap exists between these three disciplines. Much of the activity that occurs during our conversations with God is actually spiritual reflection. The main distinction is the extent to which we are thinking our own thoughts or seeking to hear His thoughts. Often a time of meditation will move quite naturally into a discussion with God and hearing from Him, and other times our hearing from God will cause us to reflect on what He has said.

In practice, spiritual reflection is an excellent way to begin our time of connection to God, with the expectation that He will join us and begin to teach us in the process.[111] For those who seem to have difficulty hearing God or discerning His voice, this approach to focusing on Scripture and life issues can be a lifeline to finding truth.

Other Practices and Guidelines

Like the practices described above, there are many other spiritual disciplines that provide a space for engaging with God and internalizing truth. Practices sometimes referred to as disciplines of *abstinence* are those in which we voluntarily remove something from our life that we normally have, for the purpose of discovering our dependence and God's sufficiency and exploring our identity apart from those supports. Examples include solitude, silence, fasting, and chastity. Disciplines of *engagement* call us to some intentional activity in order to stretch us and expose our self-oriented way of life. Examples of these are acts of service, confession, and heart-to-heart fellowship with others.

All of these disciplines require careful attention to our inner responses as well as the willingness to explore what God wants to teach us through those experiences. For example, a personal retreat may go through several stages in a single afternoon. We may initially be glad to have the quiet and peace, only to be followed later by periods of boredom or frustration or a barrage of intruding and distracting thoughts that prevent any peace at all. Awareness of any one of these feelings may lead us into wrestling with God about the reasons for our struggle.

The beauty of solitude is that it strips away many of the things that we use to order and structure our days as well as things that give us a sense of who we are. Without anyone else to influence our experience or any of the activities that normally hold our attention, we are better able to hear God and listen to our inner longings in ways that are virtually impossible in the

---

[111] An excellent example of this progression can be seen in Psalm 143: 5-8, 10.

busyness of our daily life.[112] In the same way that solitude opens the door for God to work with us in ways that we are not otherwise available to Him, so also each one of the classical disciplines provides a unique context within which to engage God for change.[113]

Difference Between Dead Practices and Life-Giving Practices

In order for spiritual disciplines to be life-giving encounters with God instead of dreadful dry rituals to be endured, we must be absolutely clear about how disciplines actually "work." Most importantly, *spiritual disciplines will not in and of themselves make us more Christ-like*. I am not a better Christian because I have daily devotions. If that were the case, spiritual development would be based on human effort. Expecting spiritual disciplines to make me a better person simply because I practice them will destroy their effectiveness and leave me disillusioned about their value. Many Christians have more or less given up on these practices because they expected just such a direct cause and effect.

A primary function of a spiritual discipline is to do something that is within our power in order to make a space for God to do something that only He can do, that will then change us in ways that we could not have achieved by our own efforts.[114]

Making time to be with God is something I can do. What God can do with me within that space is unbelievably redemptive. My act of devotion has no such redemptive quality. I can make a space to hear His voice. But it is His voice that makes my soul come alive. As God speaks truth into the depths of my being, He changes how I perceive my reality, my identity, and my purpose. All I can do is make a space for Him to do what He does and trust Him enough to let down my defenses and allow the Spirit to work in my heart. This orientation is absolutely crucial to our approach, because without a proper foundation for engaging in spiritual disciplines, they become distorted and fall flat, and fail to foster transformation.

Becoming more teachable and being genuinely receptive to the work of God is one of the bigger problem areas for most people. One thing that

---

[112] Palmer, *To Know As We Are Known*, pp. 122-123, has an excellent description of the impact of solitude.

[113] For a more comprehensive discussion of life-giving spiritual practices see Takle, *Forming: A Work of Grace*.

[114] Willard, *The Divine Conspiracy*, p. 353.

many find helpful is learning how to ask better questions. We are often prone to ask fairly safe questions like, "What was Peter thinking when he started to sink?" Even when we dare to ask how the text applies to us, we tend to think more in terms of what we should *do* differently, rather than ask what might need to change *inside* us in order to change our character, such as, "When was the last time I stepped out on faith and got smacked around by waves? How did I react? And why?" The more willing we are to ask God to help us with hard questions, the more God can mentor us.

Another part of asking better questions is to ask the Holy Spirit for answers instead of looking to our own reservoir of knowledge and our powers of reason. That usually means asking very open-ended questions of the Spirit, such as, "What have I been reluctant to hear about this issue?" or "What have I been unwilling to see?" Other times, our questions may be very specific, such as, "Lord, every time my boss tells me I did something wrong I spend days obsessing about it and feeling overwhelmed by shame. What is it that makes this so devastating, and how is it that I forget so quickly who I am and where You are in the process?" If that does not seem to lead anywhere, then ask it differently, or ask Him how to ask for help. Recognize that belief is hard work, and to challenge our existing beliefs requires insightful and even difficult questions. Asking good questions is as much a learned skill as listening for answers.

> Spiritual disciplines do *not* change us.
> They only make a space for engaging with God.

Remember that His thoughts are *higher* than our thoughts (Isa.55:9). That means, by definition, no matter what we might be pondering at the moment we are probably missing something. God sees the situation differently than we do. Therefore, some of the most important questions we can ask are, "What am I missing?" or "What else have I not seen yet?"

When considering how to make more space for God in your thoughts, allow yourself to be a bit creative. Even little experiments can be very powerful experiences.[115] On one occasion I heard Dallas Willard suggest the following: every morning as you are waking up and every night as you are

---

[115] A good starting point is Smith and Graybeal, *A Spiritual Formation Workbook*.

drifting off to sleep, turn your thoughts to "the Goodness of God" and hold those thoughts for five to ten minutes. Think about God's character and how our lives are different because of who He is, and let that turn over in your mind in whatever ways the Spirit might lead. That's all. My first thought, of course, was that such a simple practice would not be very helpful. But I since I had a lot of respect for Dr. Willard, I decided to try it for a while. Much to my surprise, after about three weeks I began to notice my heart shifting toward an expectancy of God's goodness in my life that I had not felt before. Instead of feeling the weight of life most of the time, I began to feel God's care for me and the joy of His presence with me. In the process, I learned not to trivialize such basic practices or underestimate their value.

Then too, remember that we all have an incredible capacity for self-deception. Those who undertake deliberate formation soon discover how easy it is to adjust our expectations, talk ourselves out of doing something important, or imagine that we are far stronger than we really are. The best defense against these misconceptions is realistic humility and utter dependence on God. On the one hand, we must never take ourselves too seriously or dismiss our training as too trivial. On the other, we must guard against being overwhelmed by the work that is before us, and trust that God knows how to navigate the path we need to walk.

The basic guideline is to be persistent and deliberate in your effort to remain open and teachable, and to take responsibility for finding and creating ways to learn. Following after truth is a lot like choosing from a variety of experimental courses, except in this class you have unlimited resources at your disposal and a twenty-four/seven personal mentor to guide you. All you need to do is cooperate with your mentor to personalize the ways in which you make a space for engaging with Him. The process will bear fruit that is worth so much more than the effort involved.

Being Intentional

Given the above vision of transformation and the means to achieve it, the greatest remaining barrier to overcome is actually making the choices necessary to begin. Intentionality is more than a mere desire to live the Kingdom life. The process of Christian formation and internalizing truth requires us to take specific steps. A pivotal point in this process is that of being *deliberate* about our pursuit of God.[116] That means we must give Him *time* and focused *attention*, and do so *persistently*. We need to add God to our day-timer, if necessary, to insure there is adequate space dedicated to building our relationship. It is not enough to simply *want* to experience the work of God in our life. We have to intentionally rearrange our life to make a place for deliberate engagement with the Holy Spirit.

Making this a reality requires several steps. First, we need to have a regular meeting time with God, preferably the same time every day. In spite of whatever negative experiences people may have previously had with their devotional time, actual planned time with God is an important part of participation. Of course it helps to catch a vision of what meeting with God could be like and not confuse this with some dry, lifeless activity we must endure. Spending time in the presence of God is a joyful and life-giving experience.

There is no hard and fast rule about what we must do during that time, but we need to connect with God daily, just as we need to eat food every day to maintain our health. This in turn may mean going to bed earlier, watching less television, or even developing new schedules for the children. We really do need to rearrange our life to make the necessary space, because we are simply not designed to go for days and weeks without receiving life from God.

Second, we need to be deliberate about maintaining our connection with God throughout the day. One approach is to write a few words on a note card that capture what we received from our time with God and carry it with us, taking a few minutes here and there to re-read the card and recall what we received earlier in the day.

For example, on one particular morning I was struck by the idea that I am a child of the King. So in a classy font I typed up, "A Beloved Son of the King," copied it several times, printed it out and cut the lines apart. I then taped up at a copy of the statement in every room of the house so I would see it all the time. For many weeks it continued to serve as a constant reminder of my identity in Christ.

---

[116] "You will seek me and find me *when you seek me with all your heart*" (Jer.29:13).

214   *Internalizing Truth*

Third, we need an occasional time away so we can be alone with God for an extended period of time, ideally an entire day or at least three or four hours if possible. The goal is to have a significant block of time for Him to minister to our heart. Some people will find this very difficult at first attempt, and may require help in order to learn how to do this well. But the time can be absolutely transformative and life-giving. One of the more interesting statements ever made about the early disciples was that those who were observing Peter and John could tell "these men had been with Jesus" (Acts 4:13). The wisdom that the Jewish rulers saw in them came from spending quality time with their Teacher.

For people with particularly exhausting schedules that are really difficult to budge, these extended times can provide an important resource to supplement daily quiet times. Consider that fact that God gave the law to an agrarian people who probably worked sixteen-hour days just to survive. His solution was to require them to set aside an entire day of Sabbath once a week to connect with God and pay special attention to their spiritual lives. For us that could mean extended Listening to the Word and Dialoguing with the Spirit. Then whatever gems come out of that time can be carried around for the rest of the week and used as a focal point for on-going reflection.[117] Since truth often takes time to emerge and time to be internalized, this is an excellent practice that allows single elements of light to penetrate deep into our soul over time.

Finally, we need to be alert for the teachable moments brought to us by life in the world. Good parents often run into these serendipitous events with their children, where they find themselves in the middle of an experience that lends itself to a few choice words of instruction that stick with their kids for years to come. God can do the same with we if we are intentional about our observations. Teachable moments include everything from particularly joyful times to confusing and difficult events. The key is to take these moments to God at the earliest possible opportunity and ask Him what it is He can tell us about what we are feeling and experiencing. He can use those experiences to impart truth that goes deep into our soul.

---

[117] "Talking about them when you sit at home and when you walk along the road, when you lie down and when you get up" (Deut.11:19).

Rowing or Sailing?

Participating with the Spirit is a lot like sailing. Most of us have learned to live the Christian life much like a person who is rowing against the current. The harder we try the more tired we become, and still the boat seems to have a mind of its own. But raising the sail and orienting it to the wind can move the boat forward in ways that we could never accomplish by rowing. There is still much we can do, and much that we can learn about aligning the sail with the wind.

Working with the Holy Spirit for the purpose of internal change is very similar. Learning to engage with God is like aligning the sail. Catching the wind is like having His life flow into us by virtue of our close relationship with Him and internalizing the truth that He brings. Our life then moves forward without the continuous effort of "rowing" against our internal inclinations to go elsewhere.

We need to become active students of His teaching in ways that open us up to the truth of God. That truth can then penetrate our heart and mind and transform our implicit beliefs, which in turn will change our inner responses to life around us. Over time we will become more and more inclined to live by nature the way that God designed us to live.

Life 101

Kingdom life as described in the New Testament is a beautiful thing. Yet many Christians give up on that vision because no matter how hard they try it seems permanently out of reach. They may have all kinds of reasons why they think their growth has slowed down to a crawl, but the truth is that they have never been trained in how to engage with their mentor in ways that transform their soul. It is as though they have been trying to build a house with nothing but a hammer. Having the right tools makes a big difference in the results.

Because most of us have been taught to crank out the Christian life though hard work, we need to go back to square one and admit that we know far less about this process than we thought. We have been misled as to the true nature of the problems we face, as well as how to move forward. There is much that we must unlearn and relearn if we are to get to know our God experientially and how to receive more life from Him instead of trying to make it happen in our own strength. Somewhere down deep inside, within that new life that God gave to us, we all believe there must be a way to become more of what God intended us to be. It is time to rediscover that life! And learning how to engage with God for truth that leads to transformation is one of the most powerful means we have toward that end.

Chapter 11
Realigning Our Christian Development

Truth in Biblical terms is seeing reality the way God knows it to be. That includes everything about life, others, and ourselves. The more our thoughts fall into line with His thoughts, the more we will be like Him.

For this reason, truth as it is described in this book is one of the most accessible and powerful means of transformation available to us, both in terms of healing our old patterns and in establishing new ones. In short, learning to internalize truth plays a vital role in the process of sanctification.

> *Being transformed into His likeness with ever-increasing glory, which comes from the Lord, who is the Spirit. (2Cor.3:18)*

Redefining Sanctification in Accessible Terms

Given a basic understanding of the nature of truth and belief, we are now in a position to move beyond traditional models of discipleship and see how truth fits into the larger picture of sanctification, which is *the gradual process of incremental transformation resulting more and more in a Christ-like character*. To begin, let us break that definition into its component parts.

Gradual Process. Undoing the malformation from this world and being re-formed in Christ-likeness is a life-long process. There is decidedly more work to do than can be accomplished in a single lifetime. That does not mean we have no control over the process or that it is so gradual that we are more or less unaware of what the Spirit is up to at any given moment. Extensive time is needed not because of the pace at which change can happen, but rather because of the extent of malformation that actually exists within us. There is truly far more damage in our soul than we can imagine. Still the process can be a continual experience of new life and growth that brings great joy and satisfaction every day.

This is also why we need so much grace in regard to where we are at any given moment in time. We are unfinished works of grace. And if we hold ourselves to a perfect standard in a way that is shaming and condemning, we will live with a continual burden of failure that can only lead to a distorted view of who we are in Christ. Grace means we get the relationship first. Then we work on the "stuff" within the context of that relationship. We do not have to pretend we are fully formed in Christ. The good news of the kingdom is that we can live life with God before the job of transformation is completed![118] And our life in Christ continues to deepen and grow with every thought that is transformed from death to life.

Incremental. We replace our faulty beliefs one at a time. Some are changed in a single moment. Some require days or weeks of weakening before giving way to the truth. Many of the means of internalization may even initially appear to be doing very little toward reforming our heart and mind. Yet each minor step is one more piece of the larger goal, like the Israelites taking the land one city at a time.

Growth is also incremental in the sense that a little growth improves our connection with God which in turn leads to more growth which deepens our connection to Him, and so on. Sometimes it takes several smaller steps of healing and growth to prepare us for a larger one. Rather than attempt a total makeover in a single power-encounter, we must learn to seek and appreciate the significance of very elementary alterations in such things as our perceptions of God, the attitudes of our heart, our identity as His apprentice, and our relationships with other people.

Transformation. This process is not just about filling in missing pieces, but about one change after another, from a way of darkness to a way of light. The misbeliefs we hold must be replaced by the truth of God and allowed to alter our very character. Perhaps the best image for this is that of death and resurrection. As we die to the ways of darkness we become alive to the ways of light. When Paul said, "Just as you received Christ Jesus as Lord, continue to live in Him" (Col.2:6) he was referring to a way of encountering Christ over and over that is similar to the way a person experiences their

---

[118] "Blessed are the spiritually impoverished, because they precisely the ones the kingdom is for!" (Mt.5:3, paraphrase).

initial rebirth of the spirit. If we are engaged with the Holy Spirit in an on-going apprentice relationship, we can expect transformation to become commonplace in our life. And we will experience these changes on multiple levels, sometimes as rapid shifts in values and beliefs, and sometimes as more gradual movement in attitude and character.

One day Bonnie came across the verses about "do not worry, saying, 'what shall we eat' or 'what shall we wear' … for which of you by worrying can add to your height?" As she reflected on this, Bonnie realized that she had a lot of anxiety about her everyday provisions. In talking with God, it dawned on her that about 98% of life is made up of things over which she had no real control. Which meant trusting God was absolutely necessary, and her anxiety was wasted energy over the illusion of being able to provide for herself. The truth came at a teachable moment, and gave her profound peace about her financial situation.

About a week later she revisited this issue and God continued her training by revealing that she rarely felt generous and was often very protective of her modest possessions to the point of being stingy. This led her to the realization that she had often felt "taken from" as a child and had never developed a sense that she could say "no" without feeling guilty. Her protective attitude was a reaction to repeated experiences of loss. These insights provided key focal points for her discussions with God in order to continue to seek more healing and liberty for her soul.

So it is with transformation, where one good thing leads to many more. Each step opens the door to the next, reveals more of what we need, and gives us hope that life can be different.

Christ-like Character. Our goal is not just to abstain from sin, but to actually develop more and more into the likeness of Christ.[119] We do not have to wait until we die before we take on elements of Christ's character, but can see this process happening throughout our lifetime here on earth.

---

[119] "We are being transformed into His likeness with ever-increasing glory" (2Cor.3:18); "Become mature, attaining to the whole measure of the fullness of Christ" (Eph.4:13). "And everyone who has this hope is already in the process of becoming more like Him" (1Jn.3:5 paraphrase).

God's intent is to mold and reshape us more and more into the image of Christ. This is the very essence of sanctification.

As stated earlier, we cannot truly follow His example unless we first take on His character. When Jesus says "love your enemies" (Mt.5:44) He asks us to do something that our flesh rebels against because we can list at least a dozen good reasons why we should retaliate or demand justice or make them suffer for their actions. Only when our heart is changed and we see our enemies the way Christ sees them is there any hope of our actually loving them. Sanctification does not mean we acquire the self-control to restrain from acting on vengeful impulses toward our enemies. Rather, we take on enough of the character of Christ so that we no longer harbor those feelings of anger and hate. Instead, our enemies have value in our eyes and we care about their spiritual well-being. This same perspective can be applied over and over to all of the teachings of Jesus.

Internalizing Truth

To be transformed from the inside out is at the very heart of what separates the New Covenant from the Old.[120] Paul argues very forcefully in the first half of Romans that the law written on scrolls was never able to produce the change in us that God desired. So He chose to write His word on our heart and mind. When we treat the Word of God like a collection of principles to be followed, we effectively revert back to following an external code of conduct, a way of life that has proven to not work. We must instead find out what God intends to do with our heart and mind and learn how to participate with Him in the process of change. As our core beliefs begin to line up with the mind of Christ, we become more and more Christ-like in our character, and holiness becomes a way of life.

---

[120] "I will put my laws in their minds and write them on their hearts" (Heb.8:10).

Three Major Dimensions to Christian Development

We are now ready to pull together a coherent picture of Christian growth and development that includes, among other things, how the Holy Spirit transforms us through His ministry of truth. From our perspective as apprentices of Kingdom life, participating with God for the purpose of internalizing truth can be divided into three major areas.

The first area is that of *proactive* formation, in which we deliberately seek to be taught by the Holy Spirit by connecting with Him intentionally for that purpose. As discussed in the last chapter, we can participate in this aspect of sanctification by engaging with God within the context of those spiritual practices that have proven effective over the centuries. In this way, we work truth into our heart and body to replace the assumptions and practices that we have acquired through years of malformation.

The other two areas are more *responsive* in nature. One has to do with addressing the sin in our life, and the other has to do with healing wounds we have received from living in a broken world. When either area comes to the forefront of our life, we can enlist the Holy Spirit in the process of deliberately rooting out the exact nature of the faulty beliefs involved and receive healing through hearing God's perspective on what we are dealing with. In this way we can "put to death the misdeeds of the body" (Rom.8:13).

Proactive Formation

Once we see that the struggle between good and evil in humans is deeply connected to the issues of belief, truth, and deception, we arrive very naturally at an *optimistic* doctrine of transformation. If one of our biggest problems is a mind that has been malformed by deception and faulty values, then with the Holy Spirit as our mentor, we can deal with our true core issues and experience substantial character change.

Engaging with God in real and purposeful ways for His mentoring and guidance will predictably impact our soul positively, just as continuous distance or alienation from Him impacts us negatively. Additionally, as we draw closer to the Light, our distortions and flaws become more and more apparent. We may not like what we see, but if we truly get to know the love of God and can get over the mistaken goal of trying to look good in front of Him, we will soon come to the point where the discomfort of exposure in His presence is no longer a threat to our self worth. We can even invite His searching with joyful anticipation, as David did in his famous Psalm. [121] What a relief to melt in His arms every time something new comes to the surface, and every time something old comes back to accuse us of failing! These are some of the most teachable moments and the times when we need Him more than ever. Such unique, personal moments of exposure that come as a result of proactive formation may then lead us to the next two areas.

Addressing the Sin in Our Life

Wherever sin is exposed in our life we have at least two choices open to us – to move toward healing and reconciliation to God, or move away from Him and hide like Adam and Eve did. Proactive Christian formation will predictably bring our failings to light and present us with this choice on a regular basis. The question is what can be done with these experiences so they become opportunities to break the cycle of sin in our life, rather than additional entries in the list of repetitive failures.

As we said earlier, much of the "discipling" in recent generations bears a strong resemblance to behavior modification couched in spiritual terminology. We are given lists of things to do and not do. If we sin we are told to be really sorry, repent, and try harder next time. Inner healing, if it occurs at all, is either accidental or considered to be non-essential.

The problem with this approach is that it attempts to enter the *sin cycle* after the transgression has already occurred. The cycle itself looks something like the diagram on the next page, with *repentance* being the place where we attempt to interrupt the process. We begin with a period of stability, which to a great extent is something of an illusion. Often all that is required is a single trigger to set the whole thing in motion. It may be a comment from another person, an accident, or some unexpected interruption in our day. Our implicit beliefs get stirred up and dump their impressions into the present moment and we react almost without thinking.

---

[121] "O Lord, you have searched me and you know me...Such knowledge is too wonderful for me...Search me, O God, and know my heart" (Ps.139:1).

The next thing we know we are asking God to forgive us for breaking down and failing yet again. This process can repeat almost endlessly.

Getting caught in this sin cycle and trying to interrupt the process at the point of repentance leads to spiritual exhaustion, despair, and resignation. The cycle itself is actually rooted in self-effort and an approach to prayer that essentially says "God, please help me in my effort to be different."

Repentance in regard to what we have done is certainly a part of restoration, but it is not the whole of it. In most instances, we need God to replace the underlying beliefs that we have held that led us into the sin. If we do not know what those implicit beliefs are, then we need to engage with the Holy Spirit for the purpose of exposing them to the light of truth so that He can give us His perspective. This approach to dealing with sin gives us great freedom and real hope for change.

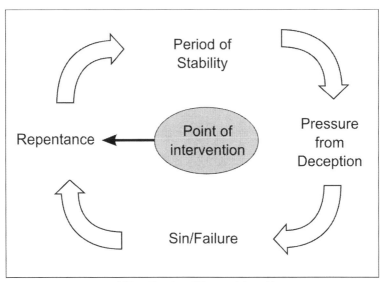

The Cycle of Repetitive Sin

However, the ideal place to intervene is at the point of *deception*. To break any pattern of sin, the critical task is to unmask the faulty beliefs that drive the behaviors and replace them with truth. As we participate with the Holy Spirit, He will reveal what we need to know, and as we internalize that truth our life will change. Over time the malformation is replaced with a renewed mind and our character grows up into its true nature.

Daniel's life-long conflict with his family is one example of how this can work. For nearly fifty years, Daniel had held deep resentments toward his parents and two of his siblings because of his early family life. This issue had come to a head many times and Daniel had prayed, cried, repented, and done everything he could to let go of his anger and hate. But every time he found himself in the same room with any of them, all the feelings of resentment would come flooding back and it was all he could do just to clench his jaw shut and remain civil.

One day God gave Daniel a picture of his family out in about twelve feet of water with everyone thrashing around trying to get some air. In order to breathe, each person would grab another and push them under, and they in turn would then get pushed down by someone else. As Daniel contemplated the image, it suddenly dawned on him, "They're not being mean…they're desperate!"

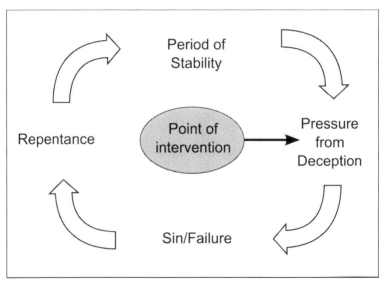

Breaking the Cycle

This revelation broke his heart, and he no longer felt bitterness and hate. Instead, he felt compassion for his family and longed for their healing. Daniel's problem was not about disobedience or a failure to honor his father and mother. His problem was that he had believed all his life his family was mean-spirited and deliberately evil. When he saw them through the eyes of heaven, his heart changed and his resentments were transformed into compassion. This is how renewing our mind can set us free in ways that simply trying harder to do the right things cannot.

There is so much God can do to break the power of sin in our life, if we move toward Him at the time of our distress and invite Him to expose the buried beliefs that drive our behavior. Only then can we receive the depth of healing that can alter our desires and change how we act, not by trying harder, but by becoming a different person from the inside out.

Healing Wounds Acquired from Living in a Broken World

Deception works in ways other than just causing us to sin. Our faulty thinking about the wrongs that have been done *to* us can be very destructive as well. Those implicit beliefs need to be changed in order to free us of the pain and bondage that keep us stuck long after the initial event. For example, if a husband has an affair, the wife who is betrayed may seriously wonder whether God cares about her or whether her life has been ruined beyond redemption. Such powerful feelings of abandonment and rejection cause very deep wounds which the enemy twists and distorts into beliefs that lead a person to abandon hope or doubt God's love for them.

Often years after going through a traumatic event, there are lingering emotional and spiritual consequences that appear to be a direct result of that experience. While it is true that trauma can result in long-term pain, it does so primarily through indirect means (unless there are continuing physical problems). Most of the pain we still feel years after a traumatic event comes not from the experience itself but from the ways we have interpreted that experience – beliefs that tell us terrible things about who we are, who God is, and what we can expect from life and others. Those lies are the real source of bondage, because we believe them deeply and live as if they were true. Our earlier experience becomes something of a container for the lie,[122] but the experience itself is no longer the main cause of the present pain. The lies we believe are the real source of our distress.

For example, a woman who had been date-raped in high school was never able to recall that experience without feeling a great deal of pain and shame because she felt as if she had become "damaged goods." When she

---

[122] Smith, *Beyond Tolerable Recovery*.

asked God how He could possibly still love her, He called her His "beloved" and helped her to see herself as beautiful and pure. Having nothing about which to be ashamed, she felt restored to her former purity and wholeness. After God altered her understanding of who she was, the memory no longer held the terrible pain that it once had.

Changing what happened is not really possible, because the events actually occurred and are part of a person's history. Unless there are significant facts missing in regard to the incident, there is usually no way to go back and reconstruct the event. What *can* be changed are the person's *interpretations* of the experience, the *conclusions* reached about his or her life, and their perceptions about God's heart in the matter. When these areas are transformed, even the way they experience the memory will change. For all of this to happen, they need to hear and see God's perspective since no human viewpoint will be of much help. Only His voice has the power to give life to the words of truth that are needed.

We are all affected by deception in this way, because we all have dozens or even hundreds of woundings that opened doorways to distorted interpretations of our life. Most of us carry far more of these distortions than we realize. Healing from even a few of these faulty beliefs can result in a great deal of spiritual freedom and forward movement.

Nearly all dynamics associated with dysfunctional family patterns are rooted in lies that were internalized by the family members from childhood wounding, usually in both parents and children. Whether each succeeding generation internalizes their parents' worldview or rebels against it, the resulting beliefs about life and self remain faulty, and the problems persist. When people learn how to engage with God for truth, the Holy Spirit can speak into these systems with the insight necessary to break the cycle.

Receiving healing for our wounds can be amazing and wonderful in and of itself. But that's not all. In addition to the immediate healing that we receive, we get first-hand experience of the care and compassion God has for us in our helplessness. This in turn builds trust in our relationship with God, which strengthens our whole venture of spiritual formation. We also see more clearly how much of our life difficulties are intertwined with the work of deception. Repeated healings bring a tremendous sense of relief that we are not condemned to life-long bondage, and great hope that we truly can become more and more Christ-like and live the way that God intended. In summary, healing is not intended by God to be an end in itself, but a doorway to closer intimacy with Him and a heart of love for others (1Tim.1:5).

Foundational Truths We All Need to Believe

Our re-formation is accomplished in part by God's amazing ability to tailor His truth to the particular ways in which we have been malformed by deception. Much of the healing we receive comes from these custom-made gifts of truth that we can learn how to receive from Him.

At the same time, there are certain foundational truths which help to guide this whole process. A few of these stand out as particularly important, partly because of their crucial nature and partly because their significance has often been overlooked. We shall attempt to identify some of these over-arching truths here.

The Work is Never Done

Because of the extensive deception and malformation we have all internalized in the past and the continuous confusion we encounter day by day, we will never finish our restoration in this life or outgrow our need to hear God's truth for us. Even if we gave our full attention to Christian formation, we would come to the end our life with a lot of unfinished work still ahead of us. Surprisingly, this is good news on at least three fronts.

First, this frees us from the condemnation of being unfinished. *Of course* we have holes in our life and things that are not right! This is exactly what we should expect to find. God knows this, too, and has made a point of it so that we would not get too caught up in trying to arrive at some place of perfection.[123] Life in the kingdom of God is not about being perfect, it is about being restored. On that basis, all who seek God's light and restoration qualify as residents of the kingdom, no matter what their state.[124]

---

[123] "We have this treasure in jars of clay" (2Cor.4:7).

[124] "Blessed are the spiritually impoverished, because they precisely the ones the kingdom is for!" (Mt.5:3, paraphrase).

Second, even a little light can make a tremendous difference in a dark place. The joy of forward movement in this world is so great that the inability to complete the task becomes almost irrelevant. The prospect of this happening hundreds of times in our lifetime is real cause for rejoicing.

Third, we must never take the self-righteous stance of believing we have "arrived" or that we already know what we need to know. That would be the epitome of self-deception. Remaining teachable and learning how to learn are incredibly important skills that will serve us well throughout our lifetime as apprentices of Jesus.

Transformation is Really Possible

To be set free in some area of life simply by hearing the voice of God may sound impossible to those who have struggled unsuccessfully for any length of time. The fact is we have been deceived about the inaccessibility of transformation due to the poor strategies we have employed in the past. Rather than being taught how to engage with the Holy Spirit for transformation, most of us have been taught to feel really sorry and try harder. The task before us is to learn how to participate well with God in our own formation, much of which revolves around renewing our mind by internalizing truth through engaging with God.

The Primary Battle is Internal

One of the greatest frustrations for Christians comes from fighting the wrong battles. Many find themselves continuously at war with the mishaps around them: the accidents, illnesses, and other tragedies of this world. They want to believe that following God will somehow protect them from the pain of this messy planet or provide them with the power to fix whatever goes wrong. However, the real battle God wants us to learn about takes place in our heart. We need to participate with the Holy Spirit and allow Him to vanquish all of the doubts and lies that keep us in bondage to the external circumstances of our life.

Secondly, many of those who *do* recognize that the battle is inside us see it primarily as an attempt to repress an old fallen nature, whereas the real struggle is to nurture our true identity which we have received from God. Notice the tenses in the following quote: "Since you *have taken off* your old self with its practices and *have put on* the new self, which is *being renewed* in knowledge in the image of its Creator" (Col.3:9-10). According to Paul, we have a new nature that is still in the process of being renewed. That is where our hope lies. We are new creatures, but we still have unfinished work to do in our formation. As we learn how to participate with the Spirit in our own renewal, we will see the kind of growth and change that our new nature was designed for.

Finally, this process of renewal and identity development can only take place within the context of a genuine functioning relationship with God. The problem here is that despite all the effort made at Christian education, there are precious few places in the Christian world that teach us how to build a real and vital relationship with God. Instead, they teach us how to manage our behaviors and attitudes and how to study the Bible, and call that a relationship.

Until we revisit this wholesale distortion of the nature of our relationship to God, we will continue to promote an external Christian lifestyle at the expense of helping people truly engage with God.

Most of Our Distortions Have Common Themes

Most of the distortions we carry around involve a very small set of recurring themes with slight variations. Although it is important to seek out the nuances of our lies and distorted vision, it can be helpful to know that most of our problems involve either distortions about who God is, distortions about who we are, or some distorted understanding of our relationships with others.

In practice, most of the lies about our identity also turn out to be related in some way to lies about God. For example, if deep down I believe that my life will never matter, most likely I also believe that God has abandoned me at some level. In any case, the lies related to how we perceive ourselves, how we perceive God, and how we are to relate to one another are truly destructive, and they can cripple us both spiritually and emotionally.

Lies about who God is can destroy all hope of recovery, because they distance us from our only real source of hope. Lies about who we are lead us invariably to self-condemnation and self-hate. Furthermore, there are hundreds of variations on identity lies, and we will undoubtedly continue to encounter them for the rest of our life. To combat these distortions, we must become thoroughly convinced of the goodness of God in our life and the truth of who God has created us to be.

Finally, we need to remember that renewing our mind is a God-sized problem, not something we can resolve by thinking hard about things. To the extent that we allow the Spirit of God to lead us through the healing of our identity and our images of God, we will be able to relate to God and trust His work in our life. To whatever extent we think we can figure it out independently, we cut ourselves off from the very source we need.

We Need to be Honest with God to Hear What We Need

It is perhaps a bit ironic that Christians often have difficulty with prayer precisely because they are trying too hard to pray "right." They have a sense that because God is all powerful and awesome, they should approach Him with severity and reverence, and that includes the idea that there are only certain ways to talk to God and only certain kinds of things He wants to hear. Christians often pray what they think they *ought* to pray instead of telling God what is truly on their heart. They may be bitterly disappointed that God did not stop something from happening, yet pray only for God to help with the mess, and even then without much hope of Him actually doing anything. They express neither their disappointment nor their doubts.

Of course God knows what is really in their heart, so the display of reverence cannot be just for Him, even if the person has been taught that this is what God requires. Instead, this kind of prayer actually conveys distrust in God and an unwillingness to tell Him what they truly think and feel. This is a highly guarded relationship that attempts to hold back from full engagement. By approaching God in this way, they actively resist any input He might have regarding their real situation.

The Biblical authors did not have this problem. The Psalms are radically honest, often containing two opposing viewpoints as if the writer was torn between two beliefs or changed his mind in the middle of his engagement with God. But he held nothing back and that is the beauty of his prayers. We need to learn how to pray like this, to wrestle with God like Jacob, or challenge Him like Job when we cannot understand what is going on. Only then can we be fully aware of our own heart and truly open to his response.

God is incredibly respectful of the boundaries we set in the relationship. If we want limited contact and sanitized discussions, then He will accommodate our limitations and allow us to play at Christianity. But if we bare our soul and trust Him to respond, He will run to us with open arms and declare to us the very life we so desire.

Common Barriers to Truth

Even when we know the best means for engaging truth, there will still be times when things get in the way and derail the process. There are many reasons why this is so, but there are four barriers in particular that are very significant and fairly universal.

We Fail to See the Extent of Our Own Mistaken Beliefs

Many simply fail to see the pervasiveness of the spiritual problem in which we are all enmeshed. People can look straight at the evidence and still miss it completely.[125] Christians are often quite convinced that they only need a little extra knowledge or motivation to give them the edge they are missing. Knowing a lot of doctrine and Biblical information (as valuable as it is) can actually contribute to this delusional thinking.

Mistaken implicit beliefs come in many forms. One of the most common is simply the failure to see where the problem actually lies. Jennifer's story is a good example of this. As a journalist, her work was continually subject to the review of her editor. More often then not, her first draft of an article would come back all marked up for revisions and she would feel deeply hurt and angry every time. Convinced that her boss was simply the kind of person who had to have his say, she became bitter and resentful of his input. She knew this was wrong and prayed for forgiveness many times, but could not seem to change her attitude.

When she finally came to the end of herself and asked God what she was missing, she was reminded of her father who never had anything good to say to her and for whom she was never good enough, no matter what she did. Suddenly, she realized that her editor was tapping into that reservoir of resentment which she had stored up against her father for criticizing her all

---

[125] "They may be ever seeing but never perceiving" (Mk.4:12).

those years. After she cried out to God for what her father's critical spirit had cost her and began to receive God's healing for the wounds in her soul, she discovered that her editor's comments no longer bothered her and she eventually developed a healthy respect for his ability to craft news items.

The reason Jennifer had never been able to overcome this problem in her workplace was because she believed the problem was an overbearing boss and an unforgiving spirit in herself. When she finally saw that the root problem was her own misinterpretation of the situation due to unresolved issues in her past, she was able to find the healing necessary to separate constructive criticism from her self-worth. Unfortunately, many people find it hard to believe that the reason they get derailed might actually be the distorted understanding they have of their own life.

Another form of disbelief is expressed by the wholesale dismissal of transformation as something merely visionary, or as something which happens only to addicts and hookers when they get saved. The overall lack of teaching on transformation and the general lack of experience of being transformed leads many to believe that it is extremely rare at best, and that there is nothing we can do to foster it. Such disbelief is sufficient in and of itself to discourage people from seeking the changes they need. Of course, this only adds another layer of deception on top of the distorted ideas we already have, making transformation even more elusive.

Then there are Christians who mistake their malformation for ingrained personality traits that cannot be overcome. They believe "this is just who I am" and cannot see the extent to which they have been formed by long-term alignments with deception. Consequently they fight the wrong battles.

There is something inside us that resists the notion that the average Christian can be severely malformed by lies and misbeliefs. The idea may seem preposterous, even unthinkable. Ironically, it is the very pervasiveness of the problem that allows it to hide in plain sight. As such, the extent of the darkness has itself become a major barrier to belief in the truth.

Lies Appear Stronger Than They Really Are

Another major barrier to truth is the way that lies appear to be an intractable part of our DNA instead of the invading virus they really are. Deception in the human soul often takes the form of a great spiritual logjam. During the great logging days when logs were floated down the river to the sawmill, they would occasionally get stuck and create a large dam that got worse with every additional log. Attempting to break the logjam was extremely difficult and dangerous because of the tremendous forces involved. Part of the task required removing key logs that held the whole thing in place. Often a log would be pulled out of the pile with no visible effect on the rest of the logjam. However, when a key log was cut out or removed, dozens or hundreds of logs could break loose at once making the whole logjam collapse.

The lies we believe are often interwoven and mutually supportive like the logs in a logjam. We may feel some temporary relief after identifying a lie, but if we see relatively little progress, we may conclude that lies are not a very serious problem and that correcting lies has minimal impact on our life. What's more, we can then be deceived into thinking that the distortions we sense in our soul are hard-wired into our being and cannot be removed.

God is the only one who knows which logs need to be removed and in what order. We may need to persist until we experience the removal of a few key lies and the resulting release from spiritual bondage before we begin to grasp the nature of what we are actually dealing with and really come to trust this process of renewal.

Viewing Spiritual Growth as a Hidden Process

One often hears that spiritual growth is a process. If by that we mean growth is continuous and never ending in this life, then it is a true statement. But if by process we mean that spiritual growth has more to do with time than with our actual participation, or that it happens so slowly we are hardly aware of it, then the phrase may actually be more of an attempt to explain our lack of growth than a description of the realities of spiritual development. Leaving change to some abstract notion of the Holy Spirit working in mysterious ways behind the scenes will eventually foster disillusionment and keep us from participating well in our own restoration.

Yes, spiritual growth *is* a process, one that we need to engage in actively and consciously, just as building a successful marriage is a conscious, active process. The reason it needs to be identified as an ongoing process is because we need to separate growth from any notion of *arrival* or completion. Behind a lot of training programs is the unspoken idea that intentional growth is some kind of phase you go through before joining the ranks of those who minister, after which your growth will slow down and become less focused and less discernible. And while this may be an observable phenomenon in many of our churches, it is only because we have seriously misunderstood growth and transformation. The spiritual plateau we experience is not a symptom of arrival, but it may well be stagnation from a misdirected approach to spiritual growth. Viewing the work of the Holy Spirit as a hidden process is a tremendous barrier to genuine change.

Difficulty Engaging in Self-Examination Without Condemnation

One of the tasks everyone needs to learn as part of natural development is the ability to maintain some presence of mind or stay connected to other people while experiencing strong negative emotions.[126] While some emotions may be more difficult to regulate than others, for many people there is at least one emotion difficult enough to manage that it has the ability to significantly impair the ways in which they think and act.

The emotion that most commonly interferes with hearing and receiving truth is *shame*, because truth can be very revealing about our inner character. Although there is such a thing as healthy shame, most of us are more familiar with the toxic variety, a painful experience of feeling condemned as unacceptable to God and others.

Many people have great difficulty dealing with shame. For those who find shame particularly painful or difficult to recover from, anything that might trigger their shame is resisted or avoided if at all possible. That makes it extremely hard for people to hear even the most constructive and helpful criticisms, let alone consider that they have serious internal misbeliefs that are out of step with God's view of the world. Such a person may find self-examination unthinkable or intolerable, because every exposure of underlying problems is interpreted as more condemnation.

Working through this barrier can be a difficult task. In some cases, the shame itself can be approached as a system of false beliefs about who the person believes he or she is. With proper counseling and ministry, the lies

---

[126] Wilder, *The Complete Guide to Living With Men.*

supporting this negative self-image can be healed and their experience of God's love for them can become great enough to overcome their fear. With others, it may be necessary to first help them build up their capacity to hold shame without shutting down and going away. Only then will they be able to tolerate the level of self-examination that is part of hearing the truth they need for growth.

There are several keys to helping someone who is easily overwhelmed by shame. Most importantly, they need to rediscover the character and grace of God and His intense love for them. All too often people are given the impression that the Christian God is an incredibly severe judge who is perpetually on the verge of annihilating them, that it is only the constant advocacy of Jesus which gets them past His Father's wrath and into heaven. Such a view of God is evil and destructive, and terribly out of step with the Father's heart.[127] When people encounter God as He truly is, they discover His desire for their well-being and learn to allow His presence in their life. As it turns out, the scariest thing about God is also the very reason why we have hope: His holiness. It is precisely His holiness that makes Him the perfect healer and mentor, and why He has moved heaven and earth to bridge the gulf between us. While He is a fearsome being, *He is on our side*!

Those who have been trained in a judgmental religious environment may need to be reintroduced to the Kingdom of God as good news instead of the harsh, condemning message they have been taught. Some segments of the Evangelical world have long perpetuated a message of hate and judgment that destroys the credibility of the Christian message and teaches an unforgiving, perfectionist dogma that condemns every wrong move and thought, and gives no space to a meaningful relationship between God and highly flawed human beings.

Summing Up Christian Formation

At its core, Christian formation is about renewing our heart and mind over time to become more and more like the mind of Christ. As we begin to recognize the extent of the damage done by malformation and the degree to which that impacts our life, it becomes clear that the path of reconciliation

---

[127] "Anyone who has seen me has seen the Father" (Jn.14:9).

to God includes endless encounters with truth in teachable moments, and that everything we are involved in provides opportunity for growth. Furthermore, we can make space in our life to engage God deliberately in ways that are life-giving and transformative. The question is whether we can learn to internalize truth and submit to the ongoing task of becoming apprentices of life in the Kingdom.

Some Final Thoughts

We were never designed to live with the experiential knowledge of evil. It is far too toxic and takes a tremendous toll on our soul and our sense of self, God, and others. Most of all, it blinds us to the realities of the spiritual world, including the means by which we can receive our sight and be set free. Becoming a Christian opens the door to a relationship with the One who knows how to navigate this life we have, but at that point our task has only begun. Becoming more like Christ is a life-long process that requires far more than our best effort and good theology. We need to be transformed from the inside out in virtually every area of life.

But how do we do that? Anyone who has tried to live the Christian life knows from experience that we are simply not up to the task. The great question we must all face sooner or later is this: *What is it that keeps me from growing and changing the way I see promised in the New Testament?* Tragically, the answers most commonly given to this question today are either terribly misguided or entirely non-existent. Instead of being helped toward the kind of relationship with God that will transform our heart, most of us who have looked for hope have found only disappointment, or worse. But the real reason we cannot see the way forward is that the very things we have come to believe about transformation are themselves deeply flawed!

Our greatest problem is not that we do wrong things or need better rules to live by. Rather, our way of perceiving both reality and our relationship to God and the world has been terribly corrupted.

That is why discipleship programs that concentrate on controlling our responses to life have such limited results in transforming people's lives. Traditional wisdom has often stressed a behavioral approach to Christian growth. The idea is that if you do something long enough it will eventually become a natural part of you, a kind of "fake it until you make it" philosophy of change. In contrast, sanctification or spiritual transformation is something that the Holy Spirit does in the heart of the believer so that the person is different than before and sees the world through the lenses of new core beliefs. We live differently *not because we manage to do it well enough, but because we are becoming the kind of person who lives that way naturally.* Unless our practical teaching is rooted in transformation – accomplished by direct participation with the Holy Spirit – we will continue to teach discipleship that is fundamentally a program of self-effort.

As stated earlier, transformation is a multifaceted process which comes from engaging one or more life-changing sources of change such as truth, love, and other corrective experiences. Of those causes, truth is perhaps the most easily accessible, touching nearly every aspect of our life. From the Garden of Eden to the final battle, the Father of Lies is bent on bringing about destruction through the skillful use of a very powerful tool, *deception.* At the same time, God seeks to redeem all who will believe and live in the truth. It would not be too much of a stretch to say that truth and deception form one of several major unifying themes in the Bible.

In light of the overwhelming attention that Scripture gives to the issue of deception, it is rather surprising that it has received so little attention in our pulpits and our systematic theologies. A thorough grasp of the nature of deception is crucial to our understanding of evil and how to overcome sin and its effects in our lives. Christians have always accepted the idea that what a person believes can change one's eternal destiny. *Should it be so much of a leap to see that what one believes also changes choices, behavior, and character?*

Neither truth nor lies have the capacity to *force* our behavior. A lie has power only when it is *believed.* If unmasked for what it is, a lie becomes impotent. Similarly, truth will not set a person free unless it is internalized at the deepest levels. This is why *belief* is such critical work and why intimate knowledge of the truth is so important in the Scriptures. Only through the exposure of what is false and the internalization of what is true can the power of truth be released into our life. In the final analysis, the entire kingdom of evil is a house of cards. It is powerless wherever the truth of God is received and allowed to do its work.

My prayer for the body of Christ is that we would begin to see life better through the eyes of heaven and learn to live in vibrant relationship to God, whose very presence and words of truth can set us free.

Addendum

- A Model for Healing Distorted Beliefs

- A Working Vocabulary of Belief

- The Progression of Sin

- Bibliographies

A Model for Healing Distorted Beliefs

Through much experience, Christian counselors and ministers who work with inner-healing prayer have found that there is a fairly effective way of helping people to engage with God to permanently alter the underlying beliefs that cause so much pain and faulty living. The model for prayer outlined below is an adaptation of several of these approaches.[128] Please bear in mind that this is a very brief description of this kind of prayer. The reader is encouraged to check out additional sources in the bibliography for a more in-depth discussion of inner healing prayer, which can go even beyond our need for truth.

1. Ask Jesus to open your heart to His presence. It may be helpful to remember a time when you were keenly aware of His presence and ask God to stir up your memory of that time. Or you might recall something for which you can feel authentic appreciation, and from there allow yourself to feel grateful for God's involvement. When you sense the presence of God, ask Him to come closer and reveal Himself to you.

2. Discern what needs to be addressed. If you have a specific issue you want healing for, ask God if this is the time and place for that. Otherwise, ask God if He has something else He would like to talk about. If you are having difficulty perceiving God's presence, consider asking God for help with that.

3. Once you have named the issue to be addressed, identify the emotions that are associated with it. Describe any reactions, beliefs and intentions that go with the upset, and any means by which the issue may get triggered in your life. Also consider any coping patterns you may have developed over time to try to deal with this area.

4. Ask Jesus to help you bring the issue into focus using your memory of either an actual event or the people involved. Sometimes it helps to partially re-experience the problem with its distressing emotions (while

---

[128] Adapted from Koepcke, et.al., *Bringing the Life Model to Life*, p.25; Lehman, *A Brief Introduction to the Emmanuel Approach*; Smith, *Beyond Tolerable Recovery*.

staying connected to God). If you have identified a faulty belief that is involved, the more "true" that it feels, the more deeply the real truth can penetrate. If you are working with a life theme rather than a specific event, ask God to help you identify an image or icon that best captures the issues involved.

5. Check to make sure you can still sense the presence of God.

6. Ask God what He wants you to know about this issue and be open to whatever He might say or do at that point. He may reveal truth in the form of words or images, or He may reveal His heart toward you, assure you that you are not alone, or whatever it is that you need in that moment. If you are not receiving anything, check to see if you can sense His presence, or ask Him questions about the issue that will help to expose the underlying fears and implicit beliefs. Continue working with God until you sense a breakthrough.

7. Check for peace and rest in the event. If you have experienced His peace, the work is probably done for now. If the emotion has simply changed, say from shame to sadness, then there may be more that needs to be addressed. Go back and see what else needs God's touch.

8. Give thanks for the healing that has occurred.

The most important factor in all of this is staying connected with God. If at any point it becomes difficult to sense the presence of God, then everything else becomes secondary to finding out what is preventing us from sensing His presence. Sometimes all that is needed is to notice that we have lost track of God and seek Him out again. Sometimes we will discover one or more obstacles in the way of perceiving His presence such as fear of God, fear of pain, anger at God, vows we have made related to the issue or in regard to God, disbelief about healing or about God, and so on. These obstacles then become the paramount issue to be addressed, taking them back to God just as the original issue was taken to Him, and asking how He wants to address them.

For example, if you discover that you are angry with God for not preventing a certain event from happening, it is more important to deal directly with God about your anger than it is to seek healing in regard to the event. Or if you find that you do not believe He wants to heal you, tell Him what you feel and ask Him what you need to know about your disbelief. In any case, the primary concern is to remove whatever it is that prevents you from being close to God or receiving from Him.

Looking back at the entire process, notice the level of participation that is required by the person as well as God. This is not a passive process. Seeking out the best evidence for a faulty belief can mean recalling a very painful event where the belief became anchored in your emotions. You may need to be willing (and able) to hold significant levels of discomfort while remaining open to the voice of God.

Please note in some instances the trauma may be so intense that it is not possible to go back into the memories. In that case, God will often help us identify an icon or metaphor which can give us a way of referring to that trauma without revisiting all of the horrible details.

For example, God gave one woman I know a picture of herself as a dead person, which captured fairly well the aftermath of all the traumas she had experienced. As God breathed life into this dead image and raised her up, the woman experienced God's love and care for her so strongly that she was truly freed from the pain of those events. In doing so, she did not have to walk through all the terrible details related to those events.

The point is that we need to be emotionally connected to whatever it is we want healing from, but we do not need to be overwhelmed by the memories or re-experience the traumas in order to receive healing. This is why it is usually best to work with an experienced prayer minister in order to resolve some of our more difficult issues, as they can help guide the process and offer intercession on our behalf as we seek God's help.

Even in less traumatic areas it is often helpful to have another person present with you and interceding for you (even out loud, occasionally) while you pray for healing. But it is very important that the "minister" not attempt to provide the truth which they think you need, either directly or indirectly. You need to receive guidance and the truth directly from the Holy Spirit. That is the Spirit's job and it is usually not helpful to try and do it for Him. His words have the force of life, whereas ours do not.

There are often multiple lies embedded in single events, and there can be multiple events woven together to arrive at one or more lies. Dealing with these complications and listening to God while in distress is a learned process for both the minister and the one being ministered to. That is why it is important to work through all of the distress surrounding particular events, and why we should not abandon this process when we run into what might seem like a dead end. Patience and persistence are valuable assets in any aspect of spiritual formation, and especially when addressing painful wounds.

Learning to engage with God to reinterpret your life experiences from His point of view is one of the most exciting and life-giving experiences we can have. We discover more of God's heart for us and find a freedom we never thought possible. May God richly bless your pursuit of His gifts.

For more information on inner healing, I recommend the resources in the bibliographies and on the following websites:

www.KingdomFormation.org
www.kcLehman.com
www.HeartSyncMinistries.org

A Working Vocabulary of Belief

This is a list of common terms and definitions that when taken collectively, help to show how much our perceptions and interpretations of life are driven by our internal system of values and implicit beliefs.

belief: the readiness to act as if something were true.

confusion (esp. spiritual): unable to separate truth from error.

contentment: a calm feeling from the belief that I have enough.

conversion: a change from one set of beliefs to another set of beliefs.

deception: anything that obscures the truth, including lies, distortions, confusion, and repression of the truth.

despair: an intense emotion rooted in the belief that something important is hopeless.

discernment: separating truth from error; seeing things from God's perspective.

disobedience: acting contrary to a prescribed manner, due to a belief that one's interests are better served in another way.

faith: trusting that what God said is true and real and for our good.

fear: an emotion arising from the belief that I could get hurt.

gratefulness: an emotion from the belief that what I have was a gift, not earned.

hate: an emotion from the belief that another is worthy of contempt or should feel pain or die.

hope: an emotion based on the belief that something good will happen.

hopelessness: an emotion from the belief that a necessary good cannot or will not happen.

humility: a settled belief that I am a limited, small creature in the hands of a big God.

legalism: the belief that following a prescribed manner of behavior makes me more spiritual; the belief that righteousness is earned by doing the right things.

lust: desire that is stirred up by distorted perceptions of the object; desire that has been drawn to an object due to faulty beliefs about what that will do for the person.

obedience (to Jesus): acting on the belief that the One asking me to act holds me in His heart and has my best interests in mind.

repentance: change of mind from what is faulty to what is true; turning to God for a change of heart that is greater than what we can do on our own.

revelation: in-breaking of truth not previously known or acknowledged.

righteousness: a condition of the heart; an act of faith in what is true.

salvation: being rescued from the kingdom of darkness and received into the kingdom of light.

sanctification: among other things, ongoing or continuous in-working of truth; becoming your true self.

self-hate: lie-based self-image that sees the self as unacceptable and unlovable.

sin: faith in a lie; acting in unbelief; aligning with or giving in to a mistaken belief.

temptation: mistaken belief that what is offered may provide some benefit.

unbelief: belief in a lie; not believing what is true; readiness to act as if a faulty belief is true.

The Progression of Sin

The following terms describe various forms of deception that can form the basis for sin:

lies	ignorance
spiritual confusion	unbelief
perverted truth	corruption
false assumptions	false conclusions
darkness of the mind	misinterpretation of experiences
missing the important	mistaken goals such as:
misinformation	being right all the time winning
distortion	being important
denial	pain avoidance
doubt	

The above forms of deception lead directly to the following inner problems:

idolatry	hatred of self
hatred of others	lust / envy / coveting
poor choices	poor judgment
contempt	secrecy
distrust	anxiety
pride / arrogance	valuing of what is bad

Those inner problems then give birth to virtually every visible form of sin, including:

abuse	violence
adultery	relational breakdowns
materialism	marginalizing others
selfishness / self-centeredness	divisiveness / lying
cheating	stealing
abandonment	neglect
blaming / shaming	war
murder	

(Notice how all of this is driven by deception)

Bibliography of Footnote References

Clinton, Dr. Tim; Sibcy, Dr. Gary. *Attachments: Why You Love, Feel, and Act the Way You Do* (Brentwood, TN: Integrity Publishers) 2002

Cloud, Henry. *Changes That Heal: How to Understand Your Past to Ensure a Healthier Future* (Grand Rapids: Zondervan) 1993

Cloud, Dr. Henry; Townsend, Dr. John. *12 Christian Beliefs That Can Drive You Crazy: Relief From False Assumptions* (Grand Rapids: Zondervan) 1995

Crabb, Larry. *Connecting: Healing for Ourselves and Our Relationships, A Radical New Vision* (Nashville: Word Publishing) 1997

Crabb, Larry. *The Safest Place on Earth: Where People Connect and Are Forever Changed* (Nashville: Word Publishing) 1999

Curtis, Brent; Eldredge, John. *The Sacred Romance: Drawing Closer to the Heart of God* (Nashville: Thomas Nelson) 1997

Dieter, Hoekema, Hortan, McQuilkin, Walvoord. *Five Views on Sanctification* (Grand Rapids: Zondervan) 1987

D'Souza, Dinesh. *What's So Great About Christianity* (Washington DC: Regnery Publishing) 2007

Edman, V. Raymond. *They Found the Secret: 20 Transformed Lives That Reveal a Touch of Eternity* (Grand Rapids: Zondervan) 1984

Friesen, James; Wilder, E James; Bierling, Ann M; Koepcke, Rick; Poole, Maribeth. *The Life Model: Living From the Heart Jesus Gave You* (Pasadena: Shepherd's House) 2000

Grenz, Stanley. *Theology for the Community of God* (Grand Rapids: Eerdmans) 1994

Koepcke, Rick; Koepcke, Ruth Ann; Poole, Maribeth; Wilder, E James. *Bringing the Life Model to LIFE: The LIFE model Study Guide for Individuals and Small Groups* (Pasadena: Shepherd's House) 2002

Larson, Scott, ed. *Indelible Ink: 22 Prominent Christian Leaders Discuss the Books That Shape Their Faith* (Colorado Springs: WaterBook Press) 2003

Lehman, Karl. *A Brief Introduction to the Emmanuel Approach* (www.kclehman.com) 2007

Lewis, C. S. *The Screwtape Letters* (New York: Macmillan Publishing) 1961

Lockyer, Herbert Sr, editor. *Nelson's Illustrated Bible Dictionary* (Nashville: Thomas Nelson Publishers) 1986

Moo, Douglas. *The Epistle to the Romans (The New International Commentary on the New Testament)* (Grand Rapids: Eerdmans) 1996

Moon, Gary. *Renovation of the Heart* study series (Franklin Springs, GA: LifeSprings Resources) 2003

Mulholland, M. Robert, Jr. *Shaped By the Word: The Power of Scripture in Spiritual Formation* (Nashville: Upper Room Book) 2000

Palmer, Parker J. *To Know As We Are Known: Education as a Spiritual Journey* (San Francisco: HarperCollins) 1993

Phillips, J.B. *Your God is Too Small* (New York: Collier Books) 1961

Smith, Ed. *Beyond Tolerable Recovery* (Campbellsville, KY: Alathia) 1996

Smith, James; Graybeal, Lynda. *A Spiritual Formation Workbook: Small-Group Resources for Nurturing Christian Growth* (San Francisco: HarperCollins) 1993

Takle, David. *Whispers of My Abba: From His Heart to Mine* (NC: Kingdom Formation Ministries) 2011

Takle, David. *Forming: A Work of Grace* (NC: Kingdom Formation Ministires) 2013

Thompson, Curt. *Anatomy of the Soul* (Wheaton, IL: Tyndale) 2010

Townsend, John. *Hiding From Love: How to Change the Withdrawal Patterns That Isolate and Imprison You* (Colorado Springs: NavPress) 1991

Wilder, E James. *The Complete Guide to Living With Men* (Pasadena: Shepherd's House) 2004

Willard, Dallas. *The Spirit of the Disciplines: Understanding How God Changes Lives* (New York: HarperCollins) 1988

Willard, Dallas. *The Divine Conspiracy: Rediscovering Our Hidden Life In God* (San Francisco: HarperCollins) 1998

Willard, Dallas. *Renovation of the Heart: Putting on the Character of Christ* (Colorado Springs: NavPress) 2002

Willard, Dallas. *Knowing Christ Today: Why We Can Trust Spiritual Knowledge* (New York: HarperCollins) 2009

Wright, N.T. *The New Interpreter's Bible: Acts - First Corinthians (Vol. 10)* (Nashville, TN: Abingdon Press) 2002

Additional Reading on Deception

Lewis, C. S. *The Screwtape Letters* (New York: Macmillan Publishing) 1961

McCallum, Dennis: *The Death of Truth* (Minneapolis: Bethany House) 1996

Peck, M. Scott. *People of The Lie: The Hope for Healing Human Evil* (New York: Simon and Schuster) 1983

Phillips, J.B. *Your God is Too Small* (New York: Collier Books) 1961

Cloud, Dr. Henry; Townsend, Dr. John. *12 'Christian' Beliefs That Can Drive You Crazy* (Grand Rapids: Zondervan Publishing House) 1995

Additional Help on Internalizing Truth

Johnson, Jan. *When The Soul Listens: Finding Rest and Direction in Contemplative Prayer* (Colorado Springs: NavPress) 1999

Takle, David. *Whispers of My Abba: From His Heart to Mine* (NC: Kingdom Formation Ministries) 2011

Takle, David. *Forming: A Work of Grace* (NC: Kingdom Formation Ministires) 2013

Willard, Dallas. *The Spirit of the Disciplines: Understanding How God Changes Lives* (New York: HarperCollins) 1988

Willard, Dallas. *Renovation of the Heart: Putting on the Character of Christ* (Colorado Springs: NavPress) 2002

Group Discussion Guide

For Personal Reflection and Group Discussion

The Truth About Lies and Lies About Truth is a thought-provoking and paradigm-challenging book. Because of that, and because of the density of the material in this book, your group should have no difficulty generating discussions. In fact, most groups will need more than one meeting to discuss each chapter. About all you will have to do in order to launch a discussion is ask one question:

"What things in this chapter caught your attention?"

We have found that attempting to direct these discussions with anything more specific than that tends to inhibit people's participation rather than encourage it. Consequently, most of the questions in this guide are intended for personal reflection and preparation for group discussion rather than for directing the group itself. Hopefully these questions will generate additional critical thinking that will be helpful in discussing the material, as well as assist in connecting the reader's actual life experience with the ideas in each chapter. As a group leader, be sure to encourage your group members to spend some time thinking about their responses to the questions prior to each meeting.

There are also a few exercises suggested in the guide. If you have the time, it can be very valuable to do them together and then discuss the reactions people have to them. Exercises that require a time of reflection may need at least 15-20 minutes of group silence while everyone works on their own response.

How Long Will the Study Last?

We would suggest at least an hour minimum (preferably 90 minutes) for each discussion time. If your group needs to keep pace with a quarterly church calendar or accommodate other time constraints, we would recommend one of the following plans:

For a 13-week group (one quarter):

> Allow one week for each chapter, except for chapters 9 and 10, which would do better with two weeks each.

For a 24-week group (two quarters):

> Allow two weeks to each chapter, except for chapters 9 and 10, which would get three weeks each.

If your time is flexible, you may want to spend an additional week near the end of the group to discuss the "Model for Healing Distorted Beliefs" (in the Addendum) and encourage participants to spend a significant amount of time outside of group to engage with God about an item on their survey (at the end of the guide). It can be very valuable and encouraging to discuss the various results people will have with this process.

Please be aware that due to the design of the book, discussing this material over a period of time may create considerable angst in some group participants. Because the paradigm shift is so big, much of the book is devoted to deconstructing our previously mistaken assumptions about how spiritual growth takes place. Unless this process of deconstruction is fairly successful, it is very difficult to reconstruct the new paradigm without it being trivialized or misunderstood. Consequently, long before this new approach to growth is presented, you will probably have group members asking "How do we fix this problem?" Just encourage each other to be patient. The process is important and worth taking the time to thoroughly understand each step along the way.

An Invitation to The Abundant Life

1. What images come to mind as you consider the phrase "Abundant Life"?

2. What do you think about the gap we all experience between the kind of life described in the New Testament and the kind of life most of us have?

3. In your own words, how is transformation relevant to experiencing a more abundant life?

Chapter 1 – The Problem is Worse Than We Think

1. Deception in this chapter is given an all-encompassing definition:

"All of our perceptions or interpretations of reality that are incomplete or distorted in some way."

What examples can you offer from your own life or observations that would fall into this definition?

2. Our experience of deception is categorized here under two main areas:

    (a) the types or *forms* of deception that we encounter.

    (b) the *sources* of deception, or *where* these forms arise from.

Which of these areas can you personally identify with as significant in your own journey?

3. What television shows or movies you have seen in which you can identify a seriously flawed premise. For example, in *Sex and the City* the characters all believe very strongly in their right to determine morality from their feelings, and are deeply offended by any suggestion to the contrary.

4. Have you ever been amazed at some negative dynamic you saw at work in someone else's family? What process or family rule surprised you and why? How might that be related to faulty beliefs that exist in that family?

5. What are some distorted dynamics that you have identified in your own family? What underlying beliefs fuel those behaviors?

6. The New Testament paints a picture of a Spirit-filled, transformed life that many Christians find beyond reach or too good to be true. How have you witnessed people grappling with the disparity between this picture and where they see themselves? What *faulty beliefs* do you think might arise from trying to make sense of that gap?

7. What examples can you cite from your own life or people you know in which a personal injury (emotional or physical) led to a deeply held faulty belief about God, self, or life?

8. In what ways has your understanding of deception changed from reading this chapter?

Chapter 2 – The Truth About Lies

1. Have you ever thought about the idea that unbelief is actually belief in a lie? What is your reaction to that redefinition? What are some examples of this in Scripture? In everyday life?

2. Consider the following quote from page 61: "Evil must always distort and confound those realities in order to seduce people into participating in their own self-destruction." In your own words, describe the process by which we find ourselves to be active agents in the very things that hurt us and keep us trapped.

3. Read through the chart at the end of Chapter 2 and choose a line where you can identify with two or more of the characteristics shown. Give examples of when each characteristic feels true. What makes one feel more true than another? How has your experience of these changed over time?

4. How might the pervasiveness of deception lead us to a position of more humility and teachability?

5. Give two examples of experiences that made a lasting impression on you. Try to find one positive story and one negative. What did you "learn" from each experience (can be either truth or lie). After each experience, what things did you see or interpret differently than before?

6. In what way does knowing about the pervasiveness of deception actually offer us great hope instead of despair?

Chapter 3 – The Destructive Nature of Deception

1. What are the great lessons of Eden?

1a. In what other ways have you heard this story interpreted? How does this chapter change how you think about that story?

1b. How does this understanding of deception change the way we view the "choices" made by Adam and Eve?

2. Try to identify several other places in the Bible where people failed, and then work backwards to identify what faulty beliefs they might have

assumed that led them to the actions they took. How many such cause-and-effect relationships can you see?

3. What difference does it make for us if deception is one of the most significant causes for sin?

4. Identify a time when you experienced anger and conflict with another person that was actually the result of a misunderstanding. When the mistaken ideas were cleared up, what happened to your emotions? How is that related to our ideas about deception causing problems?

5. Suppose you have a negative assumption about a person that is actually not true. What kinds of relational damage might occur if you acted on your assumptions *as if* they were true?

Chapter 4 – From Deception to Malformation

1. Identify an area in your life where you often "miss the mark." Consider the issue for a while from the perspective of deception. What implicit beliefs might be lurking behind your particular area of weakness?

2. Identify an event or theme from your past (trauma, resentment, regret, a person you cannot forgive) that causes you distress whenever you think about it very long. What beliefs have you internalized about that area that generate those emotions?

3. What is your reaction to the statement that "just as righteousness is an act of faith in the truth, sin is an act of faith in a lie."

4. In your own words, describe how a lie works its way into our mind and causes *malformation*. How do areas of malformation differ from our fallen nature? How does this suggest an answer to many of the areas of our life where we feel stuck?

Exercise: Take the survey at the end of this study guide. Choose an item that rates 2 or 3. What emotions does this item stir in you? In what ways does this issue impact your life? What companion beliefs are involved?

Chapter 5 – My Beliefs May Not Be What I Think I Believe

1. What are some differences between beliefs that are internalized from experience and the beliefs we acquire through Christian education?

2. Give some examples that demonstrate the following statement: "Once we arrive at an explanation or belief about an event, it immediately appears self-evident to us that the event proves the belief to be true."

3. Think about an area in which you have experienced a head/heart split. Using our vocabulary of belief, how would you describe those opposing forces? (e.g. "In my head I believe it is wrong to covet. But my gut seems to believe that I have been deprived of things I ought to have, and I resent not having them").

Exercise: Look over the survey of beliefs that you filled out earlier. In how many of those areas rated 2 or higher can you identify a head/heart split going on inside you?

Exercise: Reread the section on *Consent*. For the next few days, try to notice all the areas in which you lend your consent but will never act on. How do these areas indicate the presence of underlying beliefs which are at odds with other beliefs that you aspire to?

Chapter 6 – How Beliefs Drive My Life

1. Using the model of how beliefs drive our perceptions, interpretations and responses, give an example of how you and another person have responded (emotionally and physically) to a single event very differently. What underlying beliefs might have caused you to arrive at different responses?

1a. Using the same model, give an example of a situation in which you would respond differently today than you would have a few years ago. What underlying beliefs or values do you think have changed in the mean time that cause you to react differently?

2. Think of a situation in which you often find yourself overreacting (e.g. when hearing criticism; when up against a deadline; when making a mistake). Mentally walk through a time when this happened, and slow the

process down. Separate your perceptions, interpretations, and responses. What internalized beliefs might be impacting each of these areas? (they may be either true or false beliefs).

3. Using the model, describe how a significant negative experience at one point in your life could continue to affect your behavior many years after the event.

4. Often when we get stuck, the advice we hear is, "Try harder. Read more. Pray more. Get more involved." What light does the model presented in this chapter shed on this approach to healing and spiritual growth?

5. "What if we could internalize truth with the same intensity and impact with which we initially internalized the lies?" How would that change the way we pursue spiritual growth, or the way we address sin in our life, or the way we address old wounds that keep us stuck?

Chapter 7 – True Belief is Hard Work

1. Without looking back at the text, what beliefs do you suppose permeated the Israelite culture after it had been in slavery for many generations? List as many as you can think of.

1a. How do you think those beliefs played out when Moses came to them and announced a plan to walk away from their oppressors? Be specific.

1b. After they succeeded in getting away, how would those beliefs have interfered with forming a new community or following Moses?

2. Assuming that we may not be aware of our own faulty beliefs, what does that say about our ability to control our responses by willpower alone?

3. What are some examples of the ways in which a child might cope with a painful environment (or dysfunctional parent) that later in life could eventually become more destructive than helpful? For example: Learning to deny your own needs may a good strategy when growing up in a family where asking for what you need is usually met with hostility. But as an adult, denying your needs can often lead to deep resentments and loss of relationships.

4. In what ways does this model of malformation help to alleviate some of the toxic shame we feel for not being as far along in our spiritual development as we think we should be? (see "Why does the work of recovery fall to the wounded?")

Chapter 8 – Lies We Believe About Christian Development

1. When have you found it to be true in your own life that the "try harder" approach to spiritual growth simply did not work?

2. What are some of the things you have told yourself (or others told you) about why you cannot live up to the standards you thought were required?

3. What reactions do you have to the diagram that demonstrates how using truth to focus on behavior actually creates an internal war with the pressure that comes from our internalized beliefs?

Exercise: Choose an item from your survey with a rating of 2 or 3. Consider the truth that since God's thoughts are higher than our thoughts, He has very different "internalized beliefs" than we do. Consequently, He is able to perceive things that we cannot, His interpretations are different from ours, and His responses would be very different as well. Ask God what He can tell you about your implicit beliefs in regard to this one item from your survey and spend a few minutes writing out whatever thoughts come to mind. Share your process with the group.

Chapter 9 – Truth is More Than True Information

1. How has your perception of "truth" been impacted by this chapter?

2. An example was given of a young man who experienced a lot spiritual growth shortly after conversion, but then it all slowed down to a crawl. In what ways can you identify with this scenario?

2a. What explanations have you heard for this common phenomena?

3. What has been your understanding of "Christian obedience" in the past? In what ways have you responded to that teaching? What is your reaction to the description of obedience in this chapter?

4. How would you describe your relationship to God? What have you been taught to expect in that regard? What has been your understanding of how we develop that relationship? How does that compare to the description of "relationship" in this chapter?

5. What reactions do you have to the "Stories of Transformation by Truth"?

Chapter 10 – Internalizing Truth

1. Have you ever experienced God speaking into your life? What was it like?

2. What has been your experience with Conversational Prayer? If you are familiar with this, how did you learn? If this is new to you, what are your thoughts about it?

3. Knowing God's voice has the power of life within it, what if you could be mentored by God Himself in regard to things that seem too painful or too difficult for you? What areas would you most want help with?

4. When have you had an experience in which the actions of another person (or a story they told) had a significant positive impact on you? How does that relate to the role of community in our spiritual development?

5. How does this chapter's description of "participation" with God differ from how you have thought about it in the past?

6. What "teachable moments" have you experienced recently? Can you recall any significant teaching moments in your past?

7. What "spiritual disciplines" have you attempted in which you eventually became disillusioned or burned out? In what ways can you relate to the discussion about the "Difference between dead practices and life-giving disciplines"?

Exercise: Spend some time reading Isaiah 55 slowly, asking God to draw you to some phrase in the chapter. When something catches your attention, write it down and then write out whatever else comes to mind about that phrase. Try listening to your heart and the Spirit of God (do not rely solely on what you can reason out). When the writing slows down, spend some time reflecting on whatever insights you have received.

Exercise: Re-read the section on Conversations with God. Select an item from your survey with a rating of 2 or 3 and ask God what He would like to reveal to you about that issue. Write out your thoughts as they come to you, without worrying too much whether they originate with you or God. Discuss what this process was like.

Chapter 11 – Realigning Our Christian Development

1. What caught your attention in regard to the various phrases that make up the definition of *sanctification*?

2. In your own words, describe the three major dimensions to Christian development. How does internalizing truth impact all three areas?

3. Of the "Foundational Truths We All Need to Believe" which ones have you struggled with the most? In which area have you had the least amount of training?

4. Which of the "Common Barriers to Truth" have you experienced?

Exercise: Read the "Model for Healing Distorted Beliefs" and ask God to help you with another item on your survey. Record your conversation with Him.

Survey – Perceptions and Observations About Life

For each of the items below ask,
"How <u>often</u> do I feel or think or act this way?"
Then rate it from 0 to 5 using the following scale:
(feel free to qualify any items by adding names or events)

0=never / 1=rarely / 2=occasionally / 3=sometimes / 4=often / 5=lots

____ I think God is disappointed in me

____ God seems very distant to me

____ I am afraid of what God wants from me

____ I worry about what others think of me

____ I worry about finances

____ I'm really hard on myself

____ Evil is more powerful than Good

____ I despair over my feelings of powerlessness

____ I feel angry at God about things that have happened to me

____ I have doubts about God's interest or concern for me

____ I'm better off alone than trying to get close to others

____ I have places in my life where I feel stuck and cannot seem to change

____ I feel judgmental or contemptuous toward others

____ I compare myself to others and feel as if I don't measure up

____ I seem to need everyone to like me and/or approve of me

____ There are people that I'm not sure I can ever forgive

____ I have trouble "forgiving myself" for certain mistakes I have made

____ I am afraid of making mistakes or failing at things I try

____ I am surprised by my own reactions to certain situations

____ I have painful regrets about choices I have made

____ If you knew me better, you wouldn't like me

____ I believe negative feedback more than positive

____ I'm really hard on myself

____ I have memories that are too painful to think about

____ I worry about wasting my life

____ I feel cheated in certain areas of my life

____ There are places in my life I do not think God can heal

There is no scoring for this survey. The purpose is to call attention to areas which may indicate the presence of underlying beliefs God wants to change.

(Keep your results. This survey will be used in various exercises throughout this discussion guide)

You may copy this survey for your use. **www.KingdomFormation.org**

Whispers of my Abba

From His Heart to Mine

by David Takle

If you want to learn more about how to hear God speak into your life, then this book is what you are looking for.

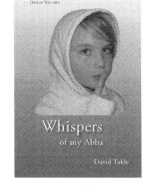

Whispers of my Abba explores conversational prayer as a mentor would, with the depth and breadth necessary to help the reader discover the joy of listening to God.

Whispers includes actual journal entries that demonstrate what it can be like to engage in conversations with God, and also contains a troubleshooting chapter on what to do when hearing God is difficult.

If you want to know more about how to have conversations with God, or if you want to give a gift to others that will change their life forever, consider this excellent resource on hearing God's voice.

Forming

A Work of Grace

by David Takle

Christian growth and development does not come from trying to act more like Jesus, it comes from becoming more like Jesus on the inside. *Forming* will show you how to engage with God and build a relationship with Him that is vibrant enough to change you from the inside out.

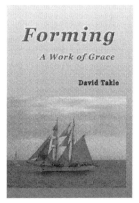

Rather than trying to row against the current of your inner life in an effort to do what you think is right, *Forming* shows you how to align your sails with the wind, engaging with the Spirit of God to change the direction of your heart, so you can go places you never could reach by rowing.

If you are tired of "row harder" approaches to spiritual growth, then you will want to read and digest every word in this book.

"I wish someone would have told me these things when I first became a Christian. It would have saved me a lot of heartache and disappointment."
– Reader in North Carolina

Forming

Change by Grace

A 12-Week Course in Spiritual Formation

by David Takle

Experience a fresh, life-giving approach to spiritual growth and restoration that will jump-start your spiritual life and change forever your relationship with God.

Forming will show you how God changes lives, and how you can participate with Him to foster the changes in your heart and mind that you always believed should be possible.

Topics include:

- What is Christian Formation?
- How do we grow spiritually?
- What is our part and what is God's part in spiritual growth?
- How is this different from traditional models of Christian discipleship?

Both seasoned believers as well as those new to the faith who have taken this course report that it has been one of the most important experiences of their entire Christian journey!

See **www.KingdomFormation.org** for more information.

57172765R00163

Made in the USA
Middletown, DE
27 July 2019